Poet, Public, and
Performance in
Ancient Greece

Poet, Public, and Performance in Ancient Greece

Edited by

Lowell Edmunds & Robert W. Wallace

with a Preface by

Maurizio Bettini

THE JOHNS HOPKINS UNIVERSITY PRESS

Baltimore and London

Copyright © 1997 The Johns Hopkins University Press
All rights reserved. Published 1997
Printed in the United States of America on acid-free paper
06 05 04 03 02 01 00 99 98 97   5 4 3 2 1

The Johns Hopkins University Press
2715 North Charles Street
Baltimore, Maryland 21218-4319
The Johns Hopkins Press Ltd., London

Library of Congress Cataloging-in-Publication Data will be found
at the end of this book.
A catalog record for this book is available from the British Library.

Contents

Preface

Maurizio Bettini

GREEK POETRY differed profoundly from modern poetry in content, form, and methods of presentation. An essentially practical art, it was closely linked to the realities of social and political life, and to the actual behavior of individuals within a community. It rendered the poet's own experience of human existence as well as that of others, but was not private poetry in the modern sense. It drew regularly for its themes on myth, which was at once the sole subject matter of narrative and dramatic poetry and a constant point of paradigmatic reference in lyric. . . . What distances it most radically from modern poetry is the medium of communication: not a written text for reading but a solo or choral performance, to the accompaniment of a musical instrument, before an audience."[1] So begins the book perhaps best known and most successful among the many that Bruno Gentili has written, *Poetry and Its Public in Ancient Greece.* And, indeed, it would be difficult to find another definition that, in so few words, succeeded in describing so clearly the distinctive characteristics of Greek poetry.

A stylistic phenomenon of recurrence strikes us immediately in this definition of Greek poetry. Gentili refers three times, in a few lines, to poetry and to *modern* culture, and he does so with a precise scheme of reference: he intends to stress the differences between our experience of poetry and the Greeks'. In other words, he knows that modern poetry, in its attention to the inner life of the poet and of his personae, often has a private character. For this reason, he is concerned to explain immediately that Greek poetry was completely different—individual but at the same time linked "to the realities of social and political life, and to the actual behavior of individuals within a community." The force of Gentili as an interpreter of Greek poetry (especially in his contributions after 1969, the year that "marked a decisive turn in" his studies)[2] consists precisely in this: when his gaze appears to be most intensely concentrated on Pindar, Sappho, or Bacchylides, at that moment his attention to the contemporary world turns out to be strongest. The vision of Greek culture presented to us by Gentili is regularly a *bifocal* one. As Rousseau said: "Quand on veut étudier les hommes il faut regarder près de soi; mais pour étudier l'homme il faut apprendre à porter sa vue au loin; il faut d'abord observer les différences pour découvrir les propriétés."[3]

In this spirit we set about to celebrate Bruno Gentili, collecting for him the essays we publish here. Research on "différences" in order to understand "propriétés," or the bifocal gaze (moderate but constant) turned toward ancient Greece and toward modernity, characterizes more than one of the contributions to this volume. Maria Grazia Bonanno finds in the cinematography of Pasolini the cue for defining a difference that can help us understand certain things neglected by Aristotle, while Robert Wallace concludes his essay on the behavior of the Athenians in the theater with reflection on how "we" usually attend a theatrical spectacle, and Lowell Edmunds concludes with the story of a French officer who experienced in prison, in Tunisia, an organization of space and social groups that recalls very closely that of the Megara of Theognis. But we are getting ahead of ourselves. Before we speak about the individual contributions, it would be well to say something more about the specific occasion—a public scholarly "performance"—on which they appeared.

The event took place in the course of a single day, February 11, 1994, in the splendid lecture hall of the Villa Aurelia, at the American Academy in Rome. To this institution we owe the generous support that allowed us to realize our plan. The title of the conference was "Poeta, Pubblico e Performance," with obvious reference to the three themes that most markedly characterize the research of the scholar whom we wanted to celebrate. The audience was numerous and responsive. Gentili sat in the first row, and (anyone who knows him will understand what we mean) his presence was not limited to an Olympian acceptance of the homage that was paid him. It was wonderful to celebrate someone who stood up, intervened, argued, in the same way as the audience that had gathered for this occasion. This is the fondest memory from that day in February, with a sun that at a certain point shone on Rome and allowed us to have lunch on the terrace and in the garden. On the shelves in our libraries it still happens that we find old miscellanies *in honorem*, in which, at the end of the volume, it was the custom to include the menu of the repast offered the guests. Not to have saved one from the conference in honor of Bruno Gentili is a shame. It should have been published.

And now we turn to the essays in this volume. In theme, they cover two fundamental strains of Greek literary production: one we could call "nontheatrical" (epic, elegy, gnomology, anonymous creation of maxims, proverbs, and apophthegms); the other is constituted by the theatrical experience of the Greeks. The picture that unifies this research is constituted by the constant dialectic among the three poles of poetic communication in archaic and classical Greece: poet, public, and performance. Naturally each scholar has carved out his own space in this triangle, accenting the "corner" congenial to him.

Giulio Guidorizzi analyzes a passage in the *Odyssey* that poses a problem for communication between poet and public: the short passage in book 20 in which a collective delirium comes over the suitors (345–49). How does the poet describe a scene that lies outside the narrative themes and the diction of epic? Guidorizzi shows that the public could have identified the suitors' state of mind as a Dionysiac ecstasy. In particular, the eating of raw meat is a semantic-symbolic sign that the public can interpret in terms of the ὠμοφαγία known to them as specifically Dionysiac (whether or not practiced in reality).

Antonio Aloni, analyzing the difficult text of the elegy of Simonides for the victors at Plataea, takes up the problem of the performance of elegiac poetry. Can we be satisfied with the thought that archaic Greek elegy had only the symposium as the site of its rendition? Certainly not: and indeed Simonidean elegy permits Aloni to adduce new data for the resolution of this complicated question, even if, as he observes at the end of his essay, the Simonidean text adds to the dossier on elegy both new cues for the solution of old problems and new problems to solve. But perhaps the most vivid aspect of the essay is found in the section that Aloni dedicates to the patronage of the elegy: "One of the many things that Bruno Gentili has taught us" is that communication in archaic and classical Greece cannot be understood unless one bears patronage in mind, especially in the case of public performances. That is why Simonides adroitly separates a nonlocalistic vision of the event from a clear emphasis on the role played by the Spartans in the Battle of Plataea. In sum, Aloni's contribution takes shape as an essay that addresses both theoretical problems of poetic genre (What kind of "performance" is fitting for archaic Greek elegy?) and themes that have a contingent, historical character (the specific patron of the poem), although both these aspects strictly belong to the significatum of the text.

Lowell Edmunds is perhaps the one who tried hardest to hold in equilibrium the three subthemes of the conference: he is concerned with the poet (Is Theognis a historical person or only a poetic persona?), the audience to which Theognidean elegy is addressed (a group of symposiasts), and the type of performance presupposed not only by the whole collection but especially by verses 19–23, which contain the famous reference to the seal of Theognis. The question is this: "Are these verses unperformable? Are they conceived as exclusively written poetry?" Following Gregory Nagy, Edmunds overturns one of the most often cited foundations of the importance of archaic Greek individuality—the "seal" of Theognis, the "name" as guarantee of unique and unrepeatable poetry: indeed, the presence of "seals" in the Theognidean manner manifests itself just when there is the intention of giving authority to collections of traditional material. The Theognidean sylloge therefore offers us a sympotic manual that incorporates gnomological material, or a collection of gnomai that incorporates a sympotic manual. As for the "seal," whoever affixed it to the collection certainly did not intend to make it correspond to the "name" of Theognis (as Edmunds mentions, seals in archaic Greece are "nonwritten tokens" and are not a good metaphor to indicate a signature). The Theognidean seal functions rather as a metaphor of protection and closing for the material of the collection and, as a whole, as allusion to the unmistakable "marks," poetic and stylistic but also ethical and political, that claim to countersign the form and contents of the sylloge. Unexpectedly, the problem of the Theognidean σφραγίς thus comes to belong to the history of semiotics. In the vision of the one who composed verses 19–23 of the sylloge, different levels of the text were strewn with a series of authoritative "signs" capable of identifying and protecting it. And to signify this subtle semiotic operation, the metaphor, semiotic par excellence, of the "seal" was chosen.

With Joseph Russo, the anonymous, collective voice of Greek cultural production (already broadly lurking in the pages of Edmunds) comes decisively to the fore. Russo's essay analyzes an aspect of literary creation often undervalued by classicists but present in the research of folklorists and anthropologists: proverbs, maxims, apothegms, or the "performance of wisdom through authoritative words."[4] As can easily be imagined, this turn "along the lines of modern ethnographic research" has certainly not troubled the dreams of Bruno Gentili: it is "in accord with his long-standing interest in interpreting ancient texts in the light of modern methodologies." The type of cultural production examined by Russo arises as an immediate reaction to particular exigencies imposed by the situational context. As such, it presents itself as fundamentally different from the creations of artistic production, which also surely respond to the promptings of situations but in a freer and, above all, more complex fashion. The adjective that best defines this type of cultural production is surely *emergent*. The main problem obviously consists in distinguishing these different categories, tracing the lines of a possibly different status for each of the three genres. The operation becomes most complex in the case of the apothegm (for which *retort* would be the basic definition), which Russo analyzes also in a diachronic perspective, while discovering notable "overlapping" between this genre and others similar to it. The difference of status, however, between this genre and the other two that Russo discusses remains clear. It is difficult, once again, not to yield to the temptation of the "bifocal" gaze. How often, in our contemporary experience, an evening with friends ends with the spirited alternating citation of famous "apothegms." If the guests are classicists, apothegms of Housman, Eduard Fraenkel, or Giorgio Pasquali will easily come to be repeated. But it will certainly not happen that modern "symposiasts" (unless they intend to emulate the learned pedantry of the *Deipnosophistae* of Athenaeus or that of the grammarians at the *Saturnalia* of Macrobius) pass an evening exchanging maxims or proverbs. The apothegm has its own autonomy. It carries with it sense and context sufficient to give it independent validity—yet another indication of the inalienable difference, functional and contextual, that separates the apothegm from its cousins.

With Charles Segal, our attention shifts to the second of the thematic strains in this collection of essays, Greek theatrical experience. In particular, Segal addresses an aspect of dramatic poetry for which Gentili has made contributions of great importance: the chorus. Through a reading that continuously circles back to Euripides' *Bacchae*, in a series of illuminating, ever closer passes, Segal causes to emerge in all its contradictory clarity the unusual role played by the chorus in this tragedy: a chorus exceptionally unsympathetic as regards the polis, one that often speaks a language (virtually) different from that of the drama's protagonists. Among the many paradoxes, cultural and religious as well as theatrical, that characterize the *Bacchae*, there is also this: the city is not at all represented by the chorus. Though Thebes is more intact than the Troy presupposed by the *Hecuba* or in the *Trojan Women*, its ruin seems greater because there is no choral voice that represents the city or the family at the end of the tragedy. Segal's essay is not limited, however, to developing this basic perspective. A section is devoted to the suggestive correspondences between menadic behavior and the ritual behavior of women on the occasion of funeral lament, thus defining a specific area of female emotionality, of its autonomy, and therefore of its potential (and feared) disorder. On this occasion, Segal's gaze becomes bifocal, as the most interesting comparisons come from the research of ethnographers on grief in contemporary Greece.

Thomas Cole studies the plot of Euripides' *Ion*, or, better, the arrangement that this mythic event assumes in the hands of the most adroit of the tragedians. The problem, "intriguing" indeed, is posed by Cole in terms explicitly defined as "post-Gentilian." By this formulation, he means that the emphasis of his analysis is going to fall not so much on the historical context as on the "probable audience when the play was represented for the first—and presumably last—time on an Athenian stage." Once again the dialectic between author and audience is that which most interests the critic, while the subject of analysis appears to be constituted more by the concrete performance of the text that is used (up) in the theatrical event than by the traits, unchanging but, for that very reason, rigid, of a text written once and for all. The center of the mythical event developed in the *Ion*, as is well known, is the uncertain genealogy of the hero. In Cole's analysis, this central aspect of the tragedy assumes the ambiguous nature of a message that offers at least two interpretations. The task of constructing the meaning of the tragedy is to some extent delegated to the public and its interaction with the intention of the poet.

Robert Wallace creates an unexpected fusion of two of the subthemes of the conference, describing the "performances" of the Greek audience at the theater. Wallace assesses the validity of Plato's idea (*Laws* 700a–701b) that from the fifth and fourth centuries at Athens there was a growing tendency to please the tastes of the audience—a tendency that would obviously have produced a decline in the quality of dramatic poetry. The conclusion is that, with certain limitations, Plato was right. In this phase of Greek culture, theatrical production had evolved in the direction of "popular entertainment." Plato, however, ignored (willfully?) the complexity of the situation. With the passage of time, Greek culture had not simply become "barbarized," but had rather become specialized, channeling itself on the one hand into elite expressions, elevated and reserved for the few, and, on the other, into forms oriented toward, and adopting the perspective, of the others. But how did the Athenians behave at the theater? Although the testimony on this aspect of theatrical life is only anecdotal, given that the behavior of the Athenians at the theater was not considered an interesting subject by ancient writers, Wallace presents us with an unexpected catalog of "bad behavior" on the part of the audience (thrown objects of every conceivable kind, whistling, applause, shouting, etc.). Inclination toward the bifocal gaze leads Wallace to suggest that our modern "good behavior" at the theater is the result of Platonic ideas (drama as a predominantly edifying affair) propagated by the innumerable followers of the philosopher.

Finally, Maria Grazia Bonanno's essay is centered on performance, theatrical but not only theatrical. She stresses the importance of this aspect of Greek poetic production in lyric poetry, with a section on "scenic presence" in the Partheneia of Alcman, and even in epic poetry. Very much to the point, there returns an old assertion of Victor Bérard (classical philology is a profession that fortunately keeps alive the memory of its forebears), according to whom "Homère fut pour les dix ou douze générations ioniennes et éoliennes . . . un auteur de scène, récité et joué par les aèdes, par les rhapsodes ensuite . . . l'épos est un drame en hexamètres, à un seul récitant."

The most engaged part of the essay ("the question closest to my heart") comes, however, in the second half, when Bonanno faces a crucial question in the theoretical scheme of the *Poetics*: why does Aristotle, in his theorization of drama, so disvalue the importance of *melopoiia* and especially of scenic *opsis*? The answer to this question rests not only on an attentive rereading of the passage in Aristotle but also on a reflection on the execution of the films *Edipo*, *Medea*, and the unfinished *Orestiade Africana* by Pier Paolo Pasolini. The gaze is, once again, bifocal, and, in such an original perspective, the "heretical empiricism" of Pasolini is well adapted to Bonanno's reuse of cinematography. I shall not disclose to the reader the solution that Bonanno suggests for this old Aristotelian problem but merely suggest that Aristotle now belonged to a phase of Greek culture so "written" that only with difficulty could he have allowed among the relevant traits of drama all that the letters of the alphabet were unable to register once and for all. In short, an unexpected return to orality, like the one that distinguishes contemporary culture, was needed to make us see newly and profoundly the distinctive characteristics of Greek literary production. And with this allusion to the "new orality" of our culture, the new orality of cinema, television, and the mass media in general, we have returned to one of the themes dearest to the research of Bruno Gentili.

Translated by Lowell Edmunds

Acknowledgments

O N February 11, 1994, the American Academy in Rome sponsored a conference, "Poeta, pubblico e performance," in honor of Bruno Gentili. Our inspiration was the wish to recognize Professor Gentili's many scholarly and academic accomplishments and to express our gratitude for his openness and frequent kindnesses to American scholars. We hoped also to further one ambition of the American Academy, by bringing together Italian and American scholars in a stimulating exchange of ideas and friendship. As Maurizio Bettini describes in his preface, the day was a stellar success. With the encouragement of the academy's Mellon Professor of Classical Studies, Malcolm Bell, and its director, Caroline Bruzelius, plans were set in motion to collect the day's presentations for publication. What follow are the results of that effort. The published papers follow the program of the conference with three exceptions. Giulio Guidorizzi and Lowell Edmunds, who served as presidents of conference sessions but did not deliver papers, have both contributed essays to the volume. Also, Bettini's conference paper on Latin metrics, "Numeri innumeri e folclore metrico: Plauto, *Amphitruo* 168–72," seemed best published separately, as uniquely on a non-Greek topic.

Our gratitude goes first to the American Academy for its splendid hospitality, and to Maurizio Bettini, who helped organize the conference. For their service as referees and other assistance, we would like to thank Victor Bers, Peter Burian, Mark Griffith, Jeffrey Henderson, Hugh Lloyd-Jones, Richard P. Martin, Donald J. Mastronarde, and Laura Pepe. Financial assistance was provided by the American Academy, Northwestern University, and Rutgers University.

L.E.
R.W.W.

*Poet, Public, and
Performance in
Ancient Greece*

The Laughter of the Suitors:
A Case of Collective Madness
in the Odyssey

Giulio Guidorizzi

IN THE contiguity between audience and poet, as Bruno Gentili has shown, lies a fundamental approach to research in archaic Greek poetry. This contiguity is evident, and perhaps in an especially significant way, in those episodes in which the subject of the song compels the *aoidos* to take account of social structures and of systems of belief that are substantially remote from epic myth. Here, the necessity of employing a traditional language intersects with that of introducing into the action elements that are known in the audience's culture, if not in its poetry. The result is situations of such poetic complexity that they depart from the schemata of the "typical scenes."

Book 20 of the *Odyssey* contains an episode that, from many points of view, is unexpected and surprising. Joseph Russo, the most recent commentator on the poem, says that it should be considered "the most eerie passage in Homer."[1] This brief passage cannot, in my opinion, be understood correctly except from an ethnopsychological point of view. Further, it is important evidence for the manner in which epic-rhapsodic poetry describes alterations of behavior in a traditional narrative technique. Finally, I believe that the episode refutes the opinion (once so generally held as to become a commonplace) that archaic Greek did not know, or at least did not describe, scenes of collective delirium, or what in the language and culture of post-Homeric times would be called "ecstasy" (ἔκστασις) or "enthusiasm" (ἐνθουσιασμός) and which today would be called "ecstatic trance."

> ὡς φάτο Τηλέμαχος· μνηστῆρσι δὲ Παλλὰς Ἀθήνη
> ἄσβεστον γέλω ὦρσε, παρέπλαγξεν δὲ νόημα.
> οἱ δ᾽ ἤδη γναθμοῖσι γελοίων ἀλλοτρίοισιν,

αἱμοφόρυκτα δὲ δὴ κρέα ἤσθιον· ὄσσε δ᾽ ἄρα σφέων
δακρυόφιν πίμπλαντο, γόον δ᾽ ὠίετο θυμός.

20.345–49

So spoke Telemachos, but among the wooers Pallas Athene roused
unquenchable laughter, and turned their wits awry. And now they
laughed with alien lips, and all bedabbled with blood was the flesh
they ate, and their eyes were filled with tears and their spirits set on
wailing.[2]

In the following verses, the seer Theoklymenos, who is present at the scene,
takes what he has seen as the starting point for a prophecy of the death of the
suitors, which will happen soon:

" ἆ δειλοί, τί κακὸν τόδε πάσχετε; νυκτὶ μὲν ὑμέων
εἰλύαται κεφαλαί τε πρόσωπά τε νέρθε τε γοῦνα.
οἰμωγὴ δὲ δέδηε, δεδάκρυνται δὲ παρειαί,
αἵματι δ᾽ ἐρράδαται τοῖχοι καλαί τε μεσόδμαι·
εἰδώλων δὲ πλέον πρόθυρον, πλείη δὲ καὶ αὐλή,
ἱεμένων Ἔρεβόσδε ὑπὸ ζόφον· ἥλιος δὲ
οὐρανοῦ ἐξαπόλωλε, κακὴ δ᾽ ἐπιδέδρομεν ἀχλύς."

20.351–57

Ah, wretched men, what evil is this that you suffer? Shrouded in
night are your heads and your faces and your knees underneath you;
kindled is the sound of wailing, bathed in tears are your cheeks, and
sprinkled with blood are the walls and the fair rafters. And full of
ghosts is the porch and full the court, of ghosts that hasten down to
Erebus beneath the darkness, and the sun has perished out of heaven
and an evil mist hovers over all. (Ibid.)

After these words, the suitors return to their senses and resume their arrogant
and violent attitude, evidently forgetting what has just happened. Indeed, they
laugh "sweetly" (ἡδὺ γέλασσαν), and one of them hurls the accusation back at
the seer Theoklymenos: "the guest who just arrived is mad!" (ἀφραίνει ξεῖνος,
360). Theoklymenos is truly beside himself, but for a reason different from the
one that the suitors derisively fling in his face. He is beside himself because his
ecstatic prophecy transforms him into an inspired visionary, according to a
schema of divination otherwise well known to Greek culture.

The poet's play of reversals is clear in the contrast of the two situations: on the one hand, the "unquenchable" and alienated laughter of the suitors is opposed to the "sweet" laughter that follows, fitting convivial behavior; on the other, the madness of the suitors (Pallas Athene "turned their wits awry") renders paradoxical their reproaches vis-à-vis Theoklymenos, who, unlike them, is perfectly capable of foreseeing the developments of the situation and is therefore wise in the highest degree precisely because of the enthusiastic madness that possesses him.

The ancient commentators were aware of the strangeness of the whole passage. The scholiast *ad locum* comments: "all that [i.e., the line of shades that set out for the beyond] does not appear to the suitors but only to Theoklymenos," an interpretation that is apparently conjectural, but the embarrassment of the scholiast can be easily understood when one considers that an episode of this kind has no parallels in the epic tradition and is therefore destined to put in crisis the analogical method on which the Homeric scholia base their exegesis.

It is clear that this scene is far from typical. A situation of psychic alienation is contrary to the Homeric manner of describing the phenomena of divination, which are usually the product of a rational prophetic skill and not of a spontaneous visionary inspiration, which has no parallels in Homeric epic.[3] But the most singular aspect of the situation is the description of the alienated exaltation of the suitors and of the pathological traits in which their hallucinatory joy is expressed. They find themselves in a state of complete mental dissociation, revealed in a series of precise symptoms that are worth examining one by one.

1. A sudden change of behavior takes place in the suitors. The crisis of laughter explodes without warning and interrupts without any apparent motivation the normal course of the symposium.

2. The crisis is attributed to the intervention of a divinity who deprives its victims of their senses. The fact that in Homeric epic a divinity unexpectedly exerts an influence on the behavior of a human is not out of the ordinary. Indeed, this is the characteristic schema in which both gods and demons are presented as acting in Homeric poems (e.g., Ate), when they intervene in the course of the action to increase the courage (μένος) of a hero, transporting him into a state of delirious martial exaltation, or, on the contrary, to "blind" him and "rob him of his senses."[4] But in this case the intervention of Athena is described in more pertinent terms that identify the specific kind of delirium by which the suitors are seized: the goddess "turned their wits awry." The verb used (παραπλάζω) serves in the Homeric language to designate the concrete or material deviation of an object with respect to its line, for example, an arrow that misses its mark or a ship that departs from its proper course.[5]

In other words, this verb (which should not be considered a simple metaphor but the reflex of a schema of beliefs) describes in terms of spatial dislocation the bewilderment of consciousness into which the suitors fall as the result of the intervention of a divinity. Body and mind (νόημα) seem to be divided, and the latter is "no longer there." In later epic cases of divine possession, the same idea is described, as victims are "struck from their senses" (παράκοποι φρενῶν).[6]

3. In contrast with other scenes of psychic alteration described in the Homeric poems, in this case the suitors lose control of their bodies and offer a disturbing pathological spectacle. Their faces are deformed; their jaws are "alien," that is, out of their control. Their laughter is unrestrainably convulsed (ἄσβεστον); their eyes are rolling and full of tears. In later culture or at least in later language, this split between the physical and the psychic sphere was called "ecstasis" or "enthusiasm" (ἔκστασις, ἐνθουσιασμός) and was attributed to the intervention of a demon or a divinity in the human psyche. It might be relevant to recall, from an author of a later period, the description of the face of someone undergoing a crisis of possession: "all those who are possessed by the gods," Xenophon writes, "offer a moving spectacle: they present the monstrous look of the Gorgon."[7]

4. The delirium is collective and seizes all the suitors at the same time. We could compare it with a contagion that spreads among them, as if each one was reflected in the alienation of the others. Once again, it is a matter of a situation foreign to the psychological world represented in archaic Greek epic. Of course, collective alteration of the personality is well known to students of ethno-psychology who deal with ritual ecstatics,[8] and to classicists who have identified this phenomenon in various, and verifiably historical, manifestations of religious trance that took place in archaic and classical Greece, especially the Dionysiac and corybantic cults.[9] But the collective delirium of the suitors in this passage is not linked to any ritual whatsoever and seems to occur spontaneously, even if the poet, as is obvious, presents it as the result of a demonic intervention in the human psyche.

5. When the crisis of collective delirium stops, in a fashion just as sudden as the one with which it began, the suitors fail to remember it. Amnesia at the end of the crisis also belongs to the universal symptomatology of the ecstatic trance, and is well documented in the ancient sources (see, e.g., Eur. *Bacch.* 1259–1301).

6. The suitors laugh and eat meat "bedabbled with blood." As we shall see, this point is important for the decipherment of the scene in the light of the audience's cultural context.

In substance, then, the access of delirium that grips the suitors presents all the characteristics of a case of collective possession: it is attributed to a demonic intervention in the psyches of the victims. It happens with no warning, without apparent reason, and suddenly, like a contagion, infects all present. It brings a complete splitting of the personality, with convulsive psychosomatic effects. Finally, when the individual who is the victim recovers his senses, he retains no memory of what has happened.

The psychological state described here can perhaps be better understood if it is linked to a series of phenomena found in all the so-called primitive cultures. That such phenomena were present in post-Homeric Greece is well known (as we have noted). Similar psychic conditions have long been studied in vast regions of Asia, from Siberia to Malaysia. The Malaysians call it *latah*, the Yakut *amurak*, the Tungus *olon*. It is a matter of phenomena that belong to the generic category that in the past was called "loss of soul." This situation consists essentially of a sudden psychomotor attack that, without any apparent cause, triggers a split in the behavior of the individual who is the victim, spreads contagiously to others, and at its conclusion leaves the individual without any memory of what has happened. "A *latah* person, when his attention is attracted by the oscillating movement of branches shaken by the wind, will imitate this movement passively. Two *latah* surprised by an unexpected noise entered into a state of reciprocal mimetic automatism in which for about a half hour one continued to imitate the gestures of the other."[10]

The most significant characteristic of this psychological condition is the access of ecokinesia and ecolalia, which seize collectively those who "lose their soul." Ernesto De Martino cites an eyewitness account, "an interesting case of collective olonism is reported by V. L. Priklonsky. One day, during a parade of the Third Transbaikal Cossack Battalion, a detachment composed entirely of natives suddenly entered the *olon* condition. Instead of following the commands of the colonel, who was a Russian, it began to repeat them ecolalically. Naturally the colonel grew angry and showered his men with abuse. They, still in the same state of *olon*, repeated the abuse, too."[11]

The collective (because of the presence of a collectivity that is primed for and predisposed to the release of the trance) sinking into a state of psychological scission, with more or less violent psychosomatic effects, and the reemergence therefrom into a state of amnesia are two behavioral models that belong to the basic structure of trance states. Ordinarily, it happens in the course of a ritual, when the trance states are organized in the course of an ecstatic rite. These can come about, however, spontaneously, and in these cases they have been well defined as "prepossessions," or "nonritualized states of possession."[12]

Is this the psychic phenomenon described in the Homeric verses? Everything seems to point to this conclusion. That such situations of "prepossession" were present in Greek culture is documented on the basis of an extensive series of reports describing sudden "assaults" of demons on the minds of certain psycholabile subjects, even outside of organized ecstatic cults (like the Dionysiac one). A significant case of this crisis of collective delirium is the one narrated by Aristoxenos of Tarentum (fr. 117 Wehrli) apropos of an inexplicable ecstatic illness that spread like a contagion among the women of the region between Locris and Rhegium: "They fell into a trance to such an extent that sometimes, while they were seated and were feasting, they heard the voice, as it were, of someone who called them and at that they bounded away, out of their minds, and no one could stop them."

To conclude the analysis let us return to a point left in suspense that represents a signal of indirect proof for the interpretation here proposed. The suitors, says the text of the *Odyssey*, ate meat "bedabbled with blood" (αἱμοφό-ρυκτα). What is the meaning of this expression? Clearly the meat served at the table in the course of a feast cannot be raw. It is roasted (as, for that matter, is often said explicitly in the course of the poem when the alimentary exploits of the suitors are described). This apparent incongruity, which surely has the purpose of fantastic evocation and which introduces the torrent of blood that the seer Theoklymenos sees flowing on the walls and that will in fact inundate the palace of Odysseus at the end of the poem, can be explained on the basis of an intersection of narrative and contextual levels.

Siegfried Laser has already intuited, without, however, drawing all the exegetic conclusions from his intuition,[13] that here the rhapsode had in mind a particular cultural schema: the bloody sacrifice of raw flesh, or ὠμοφαγία, practiced in the Dionysiac sphere. This cultural schema was well known to the audience because it belonged to their cultural or in any case ideological system. Whether or not sacrifices of raw flesh happened in reality (a subject that will not be discussed here), they belonged to the Dionysiac myth and therefore formed part of the cultural horizon of the audience that the rhapsode addressed. At the point at which the requirements of the narrative force the rhapsode to describe a scene of collective madness that attacks the suitors,[14] having at his disposal in the compositional baggage of epic-rhapsodic poetry neither the formulaic instruments nor the narrative models for describing such episodes—which, as we have said, are quite remote from the compositional models of Homeric epic—he has recourse analogically to a system of ideas that was foreign to his poetry but immediately recognizable by the audience inside its own culture. The bloody meat in substance is a semantic-symbolic signal that is immediately perceived by the audience as an element inseparable from a scene of collective madness. The suitors, "separated from their minds" (cf. 20.346), victims of a collective delirium that distorts their features because of a divine intervention, live the same experience (of course, from a formal, narrative point of view) as those who participate in an ecstatic ritual.

In this perspective, the reference to omophagy, decontextualized from Dionysiac ritual, confirms in the mind of the public the message that the rhapsode wants to transmit. They are as mad as are the followers of Dionysus in the moment in which the god takes possession of them and (to use Euripides' words) "robs them of their senses" (παράκοποι φρενῶν).

Translated by Lowell Edmunds

The Proem of the Simonides Elegy on the Battle of Plataea (Sim. Frs. 10–18 W²) and the Circumstances of Its Performance

Antonio Aloni

INTRODUCTORY COMMENTS ON THE TEXT

This chapter offers a literary-historical, rather than a philological interpretation of the proem of the new Simonidean elegy on the Battle of Plataea (11 W²), the longest and best-preserved part of the poem.[1]

The text is a largely hypothetical text, the fruit of the editors' interpretation of the material available to them and of stopgaps proposed exempli gratia by West and by Parsons. However, while it appears impossible to reconstruct Simonides' actual words with any degree of certainty, one can outline the contents of the piece with some confidence (and, even more important, outline the structure of the elegy as a whole). So, while any aesthetic evaluation of the work is out of the question (apart, that is, from an appreciation of the high quality of the proem), one can discuss the reasons behind the composition, the way in which—and the audience for which—the elegy was composed.[2]

West's text is as follows:

παι[. .]ς .[. . . cὺ δ' ἤριπες, ὡς ὅτε πεύκην
    ἢ πίτυν ἐν βήc[caιc
ὑλοτόμοι τάμ[νωcι³
    πολλὸν δ' †ἤρῶc[
ἢ μέγα πένθ]ος λαὸν [ἐπέλλαβε· πολλὰ δ' ἐτίμων,   5
    καὶ μετὰ Πατρ]όκλου c' ἄ[γγεϊ κρύψαν ἐνί.⁴

οὐ δή τίς c' ἐδ]άμαccεν ἐφ[ημέριος βροτὸς αὐτός,
ἀλλ' ὑπ' Ἀπόλλ]ωνος χειρὶ [τυπεὶς ἐδάμης.⁵
Παλλὰς δ' ἐγγὺ]ς ἐοῦσα πε[ρικλεὲς ἄ]cτ[υ καθεῖλεν
cὺν δ' ῞Ηρη, Πρ]ιάμου παιcὶ χ[αλεπτ]όμ[εναι   10
εἵνεκ' Ἀλεξά]νδροιο κακόφρ[ονο]ς, ὡς τὸν [ἀλιτρόν
ἀλλὰ χρόνω]ι θείης ἅρμα καθεῖλε δίκ[ης.⁶
τοὶ δὲ πόλι]ν πέρcαντες ἀοίδιμον [οἴκαδ' ἵ]κοντο
φέρτατοι ἡρ]ώων ἀγέμαχοι Δαναοί[,
οἷcιν ἐπ' ἀθά]νατον κέχυται κλέος ἀν[δρὸς] ἔκητι⁷   15
ὃς παρ' ἰοπ]λοκάμων δέξατο Πιερίδ[ων
πᾶcαν ἀλη]θείην, καὶ επώνυμον οπ[λοτέρ]οιcιν
ποίης· ἡμ]ιθέων ὠκύμορον γενεή[ν.⁸
ἀλλὰ cὺ μὲ]ν νῦν χαῖρε, θεᾶς ἐρικυ[δέος υἱέ
κούρης εἰν]αλίου Νηρέος· αὐτὰρ ἐγώ[20
κικλήιcκω] c' ἐπίκουρον ἐμοί, π[ολυώνυμ]ε Μοῦcα,
εἴ πέρ γ' ἀν]θρώπων εὐχομένω[ν μέλεαι·
ἔντυνο]ν καὶ τόνδ[ε μελ]ίφρονα κ[όcμον ἀοι]δῆc
ἡμετ]έρης, ἵνα τις [μνή]cεται ὕ[cτερον αὖ
ἀνδρῶ]ν, οἳ Cπάρτ[ηι τε καὶ Ἑλλάδι δούλιον ἦμ]αρ   25
ἔcχον] ἀμυνόμ[ενοι μή τιν' ἰδεῖν φανερ]ῶ[c⁹
οὐδ' ἀρε]τῆς ἐλάθ[οντο φάτις δ' ἔχε]ν οὐρανομ[ήκ]ης,
καὶ κλέος ἀ]νθρώπων [ἔccετ]αι ἀθάνατο⟨ν⟩.
οἳ μὲν ἄρ' Εὐ]ρώταν κα[ὶ Cπάρτη]c ἄcτυ λιπόντ[ες
ὥρμηcαν] Ζηνὸς παιcὶ cὺν ἱπποδάμοις   30
Τυνδαρίδα]ιc ἥρωcι καὶ εὐρυβίηι Μενελάω[ι
ἐcθλοὶ πατ]ρώιης ἡγεμόνες π[ό]λεος,
τοὺς δ' υἱὸς θείοιο Κλεο]μβ[ρ]ότου ἔξ[α]γ' ἄριcτ[ος
                            ]αγ. Παυcανίης.
αἶψα δ' ἵκοντ' Ἰcθμὸ]ν καὶ ἐπικλέα ἔργα Κορίν[θ]ου   35
νήσου τ' ἐcχατιὴν] Τανταλίδεω Πέλοπος
καὶ Μέγαρ' ἀρχαίην Ν]ίcου πόλιν, ἔνθά περ ὤ[λλοι
                      ]φῦλα περικτιόνων
. . . .   .θεῶν τεράε]ccι πεποιθότες, οἳ δὲ cυν[όντες¹⁰
ἷκον Ἐλευcῖνος γῆς ἐ]ρατὸν πεδίον¹¹   40
Μηδείους γαίης Παν]δίονος ἐξε[λάcα]ντες
Ἰαμίδεω τέχναις μάν]τιος αντιθέου[¹²
                    ].ς δαμάcαντ[
                    ] ιείδομεν[
                    ω]νυμον α[45

[. . . and you fell, as when a larch]
  or pine-tree in the [lonely mountain] glades
is felled by woodcutters . . .
  and much . . .
[A great grief seized] the war-host; [much they honoured you,]
  [and with Patr]oclus' [ashes mingled yours.]
[It was no ordinary mortal] laid you low,
  ['twas by Apoll]o's hand [that you were struck.]
[Athena] was at [hand, and smote the famous t]ow[n]
  [with Hera: they were wro]th with Priam's sons
[because of P]aris' wickedness. The car of God's
  Justice o'ertakes [the sinner in the end.]
[And so] the valiant Danaans, [best of warri]ors,
  sacked the much-sung-of city, and came [home;]
[and they] are bathed in fame that cannot die, by grace
  [of one who from the dark-]tressed Muses had
the tru[th entire,] and made the heroes' short-lived race
  a theme familiar to younger men.
[But] now farewell, [thou son] of goddess glorious,
  [daughter] of Nereus of the sea, while I
[now summon] thee, i[llustriou]s Muse, to my support,
  [if thou hast any thought] for men who pray:
[fit ou]t, as is thy wont, this [grat]eful song-a[rray]
  [of mi]ne, so that rem[emberance is preserved]
of those who held the line for Spart[a and for Greece,]
  [that none should see] the da[y of slavery.]
They kept their co[urage, and their fame rose] heaven-high;
  [their glory in] the world [will] never die.
[From the Eu]rotas and from [Sparta's] town they [marched,]
  accompanied by Zeus' horsemasters sons,
[the Tyndarid] Heroes, and by Menelaus' strength,
  [those doughty] captains of [their fath]ers' folk,
led forth by [great Cleo]brotus' most noble son,
      . . . Pausanias.
[They quickly reached the Isthmus] and the famous land
  of Corinth, [furthest bounds] of Pelops' [isle,]
[and Megara, Ni]sus' [ancient] city, where the r[est]
  [from] the
  country round.

[the ome]ns giving
confidence,
[and together they reached Eleusis'] lovely plain,
driving [the Persians from Pan]dion's [land, by help]
of the most godlike se[er, the Iamid.]
. . . overcame . . .
        . . .
. . .[13]

One should again point out that the papyrus's pitiful state of preservation means that any argument based on it risks circularity. Once it is established that Simonides' poem refers to the Battle of Plataea, scholars necessarily have to fall back on Herodotus's account of the same event to understand the references in the poem, and (as I indicate below) those references are often fragmentary—the name of a person or a place, the context of a possible action—which means that they can only be clarified by appeal to the fuller account. For example, the reference to Corinth (fr. 11, line 35) inevitably leads one to fall back on Herodotus (9.19.1) and decide that Simonides is describing the arrival of the Spartans and other Peloponnesians at the Isthmus. Similarly, the probable (but not certain) mention of a seer (fr. 11, line 42) leads West to identify him as Teisamenos (Hd. 9.33–36), and to recognize in fragment 14 Teisamenos's prophecy as recorded by Herodotus (9.36).

INTRODUCTORY REMARKS ON THE ELEGY

The unusual content and structure of this elegy make it possible to offer a further contribution to the recent debate as to the occasions on which elegiac poetry was performed.[14] Nowadays nearly everyone is of the opinion that almost all the elegies that have come down to us were originally intended for symposia. Usually sung to the accompaniment of an aulos,[15] the elegy was the means by which the symposium group identified itself; it was a means of reflection and self-preparation as well as an incitement to action.

The contents of an elegy might thus vary a great deal. Sometimes the elegy could be an almost abstract reflection on the values that govern the lives and behavior of men; at other times it might be the exemplary narration of past events—be they part of the remote past or contemporary events that were well known to the audience. With regard to the Ionian elegy of the seventh and sixth centuries, Vetta has drawn up a schema showing how the different types of elegy essentially reflect the spread and evolution of the institution of the symposium:

1. Callinus's elegies go together with symposia that were practically councils held by military commanders—still fairly similar to the sort of assemblies described in the *Iliad*. The Callinus elegy is "poetry of exhortation, outside a narrative context, freed from the intrusion of myths and without the intrusion of personal themes."

2. In the symposia of Archilochus and his companions in colonial military adventures, the fundamental point is the shared experience of the poet and his audience; it is that which becomes the subject of the narrative and the subsequent reflection upon it.

3. Finally there is the Mimnermus symposium, which is less directed toward action and more inclined to generalization and reflection. This is a more intimate form of symposium, from which the themes of public life, of politics and war, seem to be excluded. And if they are present, they are filtered through an attitude that is pensive, sometimes even sorrowful.[16]

This schema of symposium types could, with a few variations (different emphasis on the elements of political and philosophical reflection), cover all the symposia that we know to have been the destined audience for other types of elegy that have come down to us (from Solon to Theognis and Xenophanes).

Not all elegiac poetry was, however, destined for a symposium public. There are fragments in which the first-person voice of the poem seems to affirm a function for the elegy outside the context of a symposium.[17] But quite apart from that, there is the sizable group of historical/narrative elegies: Mimnermus composed a *Smyrneis* celebrating the foundation of that city; Tyrtaeus composed a *Politeia* (or *Eunomia*) that was, in part, dedicated to the deeds of Sparta during the Messenian wars; Semonides told the story of his native country in an *Archaeology of the Samians*; in the fifth century there were also elegies composed by Simonides—one dedicated to the Battle of Artemisium (frs. 1–4 W²) and the one now under discussion on the Battle of Plataea.[18] Later, Panyassis wrote a *History of Ionia*, which started from the mythical figures of Codrus and Neleus to then recount the foundation of the various Ionic cities on the Anatolian coast (this work—more than 7,000 lines—may have been in stichic pentameters or, more probably, elegiac distichs). Again in the fifth century, Ion of Chios wrote a *Foundation of Chios*, which there is good reason to believe was an elegiac poem.[19]

Poems of hundreds or thousands of lines, which give an unbroken narrative of historical events, are ill-suited to the atmosphere of a symposium (which might be characterized as both dialogic and agonal). In the strictly sympotic elegy—for example, that written by Theognis—brevity was an essential feature, a result of the egalitarian nature of the gathering and of the fact that the speaker and audience of the poem were continually alternating roles.[20]

What is more, while there is almost no trace of the mourning that numerous sources give as one of the most ancient characteristics of the elegy,[21] there can be no doubt that there was once a functional link between elegiac compositions and threnody. Proof of this is to be had from Page's work on the Doric elegy,[22] and also from Andromache's lament in Euripides' tragedy (lines 103–16), a piece not only recognized as a "threnos" by ancient scholars[23] but also referred to as such within the tragedy itself.[24] In effect, there is no reason why a symposium could not have been an occasion for the sorrowful and consolatory meditation upon the passing of family, friends, or companions in arms and political allies. There is, in fact, internal evidence that the lament of which Archilochus's fragment 13 W[2] is a part was destined for a symposium in which Pericles participated (particularly significant here is the address to Pericles himself). The symposium, however, was essentially a private occasion; threnody and the consolation of elegy were there exercised on a private scale. As the tradition of the Doric elegy shows, there was also a very important public role for such threnody.

In other words, along with the more strictly sympotic form of elegy one has also to consider two elegiac forms that could be destined for a wider public: the historical elegy (which is much longer than the sympotic elegy) and the threnodic elegy. The dominant function of the latter was consolatory; its forms length, diction, etc.) and content are still largely unknown to us, but we do know they varied according to occasion—from symposia to public ceremonies of mourning.

According to Bowie, the large-scale elegy recounting historical events would have been performed in public competition—above all at civic or Panhellenic celebrations.[25] This means that in civic celebrations from the seventh century onward (and, doubtless, well into the fifth century) the recital of an elegy was an alternative to the *epos*. Instead of dealing with the Age of Heroes, the work would have dealt with the more recent history of the city and its territories. Between the two poetic forms there was a temporal difference. At times, however, more or less sizable parts of these historical elegies might be used in symposia; single episodes abstracted from a longer poem might be freely rewritten and presented by an individual singer at a symposium.[26]

To be consistent with his theory of a public elegy of historical narrative, Bowie rules out the existence of elegiac threnodies to express mourning and offer consolation. However, here I think his otherwise excellent analysis falls into excessive formalism: a particular type of subject matter is associated with occasions and functions that, for a given poetic form, are predetermined by the subject matter itself.[27] A historical narrative elegy lies halfway between the performance of an epic and the ἀπόδεξις associated with Herodotus's work.[28] All three have certain features in common: they are directed to a large public and are intended to reinforce the collective memory. However, there was nothing to prevent historical narrative elegy being used in public or private ceremonies of mourning and compensation[29]—through song and remembering— for the deaths of individuals and the misfortunes of the community. And this, quite apart from formal considerations, was the essential role of the threnos.[30] It is significant that such a role was the main purpose of a particular form of elegy—the tombstone inscription.[31] While nonoral and not designed for collective consumption (in theory, at least, the reader of an inscription is always alone), a tombstone inscription is both intended for the public (anyone who is literate can read it) and serves to console the living and celebrate the memory of the dead. That these inscriptions, intended for public use, tend to be written in elegiac distichs is an indication that it was traditional to use elegiac meter for such purposes.

The new Simonidean elegy dedicated to the Battle of Plataea seems to show that historical narrative elegy and threnody were not necessarily mutually exclusive. The historical narrative was used for largely threnodic purposes to mourn the dead of the battle and to glorify their memory.

SIMONIDES' ELEGY

To understand how content and form go together to give us a "pragmatic" definition of Simonides' elegy—that is, to enable us to identify the communicative space for which it was composed—it is best to start from the features that Bowie says are characteristic of the narrative elegy destined for public performance.[32] These features are all to be found in Simonides' poem, but the particular ways in which they are employed give us a clear indication of the function and intended audience of the elegy.

Apart from length, the essential features seem to be the presence of a proem and the use of direct speech. The latter seems the flimsier of the defining characteristics: while it is true that there is no direct speech in the sympotic elegies known to us (see, e.g., Theognis's elegy), it is also true that in other works that were definitely intended for symposia (e.g., Archilochus's epodes) direct speech was used regularly.

However, the explicit testimony of firsthand witnesses and also the material that has come down to us does seem to confirm that it was only historical narrative elegy that made allowance for characters (apart from the narrative "I") to speak in the first person. This is the case with the "king" who is supposed to have talked to the main characters in fragment 13a W² of Mimnermus, and also of fragment 2 W² from Tyrtaeus's *Eunomia*.[33] As far as the proem is concerned, Bowie's source is Pausanias (9.29.4), who refers to a proem at the beginning of Mimnermus's elegy ἐc τὴν μάχην . . . τὴν Cμυρναίων πρὸc Γύγην τε καὶ Λυδούc.[34]

This outline seems to be borne out by Simonides' elegy, where there is no dialogue between narrator and addressee but there is an ample proem—the twenty final lines of which are in fragment 11 W². What is more, in West's reconstruction of the poem, fragment 14 W²—Teisamenos's supposed prophecy—is in direct speech.

Of the features of narrative elegy, however, the proem is most significant and interesting; it is that which enables us to investigate and understand the function and intended audience of the whole poem.

The Epic and the Lyrical Proem

The term *proem* is used to refer to a song or part of a song which introduces the poem—be it epic or lyrical—and puts it in context.

The so-called *Homeric Hymns* are independent proems, probably hypertrophic with respect to their original function, within the context of a festival dedicated to a specific god, to introduce a poem whose content may not have been strictly linked to the theme of the festival.[35] In the performance of epic poetry, the recital passed from a proem dedicated to the god celebrated to a traditional hexametrical tale (usually on a heroic subject)—in other words, to a section (whose length varied according to circumstances) taken from individual poems or cycles of poems, such as the *Iliad* or the *Thebaid*.

The proem to lyric poetry served other purposes. In some cases it made it possible to use, within one festival, songs that had been, or could be, performed on other occasions; in other cases—above all, with the epinicia—the proem was an opportunity for the poet to talk about himself, about the victor of the games, or about the actual festival taking place.

The typical features of the epic proem, which vary only slightly in the lyrical proem, are:

1. A double opening invocation of both the god celebrated and of the Muses, to whom the poet acknowledges his subjection and then appeals for inspiration.

2. An explicit—and, for the epos, exceptional—first-person presence of the poet, with possible references to the occasion for his poetic performance.

3. A fairly fixed procedure for moving on to the main body of the poem. In its full form, this includes:

    a. a farewell to the god(s) (normally χαῖρε is used);

    b. a prayer for the victory for the song;

    c. reference to the passage to another song (usually introduced with an expression such as αὐτὰρ ἐγώ).

Between the initial invocation of and the final farewell to the god, the epic proem contains a section that describes his or her attributes, or narrates the mythical events associated with his or her birth or the god's mythical deeds.[36] The extension of this section made it possible for the epic proem to evolve from an introductory section subordinate to the song that followed it to an almost independent poetic form in its own right. In fact, apart from those cases where the mythical section is missing or else reduced to a mere list of the god's names (*Hymn Hom.* 21–25), the length of the narrative section can vary a great deal. *Hymn* 18, for example, which is dedicated to Hermes, takes only 5 lines to tell the story of the union of Zeus and Maia from which the god was born, while the longer *Hymn to Hermes* (4) takes 570 lines to narrate the birth and early adventures of the god.

THE PROEM TO SIMONIDES' ELEGY

The elegiac proem shows significant differences from, as well as similarities to, the epic proem, particularly in the final section. First, as in epic, the addressee of the proem, Achilles, is invoked with the second person (line 19, χαῖρε). The proem narrative deals with the fundamental point of Achilles' existence, of his status as a hero—the Trojan War and the warrior's death at the hands of Apollo. The Muses are invoked at the end of the proem to assist the poet—present in the first person—in this song dedicated to the men who saved Greece from the barbarian. We do not know if the Muses had already been invoked at the beginning of the proem, but it seems likely.

Diction and theme are other areas in which the conclusion of Simonides' proem is extraordinarily similar to the corresponding section in an epic proem: the addressee is bidden farewell (line 19, ἀλλὰ σὺ μὲ]ν νῦν χαῖρε, θεᾶς ἐρι-κυ[δέος υἱέ), in terms that follow the usual wording of the farewells in the *Homeric Hymns* (e.g., *Hymn Ap.* 545, καὶ σὺ μὲν οὕτω χαῖρε, Διὸς καὶ Λητοῦς υἱέ). The farewell is followed immediately by an invocation of the Muses and the announcement of the poet's undertaking in the following song (lines 20–24); this "open" ending to the proem is introduced by the formula αὐτὰρ ἐγώ. Exactly the same transition is to be found at the end of no less than thirteen *Homeric Hymns*.

So much for the similarities. The differences consist mainly in the fact that the addressee is not a god but a hero, a demigod who could not avoid the common fate of mortals.[37]

What is more, the invocation of the Muses is complicated by the fact that they are mentioned as the source of the words of the poet who guaranteed the κλέος of Achilles and the Greeks—that is, they revealed πᾶσαν ἀληθείην to Homer (cf. the very probable reconstruction of line 17)—and thus are called upon (precisely because of that previous role) to assist the present poet in his endeavors.

So the usual model—in which the proem proceeds from an invocation of a god to the recognition that it is the Muses who guarantee κλέος, by inspiring the poet's song—is slightly modified by the introduction of a mortal in place of a god, and by the reference to the prestigious, exemplary figure of Homer. For the reading I am attempting to outline here, these are decisive differences.

The allusion to the poet of the *Iliad* and the *Odyssey* is important for many reasons. First, it reveals how, by the time of Simonides, the epic tradition concerning the Trojan War had become centered on the work of one author, behind whom there was only the divine, omniscient voice of the Muses. Simonides does not consider Homer as merely the author of two poems (which even then were already known by the names of the *Iliad* and the *Odyssey*), but as the origin of the most prestigious tradition relating the events of the Trojan War. In fact, Simonides' text seems to dwell upon two events, the death of Achilles and the fall of Troy, which are certainly not at the center of the Homeric poems.

The naming of the author of the epic stories of Achilles and the Greeks is central to the affirmation of the epos as Panhellenic poetry, which is not subject to the constant recomposition and modifications essential to local and family traditions.[38] Here one might compare Simonides' Panhellenic tendency with Pindar's (in a poetic, not political, sense) and his inclination to attribute to contemporary victors in games or military exploits a glory similar to that which the heroes of the past earned through their deeds.

The mention of Homer, however, serves not only to identify the function of the two poets (Homer and Simonides); in the specific case of this poem, the two are distinguished by their different relationships with the Muses. Even allowing for the uncertainty of the text we have, there is no doubt that Homer παρ' ἰοπ]λοκάμων δέξατο Πιερίδ[ων / πᾶϲαν ἀλη]θείην, or, in any case, the revelation of the song (lines 16–17). Simonides, on the other hand, limits himself to calling upon the Muse for help (line 21, κικλήϲκω] ϲ' ἐπίκουρον ἐμοί, π[ολυώνυμ]ε Μοῦϲα).

The reason for the difference between these two positions is to be found in the subject matter of the poems. Homer could not have been a witness to the events at Troy and therefore relied entirely on the Muses for the truth of his account; Simonides, on the other hand, did witness the Greek war against the Persians and so needs the Muse's help only to guarantee the ability of his poetry to render the truth and thus confer lasting fame on those who took part in the events narrated.

We can see a similar attitude in an Archilochus elegy (fr. 1 W²): while proudly affirming his own "recognition" of the sweet gift of the Muses, the poet distinguishes between such recognition and total dependency. (The latter is, however, his position with regard to the God of War.)[39]

PROEM AND OCCASION

From the foregoing it is perhaps possible to define the occasion for which Simonides' elegy was composed.[40] The stylistic and structural similarities between its proem and that of an epic poem indicate that this work was for public performance at some solemn occasion. This hypothesis is also borne out by the length of the poem and by the Panhellenic characteristics (exemplified by the reference to the figure of Homer) of the task the poet sets himself. This Panhellenism consists mainly in rejecting any local or biased use of the glory achieved by the Greeks who won the Battle of Plataea—hence the reference to the supreme example of poetry glorifying the united operation of various Greek powers against a common foe.[41]

Further light is thrown on the function (and thus the intended occasion) of the elegy by the "pragmatic" orientation of the proem. Unlike an epic proem, this one addresses not the Muses and a god but the Muses and a mortal, Achilles (and with him Patroclus), who appears as the addressee of the song, which records the glories of the Trojan adventure. But Achilles, the most valiant of the heroes, was not among those who took Troy; his mortal span came to an end before the heroes leapt from the horse to color the Trojan night with fire and blood. So the poet's song counterbalances the end of Achilles' existence with the event—the fall of Troy—that was made possible by his death (and which made the hero all the more worthy of glory and remembrance). There is an unbroken circularity between the κλέος of the hero sacrificed to his own destiny, the κλέος of the undertaking that Achilles and the other heroes brought to fruition at the cost of their own lives, and the κλέος that the poet's song renews and projects forward through the course of time. The song and the κλέος to which it bears witness are compensation for the terrible events that put an end to the lives of Achilles, Patroclus, and the other heroes who perished before the walls of Troy. This same mechanism can be seen in Pindar's epinicia, which often narrate the events leading up to the foundation of the Panhellenic games. The poet's song not only compensates the victorious athlete for his labors, it also renews the fame of the games, which in their turn are compensation and reparation for the original mournful event that was the *aition* of the games themselves.[42] The cyclical repetition of the games is the expression of a culture that saw athletic competitions, the contests of ancient heroes and contemporaries, as playing a central role in the "working out" of collective mourning—and of the sense of guilt that accompanies mourning. The games were above all essential in the struggle between the human desire for eternity (survival) and the inevitable caesura of physical death.

The models for this signification of the funeral games can be found in epinicia and even more in epic poetry. In Homer's poems there is a ritual continuation to the funerals of Achilles and Patroclus: the games held in honor of the dead. However brief, the account of Achilles' funeral given at the end of the *Odyssey* (24.36–94) brings out the clear link between the funeral rites, the athletic games, and the continuance through time of the dead man's κλέος. After having mentioned the magnificent gifts Thetis offers to the victors of the games held in honor of her son, Agamemnon concludes with a statement that makes the link clear (lines 93–94): ὣς σὺ μὲν οὐδὲ θανὼν ὄνομ' ὤλεσας, ἀλλά τοι αἰεὶ / πάντας ἐπ' ἀνθρώπους κλέος ἔσσεται ἐσθλόν, Ἀχιλλεῦ ("Thus not even in death, Achilles, has your name perished, but forever, among all men, you will have a noble fame").

In short, in ancient Greece the games were a fundamental occasion for affirming the survival of the dead beyond the moment of their death. So the games are a sort of nonverbal communication, fulfilling the same role as that fulfilled verbally by the epinicia and the threnos. Obviously, athletic competition and celebratory song went together, as is clear from Hesiod's account of the journey to Calchis to take part in the ἄεθλα in honor of the hero Amphidamas (*OD* 654–59).

If we move from athletic competitions to war, we can see the same ideological presuppositions behind the attribution and communication of a warrior's κλέος. The song is the compensation, the λύτρον for the πόνος, the combatant's labors. Such πόνος achieves its highest expression when it culminates in the warrior's death, which is a glorious sacrifice that makes victory possible. It is significant that, in both war and athletic games, defeat is not communicated. Just as the games had no second prizes or any other form of consolation for defeat (if anything, subsequent victory was the only consolation for a past defeat), so the voice of the poet does not sing the virtues and valorous deeds of the defeated—which must have existed.[43]

In the song that accompanies the ritual, the dead warrior's κλέος is nothing other than a present-day expression of the κλέος of the great warriors (the heroes and ancestors) of the past.[44] This is the cultural context within which one has to read threnodic poetry, whose function was the exaltation of the dead man's κλέος.

However, such identification of a contemporary's worth with the worth of an ancient hero was soon in conflict with the isonomy practiced in late archaic Greek cities; after, it appeared especially at odds with legislation that was, to some extent, democratic.[45] Public forms of mourning (and the performance of commemorative poetry connected with them) were either banned or rigorously controlled in a number of Greek cities. In democratic Athens, all those who had died in war were commemorated together in the *logos epitaphios*; while in Sparta a hero's funeral (with the appropriate poetic performances) was the exclusive privilege of kings.[46]

In the specific—and better-documented—case of Athens, we know that this contradiction had already generated a series of laws in the sixth century. Traditionally attributed to Solon (Plut. *Sol.* 12 and 21), these laws were intended to put a stop to the excesses funeral ceremonies might give rise to—and privately commissioned threnodic poetry in honor of individuals was one such "excess."

The aim was not to limit private display of wealth per se, but to clamp down on poetic performances that could have political consequences and which gave rise to competitiveness between different groups and clans—all determined to outdo each other in this particular form of public communication.[47]

It is in this context that we have to understand the spread of tombstone inscriptions.[48] Once opulent ceremonies in commemoration of an individual were forbidden (for political reasons), private citizens had to look for another way of publicly announcing and maintaining the glory of the deceased. The new medium was the tomb itself—in particular, the funeral monument and the inscription upon it (which "preserved" the dead man's name and worth).

The fact that these inscriptions are almost all in dactylic meter (hexametric and, above all, elegiac) is further confirmation of the ideological purpose behind the emergence and spread of this practice, which was intended to proclaim and preserve the dead man's κλέος.

The fact that Achilles is given as the addressee of the proem makes it possible to outline the main purpose of the elegy. An account of the Battle of Plataea, the poem emphasizes a parallel between it and the Trojan War (and, in particular, focuses on Achilles as a symbol of those who took part in both undertakings). The main function of the elegy, therefore, is threnodic; its purpose is compensation and atonement with regard to those who died at Plataea, warriors whose death raises them to the level of heroes. I will look at the question of who might have commissioned the elegy, but first I want to stress how the risks of partiality (which were inherent in threnody and all forms of ἔπαινος)[49] are avoided here by the clearly Panhellenic nature of both the mythical and contemporary events referred to. Achilles does not serve as the heroic paradigm for a particular warrior;[50] he is the model for all those who are mourned and praised—those whose death made victory over the Persians possible.

These elements combine to suggest that the original occasion of Simonides' elegy was an event commemorating the Battle of Plataea itself, one of those ceremonies that, according to our sources, were organized to celebrate the memory of those who fell in battle.

The course of the Battle of Plataea was rather odd; yet, though hardly a model of military tactics, the event did result in the death of the supreme commander of the Persian forces in Greece (who had been left in charge after Xerxes' retreat), and the numerous solemn celebrations held afterward show that the Greeks realized that, with the death of Mardonius, the threat of a permanent Persian presence on Greek soil had passed forever. According to our sources, Simonides composed various contributions to these celebrations: the two epigrams that, according to Pausanias (9.2.5), were inscribed on the tombs of the Athenian and Spartan dead are attributed to him, though with some reservations.[51]

The first inscription for the Athenians, says ("Simonides" 8 FGE = A.P. 7.253):

εἰ τὸ καλῶϲ θνήϲκειν ἀρετῆϲ μέροϲ ἐϲτὶ μέγιϲτον,
    ἡμῖν ἐκ πάντων τοῦτ' ἀπένειμε τύχη·
Ἑλλάδι γὰρ ϲπεύδοντεϲ ἐλευθερίην περιθεῖναι
    κείμεθ' ἀγηράντῳ χρώμενοι εὐλογίῃ.

If a valiant death is the greatest part of virtue,
 Fate has granted us that above all others;
Fighting to gain liberty for Greece,
 we lie here enveloped in a fame that cannot grow old.

The Spartan inscription reads ("Simonides" 9 FGE = *A.P.* 7.251):

ἄϲβεϲτον κλέοϲ οἵδε φίλῃ περὶ πατρίδι θέντεϲ
 κυάνεον θανάτου ἀμφεβάλοντο νέφοϲ·
οὐδὲ τεθνᾶϲι θανόντεϲ, ἐπεί ϲφ' ἀρετὴ καθύπερθε
 κυδαίνουϲ' ἀνάγει δώματοϲ ἐξ Ἀίδεω.

Undying fame these men gave to their beloved fatherland.
 They put on the dark cloud of death.
Yet dead, they are not dead; their valor
 Gives them glory and brings them back from Hades.

What is noteworthy about the two inscriptions is that neither explicitly names the fatherland of the dead warriors: in one case there is a reference to Greece, in the other to the "beloved fatherland" (which could be the city-state or all of Greece). In other words, the inscriptions (in all probability composed soon after the war) reveal none of the conflicts and jealousies that marked nearly every moment of the alliance between Athens and Sparta.

The same can be seen in other inscriptions which, even if not by Simonides, reveal what must have been a common point of view in the period just after the battle. One of these inscriptions is that which the Athenians and Spartans together had raised on the altar of Zeus Eleutherios at Plataea ("Simonides" 15 FGE = *A.P.* 6.50).[52] The other ("Simonides" 17 FGE = *A.P.* 6.197)[53] is that which the Spartan commander Pausanias had inscribed on the tripod the Greeks dedicated at Delphi after their victory. This latter inscription was subsequently erased by order of the Spartans; in it Pausanias is described as "commander of the Greeks" and, without any reference to Sparta or its allies, is said to have destroyed "the armies of the Persians."[54]

In short, it seems that for once the Greek cities—Athens and Sparta in particular—had abandoned their strong sense of civic identity, of city rivalry. The frequent references to Hellas or the "fatherland"—or even the "common fatherland"—seems to reflect unusual political harmony. This is not contradicted by the Spartan commander's inclination to take all the credit for the Greek victory for himself, without any reference to his city-state.

However, our historical sources would seem to deny that there was any such political idyll in relations between the Greek allies: Herodotus, Diodorus (who bases his account on Ephorus), and Plutarch all paint a picture of soured relations.[55] The allies seem to have been continually exchanging accusations of double-dealing, opportunism, fence-sitting, or even worse. Plutarch (*Arist.* 20) tells us that after the battle there was almost a brawl as a result of a discussion as to which of the allies had fought most valiantly. Plutarch (*De Herod. malign.* 872d–e) also explicitly accuses Herodotus (and thus Athens) of having given a distorted account of the battle, diminishing or totally denying the contributions made by cities other than Athens and Sparta.

One has, therefore, to reassess the political Panhellenism that is supposed to have reigned at the time of Plataea. Immediately after the battle, each of the allies—and, above all, men such as Pausanias, Themistocles, and Aristides, who had played a leading part in events—all tried to use the victory (and the unity that had made it possible) for their own ends. The references to Hellas and to "the beloved fatherland" turn out to be nothing but a cover for the scheming of military leaders (and of Themistocles and Pausanias in particular), who do not always seem to have had the interests of even their own city-states closest to heart. In fact, as a result of their scheming, both Themistocles and Pausanias would, within a few short years, lose all their power and be condemned as traitors by their respective cities. Even the alliance between Athens and Sparta—solemnly sworn in 481 B.C. (Hdt. 7.145)—soon revealed its limits; for each of the two cities, or at least for Athens, the war against the Persians became an opportunity and pretext for trying to assert hegemony over the entire Greek world. Just two years after Plataea, Athens was pushing for the establishment of the Delian League, a maritime alliance that served anti-Spartan ends; in a very short time the League was less a weapon to be used against the Persians than an Athenian tool for imposing hegemony on the other Greek city-states.

It is in this context of political ambiguity and tension that we have to understand who commissioned Simonides' elegy and what occasion it was intended for. The dates in our possession may be of some help here.

Plutarch quotes the lines describing the courage of the Corinthians (*De Herod. malign.* 872d–e) and then makes certain specific points:[56] the elegy was not commissioned by the Corinthians, nor does it narrate only the deeds of the Corinthian soldiers. This means, among other things, that the Corinthians were not the central characters of the elegiac narrative but ony appeared as one among several other allied contingents (probably in a sort of list given before the battle). What is more, Plutarch emphasizes that he considers the elegy totally trustworthy, a veritable piece of history writing. So, on the one hand, the elegy appeared to Plutarch at least[57] as impartial and free of interference from those who had commissioned it; on the other, there is no doubt that it must have been commissioned (B. Gentili has shown the fundamental role of commissions in early and classical Greek poetry; public performances and the profession of poet depended on them). However flimsy a lead, this clue is a starting point from which to identify who commissioned the elegy, who paid the poet. It is probable that Plutarch himself did not know; but his ignorance can be explained by reasons of chronology. It is more interesting that Herodotus appears not to know of the poem (or, as Plutarch insinuates, chose to ignore it); nor does he appear to have been familiar with a number of events that took place after the battle (and which are referred to by Plutarch). It is always very difficult to give the reasons why facts are passed over in silence; sometimes this can simply be a question of which sources were available to a historian. In Herodotus's case the sources were mainly oral,[58] and there is no doubt that they placed little or no importance on Simonides' elegy (or perhaps they had simply forgotten about it). All of which means, as we shall see, that it is fairly unlikely that the poem was commissioned by Athens.

Some of the characteristics of the proem that have already been outlined go together very well with the apparent Panhellenic feeling that (at least according to Plut. *Arist.* 21) marked the celebrations held immediately after the battle. The construction of tumuli to commemorate the fallen, and the erection by the victorious Greeks of a common altar to Zeus Eleutherios could have been the occasion for the elegy, given the magnificence of the celebrations, which involved the establishment of the Eleutheria, a quadrennial festival that included athletic competitions.

The celebrations were also an occasion for reconfirming the anti-Persian alliance—this time as an offensive rather than defensive pact. There are many open questions as to the actual contents of these celebrations, with regard not only to the festival and competitions, but also to the political decisions that may have accompanied them.[59] However, some of the clauses in the decree establishing the festival (sacrifice to Zeus Eleutherios, honors paid to the tombs of the fallen, the inviolability of Plataea), which Plutarch ascribes to Aristides (*Arist.* 21), are also implicit in some cursory comments in Thucydides (2.71.2; 3.58.4–5; 3.68.1)—with one small but very important difference: the place of Aristides is taken by the Spartan Pausanias. And, in effect, the dominance of Pausanias and the Spartans would seem to fit better with what we know of the situation: in 472, Aeschylus (*Pers.* 817) was still describing the victory of Plataea as Δωρίδος λόγχης ὕπο. In short, it is highly probable that the tumuli and tombs erected immediately after the battle, as attested by Herodotus (9.85), were consecrated in a solemn ceremony presided over by the commander of the victorious army—a ceremony that would have been the perfect setting for the performance of an elegy.

The occasion combined both the celebration of victory and mourning for the dead, and fits perfectly well with the subject matter and addressee of the proem: the conquest of Troy figures not merely as a great military victory but also as the altar on which the greatest of the Greek heroes sacrificed themselves (with Achilles and Patroclus the greatest of them all). The narrative of the proem would act as the *aition* for the ceremony, and the song would, at one and the same time, be a compensation for the death of the ancient heroes and of those who had just fallen in battle. What is more, each city—or, at least, Athens and Sparta—offered specific homage to its own dead through the inscriptions on the tumuli.

OCCASION AND COMMISSION

The state of the text that has come down to us makes it difficult to offer any more precise suggestions as to who might have commissioned the work. However, there is no doubt that the beginning of the narrative proper (fr. 11.25ff. W²) is happy to dwell on the march of the Spartan army from the Isthmus. The mention of its departure (fr. 11.29 W², οἳ μὲν ἄρ' Εὐ]ρώταν κα[ὶ Cπάρτη]ϲ ἄϲτυ λιπόντ[εϲ) is followed by a precise reference to the divine or heroic figures charged with protecting the expedition; and the names of the Dioscuri and Menelaus call to mind the most noble and ancient glories of the city. Immediately afterward two entire lines are dedicated to the genealogy and virtues of the Spartan commander Pausanias (fr. 11.33–34 W², τοὺϲ δ' υἱὸϲ θείοιο Κλεο]μ-β[ρ]ότου ἔξ[α]γ' ἄριϲτ[οϲ / . . .]αγ. Παυϲανίηϲ). The other allies from the Peloponnese must have been dealt with rather summarily (fr. 11.37–38 W², ἔνθά περ ὤ[λλοι / . . .] φῦλα περικτιόνων). And while the present state of the text means we have no knowledge of how the Athenians are introduced onto the scene, it is probable that they are already present by line 41 (the mention of Pandion bears out this supposition: Παν]δίονοϲ ἐξε[λάϲα]ντεϲ); their appearance, therefore, is given much less emphasis than that of the Spartan army.

Given this Spartan bias, it is worth looking at the reconstruction West proposes for lines 25–26, which would make the argument for a Spartan commission unavoidable: the reconstruction would, in fact, have the soldiers at Plataea saving "Sparta and Hellas" from barbarian slavery (οἳ Cπάρτ[ηι τε καὶ Ἑλλάδι δούλιον ἦμ]αρ / ἔϲχον] ἀμυνόμενοι κτλ). Obviously this reading of the lines is only hypothetical and any argument based on it must be treated with caution. However, it does fit in perfectly with the text we have and also echoes a connection (Ἑλλάδι καὶ Μεγαρεῦϲιν ἐλεύθερον ἇμαρ ἀέξειν / ἱέμενοι κτλ) to be found in an epigram—naturally attributed to Simonides (16.1–2 FGE = A.P.)[60]—commissioned by the city of Megara to commemorate those of its citizens who fell in the Persian wars. Placed immediately after the invocation of the Muse (line 23, ἔντυνο]ν καὶ τόνδ[ε μελ]ίφρονα κ[όϲμον ἀο]ιδῆϲ) and the declaration of the purpose of the song (lines 24–25, ἵνα τιϲ [μνή]ϲεται ὕ[ϲτερον αὖ / ἀνδρῶ]ν), the reference to the defenders of "Sparta and Hellas" makes that one city the central figure of the poem, the recipient of the glory and fame conferred by the elegy.

Fragment 13 W[2] lends further support to the possibility of a Spartan commission (even if the evidence is partially concealed by the state of the text: of its thirteen lines, only the left halves of lines 8–12 are legible, and even then with difficulty).[61] While an overall interpretation of the text is impossible, it is significant that in lines 8–10[62] a contrast is drawn between the Persians and Medes on the one hand and the sons of Dorus and Heracles (that is, the Spartans and Peloponnesians in general) on the other. In other words, here again the elegy puts special emphasis on the Spartans and their allies in the Peloponnesian League.[63]

It is difficult at this point not to try and give a precise interpretation of what those who commissioned the elegy expected of it.

While commissioning Simonides to write the inscription for the monument at Plataea and for the tripod at Delphi, the Spartans and/or Pausanias also commissioned an elegy that commemorated the dead and celebrated their victory "in situ"—a work that transformed the battle into an episode in the history of the "Greek people," made it into an event comparable with the victory achieved over Troy by the heroes of old.

In all probability neither his decades of experience as a professional poet nor his "octopus" *mêtis* could prevent Simonides from showing bias in favor of those who had commissioned the elegy.[64] This may have had something to do with the fact that only a couple of years later—even after yet another victory for one of his dithyrambs at the Dionysia[65]—the poet chose to end his career a long way from Athens. At this point it seems fairly safe to conclude that Pausanias was directly involved in the commissioning of the elegy. In this case there is a curious parallel between the subsequent fates of poet and patron. Pausanias was declared an enemy of Sparta, hounded to death, and even then subject to a sort of *damnatio memoriae* (the Athenians themselves had never been particularly fond of him); Simonides thought it best to take himself off to Sicily (or perhaps he was "helped" to reach that conclusion). Of the elegy itself there is not a trace in what is our main source of information on the Battle of Plataea—the work of

Herodotus. The explanation seems clear enough: with the waning of Pausanias's star, the oral narratives of the events connected with the Battle of Plataea (whether pro-Athenian or pro-Spartan) would have drastically reduced the importance attached to the disgraced general—and it was those oral narratives that were Herodotus's main source material. The deliberate "slighting" of Pausanias would also have meant that nonessential facts and events that were too closely connected with his name were "blacked out"—and one such event was the commissioning and performance of Simonides' elegy.

CONCLUSION

If the interpretation I have put forward is well founded, then one has to admit that the new Simonides elegy makes a substantial contribution to our knowledge of archaic elegy, though it does not resolve all the problems raised. In a certain sense one might say that the situation now is even more complicated than before.

In fact, what we have here is a narrative elegy on a historical subject, destined to serve as a threnody for public performance.

The variations in the proem—the epic schema of poetic "I" versus the "you" of a divine addressee plus the Muse(s) being complicated by the presence of a hero addressee (Achilles) and the evocation of Homer (source of the songs of the Trojan War)—are decisive in regard to the conclusions reached. Both variations have a paradigmatic value and function. Homer symbolizes the truth of his account of the Trojan War, the model of truth against which the poetic "I" measures himself. Achilles—and with him Patroclus and all the other heroes who died at Troy—is the model for those referred to in the poem; his eternal glory gives a meaning to the sacrifice of those who died at Plataea (they too share in the common fate of all heroes: courage and death). The essence of the elegy's threnodic function is the celebration of the fallen soldiers' heroic glory and fame.

I therefore believe that Simonides' elegy makes clear, once and for all, the links between elegy and the religious practices, which numerous sources tell us were involved in the mourning for and celebration of the dead.

However, the elegy does not enable us to trace a continuous, unambiguous line linking compositions such as Archilochus fragment 13 W^2 with Andromache's threnodic lament in Euripides' tragedy. And then, of course, there are the other poems—the elegies of Echembrotus, Sacadas, and Olympus—of which we have no direct knowledge and about which, therefore, it is best to offer no theories. It is possible, however, to outline a framework that embraces different forms of elegy, wtih the metrical form and the function of mourning giving rise to various types of "performance" (determined by nothing other than the nature of the specific occasion and the combined intentions of both poet and patron). Within this framework the elegy as a form can be recognized as supplying the function of the threnos (whose means and methods of performance it also takes over). Nevertheless, one should not forget that the elegy and elegiac performance were not the only means of expressing threnos.

In other words, we have no firm evidence for claiming that there was no choral threnodic elegy (or elegy *tout court*). Nor, as a consequence, can we be certain that the elegy under discussion was not choral;[66] no evidence in the text enables us to decide one way or the other. However, the comparison established in the proem between the first-person voice and Homer would seem to suggest that the introductory section at least was monodic. We have no evidence with regard to the presence—or, more important, the significance—of the first-person voice in the historical narrative.

Finally, the recent controversy over the forms of performance of the Pindaric epinician should make us very wary of any conclusion that tends to establish a cast-iron link between poetic meter, occasion of composition, and forms of performance. Created as tools for the rather abstract—though worthy—task of library classification, the categories of "genre" are on this occasion rather misleading, ignoring as they do that the ways in which the songs were performed were determined mainly by practical considerations, on the basis of flexible and pragmatic criteria.

The Seal of Theognis

Lowell Edmunds

Κύρνε, σοφιζομένῳ μὲν ἐμοὶ σφρηγὶς ἐπικείσθω
τοῖσδ᾽ ἔπεσιν - λήσει δ᾽ οὔποτε κλεπτόμενα,   20
οὐδέ τις ἀλλάξει κάκιον τοὐσθλοῦ παρέοντος,
ὧδε δὲ πᾶς τις ἐρεῖ· "Θεύγνιδός ἐστιν ἔπη
τοῦ Μεγαρέως"· πάντας δὲ κατ᾽ ἀνθρώπους ὀνομαστός·
ἀστοῖσιν δ᾽ οὔπω πᾶσιν ἁδεῖν δύναμαι.
οὐδὲν θαυμαστὸν Πολυπαΐδη· οὐδὲ γὰρ ὁ Ζεὺς   25
οὔθ᾽ ὕων πάντεσσ᾽ ἀνδάνει οὔτ᾽ ἀνέχων.¹

Kyrnos, as I practice my poetic skill let a seal be placed
upon these verses. No one will steal them and get away with it;
nor will anyone substitute an inferior verse for the good one that is
   there,
and, in this way, everyone will say: "They are the verses of Theognis
the Megarian; he is renowned amongst all people."²
But I cannot yet please all my fellow townsmen.
It is not surprising, son of Polypais. For Zeus
does not please everyone either raining or holding back.

Poet, audience, performance: Each word becomes a question for the seal of
Theognis, by which a proprietary claim, not yet defined to everyone's satisfac-
tion, is asserted. The status of the *poet,* apparently the most secure item in these
lines, has recently been called into question by scholars who hold that "Theognis" is the name not of a historical Megarian aristocrat but of a traditional
authority.³ Even if there was a historical Theognis, the Theognidea, an "anthology of anthologies," to use Franco Ferrari's expression, might go back ultimately not to the publication by a poet of a book of poems but to the kind of
sympotic handbook discernible in Athenaeus 15.694d–696a⁴ and in a papyrus
of the third century B.C. found at Elephantine;⁵ and sympotic "chains" have
been enucleated in the Theognidea.⁶ Thus the *performance* envisaged by the

collection—which is made explicit at lines 237–54—is at symposia, and the *audience* is the group of symposiasts on any occasion on which poems from the Theognidea are recited or sung and not a readership. Are lines 19–23, then, the only poem in the Theognidea that, as referring to the handbook itself (τοῖσδ᾽ ἔπεσιν, 20), is not intended for performance and unperformable? Are these lines conceived of as written?

In the context of such questions, this essay continues the discussion of the seal of Theognis, beginning with a critique of two widely held opinions, one concerning the relation of the seal of Theognis to other supposed poetic seals, the other concerning the name of Theognis as the seal to which lines 19–23 refer. The second half of this essay, building on the results of the first, presents arguments for the new interpretation referred to above: "Theognis" is the name not of the author of a book but of a traditional authority, a rubric under which disparate, heterogeneous poems were collected.

THE NAME AND THE SEAL

The seal of Theognis is not taken as a unique case but is considered a standard form of authorial self-identification in archaic Greek poetry. Pollux, writing in the second century A.D., stated that Terpandros had divided the citharodic nomos into seven parts, of which the penultimate was the "sphragis" (4.66). The discovery of Timotheos's *Persae* appeared to confirm Pollux's statement. The seven parts were discernible in this poem, and the name of Timotheos appeared in the proper place (line 241).[7] In consequence, the sphragis was held to be a normal form of poetic self-identification, and sphragis came to be predicable of all self-references and self-identifications in archaic Greek poetry.

Two principal assumptions were entailed: first, that Timotheos's self-naming had its ultimate precedent in Terpandros in the seventh century B.C.;[8] second, that Terpandros's practice established the poet's name as the sphragis. These assumptions underlie Wilamowitz's discussion of the sphragis in his edition of the *Persae* of 1903, and it was he who in effect established the sphragis as a standard feature of Greek literature. He believed that rhapsodic poetry had an earlier counterpart to the sphragis, and his evidence was the Homeric *Hymn to Apollo* 165–78, where, he said, the name of Homer would once have appeared.[9] He believed that Demodokos, Phokylides, and Theognis were guided by the same intention as the kitharodoi (even though the elegiac sphragis comes at the beginning of the couplet, in the case of the first two poets just named, or of the book, in the case of Theognis, whereas the lyric sphragis comes toward the end of the poem). The influence of Wilamowitz was decisive for Wolf Aly's article on the sphragis in Pauly-Wissowa, where we find such statements as: "Eine richtige σ[φραγίς] bildet der blinde Sänger auf den Apollon hymn. Hom. 1,165ff." Aly accommodates Hesiod's *Theogony* 22–34 and *Works and Days* 694 and also Alkman's numerous self-references to the category of the sphragis. The reflex of such views is apparent in the handbook of Greek literature most widely used in the English-speaking world, that of Albin Lesky. He reasons as follows concerning the Theognidean sphragis: "In the Delphic nome [i.e., the citharodic nome I have discussed] the seal was the part in which the poet spoke of himself. Consequently we must take the poet's mention of his own name [i.e., line 22] as being the seal of authenticity."[10]

Lesky's notion of the sphragis, which càn also be found in other standard handbooks, is open to doubt. In the first place, it should be remembered that in archaic Greek poetry the word *sphragis* occurs in relation to poetic practice only in Theognis 19. When *sphragis* is applied to other passages in archaic poets, it is a term borrowed from Pollux. We ought to distinguish between the use of σφρηγίς in Theognis and the various so-called sphragides in other archaic poets. In the second place, given this distinction, we ought not to infer from the practice of Timotheos that the sphragis is the poet's name.[11] We do not even know if Timotheos thought of his self-naming as a sphragis. Lesky had no right to the inference concerning Theognis's seal that he drew from "the Delphic nome." In the third place, the various putative sphragides in archaic poetry must be analyzed in relation to their own genres before they can be assimilated to one another. For example, from the generic point of view, there is no reason to put the *Homeric Hymn to Apollo* 165–78 in the same category as Theognis 19–23. It happens that the immortalizing topos employed by the poet of the *Hymn* (174–75) has a counterpart in Theognis. It is not, however, in the "seal." The shared tradition appears in the Theognidea in the poem in which Kyrnos is promised immortality (237–54). Both poets promise undying *kleos* (*Hymn. Hom. Ap.* 174; *Theog.* 245). The names of Kyrnos and of the Deliades will travel everywhere (ὅσσον ἐπ' αἶαν / ἀνθρώπων στρεψόμεσθα πόλεις εὖ ναιεταώσας, *Hymn. Hom. Ap.* 174–75; ἄφθιτον ἀνθρώποις αἰὲν ἔχων ὄνομα / Κύρνε, καθ' Ἑλλάδα γῆν στρωφώμενος, *Theog.* 246–47).[12]

In the preceding discussion of the sphragis as a feature of archaic Greek poetry, the importance of the poet's name has already emerged. In the case of the seal of Theognis, it is indeed the name of Theognis to which lines 19–23 are now commonly taken to refer. To cite the opinion that is probably most authoritative in the English-speaking world, that of Leonard E. Woodbury, "Evidently, he desired . . . to attach his name to his verses, and so to perpetuate himself." The seal "was not to make his book secure against omissions, interpolations, or alterations in the future; . . . but rather to stamp" his verses "forever as his property by affixing to them his name, which they would proclaim to all posterity."[13] In order to reach this conclusion concerning the seal as a metaphor for the poet's name, Woodbury had quite properly considered the uses of seals in archaic and classical Greece, which would determine the possible literal senses of *sphragis* and thus the possible metaphoric senses, and had concluded that "the seal attests ownership."[14]

This conclusion concerning the use of seals should be reexamined. On the basis of a survey of archaic gems, John Boardman stated: "The repetition of closely similar devices on seals tells . . . against widespread or serious use of them as personal signets."[15] Furthermore, contrary to the impression given by Woodbury's discussion, names of owners (in the form εἰμί plus the genitive), as distinguished from names of makers, are a rarity on gems and signet rings.[16] The list of such names that I have been able to construct includes only five items, and, in one case, the name was added long after the making of the ring.[17] The sole example cited by Woodbury, which, he says, "well illustrates" the state of affairs, is in fact exceptional: Θέρσιός ἐμι σᾶμα· μή με ἄνοιγε. The command, "Do not open me," is, so far as I know, unparalleled on a seal, and the name of the owner is, to repeat, unusual. Seals are "essentially non-written tokens."[18] In short, to place a seal on something was not, by itself, the same as placing a name on it. Nor does the nature of archaic seals, as described by Boardman, suggest that the seal was an appropriate metaphor for a signature. But it is in any case unlikely that the notion of the autograph, the signature—improbable in the absence of cursive writing—was available to be the subject of a metaphor. The use of the autograph to attest authorship did not become common until well into the fourth century B.C.[19]

The main practical function of seals, as it appears in fifth-century sources, was to prevent something from being opened or tampered with, not to assert a particular person's ownership.[20] Containers and doors were sealed as a deterrent measure,[21] as were letters (Eur. *IA* 325; Thuc. 1.132.5). A passage in Aristophanes' *Knights* shows that the steward of a household had the use of his master's signet ring (947). The steward would have used the ring to seal things that were inside the house, not for the purpose of showing that his master owned them, but to keep the other slaves, who knew full well who the owner was, from stealing them. Thersis's signet states precisely the message of the seal: "Don't open me," and Theognis's assertion that his verses will be subject to neither plagiarism nor corruption corresponds to this use of the seal (20–21). It is difficult, however, to see how Theognis could intend to seal his book and thus render it inaccessible, when at the same time he proclaims his future Panhellenic fame, which presupposes the universal knowledge of his poems. An interpretation of Theognis's seal is required that would explain its simultaneous retentive and public aspects and that would also remove any trace of anachronism from Theognis's statement. Theognis should not be found to be making an anachronistic and futile claim to something like copyright. In the archaic period, a poet had no sure way of protecting a published text, written or oral, from borrowing, contamination, and alteration.[22] Nor did he have a way to ensure that the text would always be attributed to him.

The reinterpretation to be offered here begins with the antithesis, generally agreed on, between 19–23, in which the seal is asserted, and 24–26 (there is a subsidiary antithesis between 19–21 [me] and 22–23 [everyone]).[23] One of the contrasts established by the antithesis between the μὲν of line 19 and the δ(ὲ) of line 24 is between Theognis and his fellow citizens. This particular contrast is all the clearer if the pattern of thought in lines 19–23 is understood, with van Groningen, as follows:[24]

19 μὲν	A	me (Theognis), seal
20	B	no theft
21	B	no substitution
22–23	A	Theognis
24 δ(ὲ)		Megareans

The substance of the μὲν proposition of line 19 (seal of Theognis) reappears in 22–23 (Theognis's name)[25] and in this way reestablishes the antithesis with the δ(ὲ) proposition beginning in line 24, where Theognis says that he cannot yet please all his fellow citizens. The seal appears, then, as an aspect of the opposition, fundamental and pervasive in the rest of the Theognidea, between Theognis (19–23) and his fellow citizens (24; cf. especially 367–70). The seal is thus an aspect of his stance toward his native city.

Against the background of this antithesis, some plays on words can be perceived. In line 21, the words kakion 'inferior' and esthlon 'genuine' refer primarily to poetry,[26] but they are the same words that designate the fundamental social division in Megara (cf. line 35 in the poem immediately following the one under discussion).[27] Further, in line 24, where δ(ὲ) introduces the antithesis, the verb ἀδεῖν 'please', referring primarily to the intended effect of the poetry, has a political meaning (LSJ s.v. ἀνδάνειν II) 'to seem good to' a legislative body, 'to meet with approval'.[28] We could say, then, that, through these double entendres, Theognis is suggesting the stability of his aristocratic poetry even if its teaching has not been ratified in Megara. The seal itself might have connotations of social class. In Athenian Old Comedy, in the period of the radical democracy, seals are mocked as indications of wealth and ostentation.[29] In an earlier period, would not a beautiful carved gem have been the appurtenance of an aristocrat?

Another element of the antithesis in lines 19–24 is σοφιζομένῳ (19). Theognis is saying not simply, "Let me set a seal on these verses,"[30] but "Let me set a seal on these verses as I practice my *sophia*."[31] He thus refers to his poetic skill, which entails both technical ability[32] and also a strategy for dealing with the divisions within Megarian society alluded to in lines 24–26.[33] The strategy consists in composing poetry for the *agathoi*, in a manner that only they can understand and only if they possess a *sophia* corresponding to the poet's.[34] In the case of the metaphor of the ship of state (667–82), their *sophia* enables them to decipher the code and to get the message and thus to receive Theognis's warning concerning Megara.[35] But even when the message is not encoded but transparent, as in many Theognidean epigrams and poems, the ethical character of the poetry establishes a bond with a community sharing the same values. For example, in a four-line poem on the pursuit of wealth, a trusty companion is exhorted to keep a "prudent heart" (σώφρονα θῦμον, 754); in the end, he will praise (αἰνήσεις, 756) Theognis's poetry, persuaded by "its prudent utterance" (μύθῳ σώφρονι, 756).[36] The same adjective, σώφρων, applies both to the recipient of Theognis's poetry and to the poetry itself.

Furthermore, in this poem the concept of *ainos* links Theognis and his trusty companion. Although Theognis is usually the source of *ainos*, he is here the recipient. One can compare the phrase αἰδοῖ μειλιχίη, which in *Odyssey* 8.166–77 refers to an eloquent speaker (8.172) and in the well-known doublet of this passage, Hesiod's *Theogony* 79–83, refers not to the speaker but to the audience (92). Richard Martin has explained the susceptibility of this phrase to transposition: *aidos* is reciprocal; it belongs to both parties.[37] The same principle of reciprocity will explain Theognis's assertion that he, the self-styled wielder of *ainos*,[38] will also receive *ainos* (αἰνήσεις, 756). The poetry is deployed in a setting in which *ainos* and the shared values it entails already govern the relationship between Theognis and the intended recipients of this poetry. Under these conditions, then, Theognis can assert that his seal makes theft and substitution impossible. Any of the *agathoi* will recognize a verse of Theognis in a foreign context—let us say in a gnomology of the *kakoi*. Any *agathos* would recognize in Theognis's poetry a verse that expressed the ideology of the *kakoi*. The ethical character of the poetry establishes an unmistakable bond with the intended audience. The wordplay in line 21 is thus central to the strategy of Theognis, and the seal of Theognis is not his name but lies in the poetry itself.

The contrastive basis of the seal of Theognis also has a temporal dimension:

μὲν   A   present (σοφιζομένῳ, 19)
          B   future (22–23)
δ(ὲ)   B   future ("not yet," i.e., in the future [24])
          A   present (δύναμαι, 24)

The opposition between present and future that is articulated by the μὲν–δ(ὲ) antithesis can be seen as the diachronic projection of the political conflict from which the poetry of Theognis emerges: present resistance to Theognis and his values in a city divided between the noble and the base; future acceptance of Theognis and his values by everyone everywhere, including the Megarians (n.b., "not yet," 24). Theognis is the spokesman of a once and future aristocracy. There is a corresponding projection of the political conflict onto a time scale that extends into the past: present, precipitous decline of the polis, as base upstarts gain power; past superiority of the *agathoi*.[39] The opposition of Theognis and like-minded aristocrats to the upstarts in Megara is portrayed as a reaction to a political reversal that has taken place in Theognis's lifetime before his very eyes (cf. 53–62; 183–92). The base are now above the noble (679 and context). Many, perhaps most, readers of Theognis would understand this political reversal in terms of Megarian history and of the life of a historical poet, but the pattern of thought is familiar in Greek literature—and not only in Greek literature.[40] *Sic omnia fatis / in peius ruere*, or, as Hugo Williams said, "What a strange coincidence it is that everything always changes for the worse during the course of a single lifetime."[41]

I have discussed the seal in the context of lines 19–26. Lines 27–30, whether or not it is part of the same poem, as in West's edition, also belongs to the context.

σοὶ δ' ἐγὼ εὐφρονέων ὑποθήσομαι, οἷάπερ αὐτὸς
    Κύρν' ἀπὸ τῶν ἀγαθῶν παῖς ἔτ' ἐὼν ἔμαθον.
πέπνυσο, μηδ' αἰσχροῖσιν ἐπ' ἔργμασι μηδ' ἀδίκοισιν
    τιμὰς μηδ' ἀρετὰς ἕλκεο μηδ' ἄφενος.

Well-disposed to you, I shall give you such counsel as I myself
learned from the better sort when I was still a boy.
Be wise and do not either be shameful or by unjust deeds
amass honors or accomplishments or wealth.

The δ(ὲ) at line 27 can be taken as adversative: "But to you . . . ,"[42] that is, whereas Theognis cannot be a lawgiver to his fellow citizens (24–26), he can give advice to Kyrnos (27–30). Furthermore, with εὖ φρονέων 'being well-disposed' (line 27), Theognis suggests the situation in which that advice will be conveyed. In archaic sympotic poetry, the adjective εὔφρων and the noun εὐφροσύνη describe the mood of men at a banquet,[43] and these words can even be transferred to the wine itself.[44] *Eu phroneôn* evokes an institution of the Megarian aristocrats, namely, the symposium, the private gathering of *agathoi*, as against the city as a whole. Cf. εὔφρονα θυμὸν ἔχοντας and εὐφροσύνως διάγειν (765, 766) in a sympotic context (756–68).[45] Lines 31–36 immediately following the passage under discussion refer explicitly to dining with the *agathoi* and *esthloi*. Therefore, the phrase *eu phroneôn* that Theognis uses of his relation to Kyrnos functions similarly to the verb αἰνήσεις at line 756. Although the phrase refers grammatically only to Theognis, its valence extends to the other side of the sympotic relationship and includes the acceptance expected of Kyrnos.[46]

This political interpretation of the seal of Theognis is corroborated by the only other attestation of the word σφραγίς in elegy, where it is used in a context that includes a reference to legislation. In the *Life of Alkibiades*, Plutarch says that in his elegies Kritias reminded Alkibiades of the decree (*psêphisma*) for his recall that Kritias had proposed (33.1). Plutarch then quotes these lines (= fr. 5 W²):

γνώμην δ' ἥ σε κατήγαγ᾽, ἐγὼ ταύτην ἐν ἅπασιν
   εἶπον, καὶ γράψας τοὖργον ἔδρασα τόδε,
σφραγὶς δ' ἡμετέρης γλώσσης ἐπὶ τοίσδεσι κεῖται.

Mine was the proposal that brought you back; I made it in public;
I wrote the proposal and did this deed.
A seal of my tongue is placed upon the following.[47]

The comparison of this fragment with Theognis 19–26 is justified in the first place by the verbal parallels: σφραγὶς δ᾽ . . . ἐπὶ τοίσδεσι κεῖται and σφρηγὶς ἐπικείσθω / τοῖσδ᾽ ἔπεσιν. Consider also the contrast between poet and city in both Theognis and Kritias: ἐγὼ . . . ἐν ἅπασιν and σοφιζομένῳ μὲν ἐμοὶ . . . ἀστοῖσιν δ᾽ . . . πᾶσιν. In thus alluding to Theognis, Kritias would have wished to suggest Theognis's position in Megara as the historical or ideological model for his own role in Athens. As Mauro Tulli has said, we should imagine a sympotic occasion for the poem from which this fragment comes.[48] In other words, it is the small circle of Kritias's aristocratic friends who will appreciate this allusion to Theognis. The significance of the sphragis in the fragment is thus of great interest, and the context, where σφραγίς has the defining genitive γλώσσης, will provide an indication of that significance.[49] If the seal is defined as the "tongue" of Kritias, the problem of the seal is reduced to the problem of the semantics of "tongue." Tulli has shown convincingly that in this fragment it refers to the poet's individual style.

The "seal of my tongue" is therefore the mark, the imprint of the peculiar expressive habits of Kritias.[50] It is not Kritias's name. In this poem, Kritias would have had no reason to attach his name to the decree since his name would already have been a matter of public record. The first two verses of the fragment refer to the standard Athenian legislative procedure, which would have resulted in the publication of Kritias's name on a stele in the standard formula Κριτίας εἶπε (cf. Pl. *Phdr.* 258a). The sphragis is therefore distinguished from the public speech and the public record. The lost verses would have been in a style different from the one he used before the Ekklesia, and this style, not his name, is Kritias's seal.[51] The demonstrative τοίσδεσι refers to the following verses and these bear the seal.

To conclude this discussion of the relation of the name and the seal of Theognis, I have argued that the seal of Theognis is the political and ethical character of the poetry, which corresponds to the peculiar expressive habits of the historical person, Kritias, in a poem on a particular historical event. This reading of the seal does not exclude the notion of poetic skill, which σοφιζο-μένῳ μὲν ἐμοὶ surely entails. Contrary to Woodbury, however, who maintains that Theognis is talking about an immortality of fame as poet, I place much greater weight on Theognis's political and ethical stance, which emerges clearly if the seal is understood in the larger context of the antithesis between 19–23 and 24–26. The question of performance remains. While it is now generally agreed that the poems of the Theognidea were intended for recitation at symposia, lines 19–26 seems to have been composed as an introduction to a collection of poems. Are they then unperformable? It was observed above that, on Tulli's interpretation, the poem in which Kritias referred to the seal of his tongue was intended for performance at a symposium, and I believe that the seal of Theognis could likewise have been performed. Lines 19–26 has been composed in such a way that the passage can serve a double function, that of text for performance or recitation, and that of introduction to a collection.

The passage can serve this double function because it presupposes two different but noncontradictory time frames. One, which was analyzed above, is internal to the situation represented by the Theognidea: the present conflicts in the city of Megara and Theognis's relation to Kyrnos; the future fame and success of Theognis. Understood in this time frame, lines 19–26 is as readily available for performance by a symposiast impersonating Theognis as any other poem in the collection (cf. 237–54). The quotation in 22–23 skillfully leaves the identification of the poet to a future audience. The name is an inference to be drawn from the character of the poetry. The symposiast can "be" Theognis without having to refer to himself as "Theognis." The vocative Κύρνε at the beginning of the poem is already enough to establish the Theognidean warrant (19). The poet who composed these lines wanted to preserve the immediacy of the sympotic performance (cf. 237–54), and Woodbury was right that "everyman" in line 22 means all future symposiasts. But the reader or user of the collection at any point in the history of its reception operates within a second time frame. He would not be holding this book in his hands if the predicted fame of Theognis had not been realized.[52] In this second time frame, the name *Theognis* has a different function: now it gives the identification that was deferred, temporally and spatially, in the first time frame. Lines 19–26 is an introduction that validates the use of the collection for the aristocratic symposiast.[53]

One can suggest, furthermore, that the poet of the seal wanted subtly to mark the opposition between its oral, performative aspects and its written aspects. This opposition emerges especially in lines 22–23 and by way of the relation of these lines to Homer. While it is obvious that Theognis here uses Homeric formulas, the peculiarities of reuse and its effects will bear further observation. Theognis's ὧδε δὲ πᾶς τις ἐρεῖ (22) conflates two Homeric formulas that extend from the beginning of the line to one or the other of the caesuras in the third foot, one used to introduce a quotation, ὧδε δέ τις εἴπεσκε(ν) (*Il.* 2.271, etc.), the other used to end a quotation, ὥς ποτέ τις ἐρέει.[54] The second of these formulas occurs three times in the *Iliad*. Agamemnon uses it to conclude his quotation of the imagined future vaunt of a Trojan leaping on the tomb of Menelaos (4.182; cf. 4.176). Hector uses it in the leave-taking scene to conclude his quotation of the imagined words of someone who beholds Andromache as a slave woman (6.462). Hector uses it when he challenges the Achaeans to single combat: he concludes by imagining what someone will say in the future when he beholds the tomb of Hector's slain opponent (7.91; cf. 7.87). In each of these three examples, the speaker refers to someone else; the quotation concluded by the formula refers to someone who is now safe and sound or at least alive (Menelaos) but will be perceived in the future as a victim, a hero killed in combat, or a woman taken captive and enslaved. In Theognis, the Homeric formula is introductory, not concluding; the speaker, Theognis, refers to himself, not to someone else; and the quotation refers to the future perception of him as successful and universally famous. (Hector imagines himself as gaining immortal fame as the result of the individual combat [7.91] but the quotation is in the nature of an epitaph for the slain opponent.) Theognis thus reverses the connotations of the Homeric formula.

The interplay between Theognis and Homer is, however, more complex. In two of the three examples just discussed, the quotation has an epigrammatic quality.[55] Hector's imagined future speaker is a sailor on the Hellespont who sees on the shore the tumulus of Hector's slain foe. In keeping with the epic's silence about writing, the tumulus has no inscribed stele, and yet the words of the future speaker are in the style of the funerary epigram, which was typically composed in hexameters (often a single hexameter) or in elegiac couplets, and examples of which survive in the form of inscriptions on stone. The oral poetry of the *Iliad* thus, in the voice of Hector, imagines a future oral recollection of a slain hero which, however, anachronistically—from the point of view of the *Iliad*—is in the style of an inscription. (The imagined future speaker necessarily uses the third person to refer to the slain hero, whereas the inscription, if there had been one, would have been in the first-person singular, and the passer-by would have lent his voice to, would have performed, the epitaph.) In this way, the *Iliad* is able to incorporate written hexameter or elegy.[56] Turning to Theognis, the quotation introduced at lines 22–23 takes the epic model of quotation of a future speaker and remakes it for the purpose of entitling a written handbook or collection of poems. It is not only the model or the form of the quotation that is remade. The poet of the seal reuses, in the quotation, the formula πάντας ἐπ᾽ ἀνθρώπους (*Il.* 10.213, etc.) and reverses the Homeric usage of ὀνομαστός, which is only with a negative ("not to be named," "abominable"). Theognis thus matches the epic incorporation of written hexameter or elegy with an elegiac incorporation of oral epic. One of the effects of the future quotations in the *Iliad*, namely, to make an implicit contrast between written and oral poetry, is heightened in the seal of Theognis by the elaborate interplay between Homeric model and reuse thereof.

Robert Renehan has pointed out that Theognis, like Hesiod, names himself only once and that the names of both poets are to be found in the same verse (22) of their respective poems.[57] If, as Renehan suggests, the Theognidea in this way deliberately recalls Hesiod, then the seal has in the lines under discussion (22–23) managed to combine allusion to Homer with allusion to the other great poet of archaic hexameter. The poet of the seal in effect alludes to the two as the pair that they were traditionally held to be.[58] The particular manner of the allusion to Hesiod might presuppose that the poet of the seal has counted the lines of the *Theogony* in a written text. But no matter what the poet's method of observation of the position of the name of Hesiod, the parallel position of the name of Theognis, if deliberate, subtly calls attention to a new kind of composition—that is, in writing—that can create allusions of a new, almost learned kind, unlike the allusions to Homer in the same lines, which need only the reader's or listener's, so to speak, general memory of Homeric formulas. The allusion to Hesiod is probably opaque to the listening symposiast; it is only for a reader.

The "intertextual" relation of the seal to Homer and Hesiod would be another example of how Theognidean elegy deliberately distances itself from archaic hexameter poetry.[59] From this point of view, the apparently trivial change from the Homeric ἐρέει to ἐρεῖ (22)—that is, the change from the uncontracted to the contracted form, which is normal in elegiac Ionian for the group εει[60]—may acquire an emblematic value; likewise the contraction in Θεύγνιδος. The two contractions get emphasis from their placement on either side of the caesura.

AUTHOR OR AUTHORITY?

The lines which are addressed to Cyrnus all bear the stamp of a particular strong personality. We know nothing about him except what we are told in the poems: that his name was Theognis, his city Megara. His voice is that of an embittered aristocrat, a loser in the social upheavals of archaic Greece, warning his beloved Cyrnus against the violence and vulgarity of the lower orders and later, perhaps in exile, lamenting his poverty and calling for revenge.[61]

. . . [T]he seal of Theognis had as its prime function the codification and authorization of a body of gnomological poetry as representing the accepted standards and values of the *agathoi*. The name of Theognis guarantees not the origin of these *epe* but their homogeneous political character and their aristocratic provenience.[62]

An article of faith in Theognidean studies has been the existence of a core of poems in the Theognidea that are the work of a historical, if undatable, Megarian poet who lived through one of the periods, again undatable, of political turmoil in his native city. Ever since the edition of Welcker in 1826, scholarship on Theognis has been occupied with the problem of identifying the authentic poems of Theognis in the collection. Gregory Nagy presented a radical alternative in the 1980s when he suggested that "the figure of Theognis represents a cumulative synthesis of Megarian poetic traditions."[63] This alternative would not, however, require the scrapping of Knox's view given in the first quotation above. Rather, the personality described by Knox could be understood as a creation of the poetry, a persona. This persona is that of a poet, yes, but a poet who is as likely to utter Solon's or Mimnermos's or Tyrtaios's verses as his "own."[64] The voice of this poet is not that of an original genius but, to use Ford's term, that of a "traditional authority," to which poems reflecting a certain ideology can be attached.

The interpretation of the seal that I have proposed tends to support the view that Theognis is the name not of a poet but of a traditional authority. The closest analogues to the seal of Theognis, beside the fragment of Kritias already discussed, are certain epigrams of Hipparkhos, Phokylides, and Demodokos, where the name likewise indicates the authority for the saying and not its origin. Those of Hipparkhos (1–2 D³) are quoted by Sokrates in Plato, *Hipparchus* 229a–b: μνῆμα τόδ' Ἱππάρχου· στεῖχε δίκαια φρονῶν and μνῆμα τόδ' Ἱππάρχου· μὴ φίλον ἐξαπάτα. The point that Ford has made concerning the first of these, that its gnomic content is a commonplace and that the first half of the line is therefore unlikely to be an assertion of authorship,[65] can also be made concerning the second epigram: with the *gnômê*, compare Theognis 1220. Plato makes it clear what Hipparkhos was doing: "he made a selection [ἐκλεξάμενος] from his wisdom [*sophia*], both from that which he had learned and from that which he had discovered on his own, of that which he considered wisest, and he put it into elegiac couplets and had it inscribed on stone as his poetry and a display of his wisdom [*sophia*]" (228c–d). Neither Plato nor anyone else records any example of wisdom discovered by Hipparkhos on his own. The verb that Plato uses for "making a selection" suggests that Hipparkhos was working from a collection (cf. Xen. *Mem.* 1.6.14; Pl. *Leg.* 811a2). The possibility that the phrase "memorial of Hipparkhos" indicates *original* authorship is still further diminished by the fact that it refers also to the herm on which the epigram is inscribed.[66] Hipparkhos's motives, as apart from political self-interest and the vanity implied by Plato, for wishing to establish himself as an authority are a separate problem.[67] For present purposes, it is enough to remember that the tyrants Pittakos of Mytilene, Kleoboulos of Lindos, and Periandros of Corinth, as well as the Athenian statesman Solon, the Spartan ephor Khilon, and the statesman Bias of Priene, were also poets and belonged to one or another list of the Seven Sages.[68]

Hipparkhos is a historical figure whom we can behold in the act of appropriating traditional wisdom and attaching it to his name. The relevant epigrams of more shadowy figures, Phokylides and Demodokos, point in the same direction. There are six epigrams of Phokylides that began καὶ τόδε Φωκυλίδου/εω (1–6 D³). One of these is especially pertinent to the present discussion (1 D³):[69]

καὶ τόδε Φωκυλίδου· Λέριοι κακοί· οὐχ ὃ μέν, ὃς δ' οὔ·
πάντες, πλὴν Προκλέους· καὶ Προκλέης Λέριος.

The same epigram, in an unmetrical form and directed this time against the Chians, is attributed in the Palatine Anthology to Demodokos (11.235 = 2 D³):

καὶ τόδε Δημοδόκου· Χῖοι κακοί· οὐχ ὃ μέν, ὃς δ' οὔ·
πάντες, πλὴν Προκλέους· καὶ Προκλέης Χῖος.

The epigram quoted here in the versions of Phokylides and Demodokos is traditional. Its rhetorical and logical form appears also in Demodokos [3] W².[70] The attribution to one poet or another by the opening "signature" could not have been taken as an assertion of authorship. Rather, the name is an attempt to assign the epigram to a known authority. In the case of Phokylides, his status as a traditional authority is clear. He is mentioned by Isokrates along with Hesiod and Theognis as one of the best teachers of how men should live (2.43).[71] (Cf. Xenoph. fr. B10 D–K: "the teacher of most is Hesiod.")

The phrase καὶ τόδε Φωκυλίδου/εω/Δημοδόκου has a parallel in a fragment of the comic poet Susarion (1.1 K): ἀκούετε λεῴ· Σουσαρίων λέγει τάδε. After the first two words, this line is a variant of the same introductory formula found in Phokylides and Demodokos, and the words of Susarion, a proverb (κακὸν γυναῖκες κτλ., fr. 1.3–5 K), show that here again the formula introduces gnomological material.[72] Although the epigrams of Hipparkhos, Phokylides, and Demodokos discussed above and the fragment of Susarion are not true analogues to the seal of Theognis, they nevertheless provide good evidence that the name Theognis need not be taken as an assertion of authorship. The only true analogue to the seal of Theognis is the seal of Kritias, an imitation, I have argued, of Theognis's, which does not, however, include the name Kritias.

Further evidence for my argument concerning the name Theognis can be found in another, clumsier imitation of Theognis in pseudo-Epikharmos.[73] The very clumsiness of the imitation brings out traits that were felt to be important. The poet is introducing a collection of rhetorical and gnomological materials that will be useful for all occasions (1–7). He asserts that even one of his verses can be useful (8–9). He has been blamed for his inability to speak concisely (10–11). The present work will disprove this judgment of his abilities (12–14):

ταῦτα δὴ 'γὼν εἰσακούσας συντίθημι τὰν τέχναν
τάνδ', ὅπως εἴπῃ τις· Ἐπίχαρμος σοφός τις ἐγένετο,
πόλλ' ὃς εἶ]π' ἀστεῖα καὶ παντοῖα καθ' ἓν [ἔπος] λέγων.

Having heard these charges, I compose this technical treatise
in order that someone may say, "Epikharmos was a skillful man
who uttered all sorts of clever things, speaking them line by line."

The resemblances between this passage and the seals of Theognis and Kritias are (1) use of the first-person singular, which does not appear in Phokylides, Demodokos, Hipparkhos, or Susarion, and is rare in prose prooimia;[74] (2) the emphasis on the skill of the poet as the basis of his claim to fame (τέχναν 'technical treatise', σοφός 'skillful'); and (3) use of the present tense (συντίθημι or σοφιζομένῳ, Theognis 10, and κεῖται, Kritias fr. 1.3 W²), which represents the poet in the act of composing his verses—a conceit, since the seal, at least in the cases of Theognis and of pseudo-Epikharmos, introduces a collection of material already composed and in some sense already published. (Cf. the remarks on the two time frames of the seal above.) The following traits are specific to Theognis and pseudo-Epikharmos: (1) the expectation of future fame (ἐρεῖ, Theognis line 22; cf. the purpose clause in pseudo-Epikharmos line 13, which looks to the future—again a conceit, because only the present fame of the poet could have caused the creation of the gnomology; (2) the tactful maneuver by which the poet puts the expected praise in someone else's mouth; (3) the statement of the poet's name within this quotation of someone else's words—yet again a conceit, because no one would have read as far as line 13 of pseudo-Epikharmos without knowing that Epikharmos was the purported author. In the case of Theognis, the name Kyrnos, which is the very first word of the poem (line 19) would have been as useful as the name Theognis (line 22) as an indication of the source of the collection. In sum, the imitation of Theognis by pseudo-Epikharmos provides clear evidence for both of the main contentions of this chapter: on the basis of the analysis of Theognis lines 19–30 and of Kritias fr. 5 W², that the seal of Theognis is not the name Theognis; on the basis of the discussion of the seal of Theognis in the context of the other relevant self-identifications by poets, that the name indicates not an author but a traditional authority.[75]

The difference between author and authority may seem to be slight. What difference does it make if we call Theognis the authority for the poems in the Theognidea rather than their author? The answer is that the Theognidea can, if Theognis is a traditional authority, be regarded as from its origin a miscellaneous collection of gnomic lore for sympotic and didactic purposes and not as the unfortunate transmogrification of a unified book of poems by a historical poet. The Theognidea can then be grouped with other collections of traditional wisdom. Such collections are the sayings of the Seven Sages;[76] the Life of Aesop; the mythological *hupothêkai* (i.e., the lore attributed to heroes and to Kheiron the centaur);[77] and probably the poems attributed to figures like Phokylides, who, as observed above, is linked by Isokrates with Theognis and Hesiod as the source of *hupothêkai*.

One thing these collections have in common is their use of a framing narrative or some other contextualization for their wisdom. The Seven Sages are performers of their wisdom in relation either to one another or to the peoples whom they rule and guide.[78] In popular use, the Aesopic fable was enclosed in a narrative frame, which indicated how Aesop had used the story, and which thus carried, in effect, a model for the new situation to which the fable was applied: the circumstances under which Aesop used this fable correspond to the circumstances under which it is used again; the moral of the fable, clear in the narrative concerning Aesop, is the moral that the new addressee should derive.[79] The mythological *hupothêkai* purported to collect the wise counsel given by a hero (or centaur) to a younger man. The two fragments of Demodokos reported by West as genuine presuppose a context of conflict between the poet and the cities that he is blaming. Against this background of the framing of wisdom, the relations between Theognis and Kyrnos and between Theognis and Megara present themselves not as the creative or historical basis of the poetry but rather as a traditional device for the organization of wisdom.

Another shared trait is conflict or competition, either contextualized in a corpus or tradition, or between corpora or traditions. As for the first kind of conflict, Demodokos has just been mentioned. The Seven Sages are in competition with one another.[80] Aesop is in competition with his master, the pretentious philosopher Xanthos. As for the second kind, a fragment of the fourth-century comedian Alexis shows Aesop and Solon conversing (fr. 9 K = test. 33 Perry). Plutarch refers to their exchanges at the court of Kroisos (*Sol.* 28) and also presents Aesop in competition with the Seven Sages in the *Banquet of the Seven Sages*. The only trace of this kind of poetic competition envisaged within the perspective of the Theognidea is attached to the singing of a hymn (*humnos*): the contestants are Theognis and the otherwise unknown Akademos; the prize is a boy; and the setting is a symposium following a dinner (993–1002). Competition between *hupothêkai* or between poets to whom *hupothêkai* are attributed or between poets who appear in *hupothêkai* (Solon fr. 20.3 W², against Mimnermos, is exceptional), however, is not to be expected, for reasons to be given below. As Mark Griffith suggested, the Theognidea may even allude respectfully to the *hupothêkai* attached to the names Sisyphus, Rhadamanthys, and Nestor.[81] Outside wisdom poetry, conflict, both external and contextualized, was the norm: between Homer and Hesiod, between Hesiod and Perses, between Stesikhoros and Helen.[82]

The third shared trait is a strong tendency for the same material to appear in more than one collection, and this is the reason why competition is largely absent at the level of the gnomic material. Even though Aesop and the Seven Sages are sometimes presented as in conflict, there is a whole series of sayings that are attributed to both.[83] As remarked above, the Theognidea contains poems also attributed to Solon, Mimnermos, and Tyrtaios; and this collection also overlaps with the mythological *hupothêkai*.[84] For example, the thought of the popular skolion called the logos or melos of Admetos occurs again and again in the Theognidea:

Ἀδμήτου λόγον ὦ ἑταῖρε μαθὼν τοὺς ἀγαθοὺς φίλει,
τῶν δειλῶν δ' ἀπέχου γνοὺς ὅτι δειλοῖς ὀλίγη χάρις.

Having learned the saying of Admetos, my friend, hold dear the
  better sort,
and keep away from the ignoble in the knowledge that in them there
  is little grace.[85]

In some respects, the Theognidea also bears comparison with the collections of oracles attested for the archaic and classical periods. While, unlike the other collections just discussed, they are often said to be the possession of one person, a *khrêsmologos*, they could also belong to a clan (the Peisistratids) or a city (Sparta). They are sometimes attributed to a mythological figure (Musaios, Laios, Orpheus) or a legendary seer (Bakis, Lykos). The attribution of individual oracles to sources changed, as did the contents of the collections (sometimes through malfeasance, as when Lasos of Hermione exposed Onomakritos's fraudulent addition to the oracles of Mousaios: Hdt. 7.6.3). They could be used competitively, as a scene in Aristophanes' *Knights* shows: with the oracles of Glanis, "the elder brother of Bakis," the Sausage Seller defeats the Paphlagonian (Kleon), who has the oracles of Bakis (999–1099).[86]

CONCLUSION

The material just surveyed reflects two mutually reinforcing practices that undoubtedly go back to the archaic period. One is the educational use of *hupothêkai*. An Athenian red-figure kyathos of around 500–490 B.C. shows two young men listening to a third reading aloud from a papyrus roll. Next to the reader, on a chest, is another papyrus roll, on the side of which is written XIPONEIA, which is taken to mean the Hupothêkai (Precepts) of Kheiron.[87] It is a school scene, of which there are several other examples. The practice is attested in Xenophon, who ascribes to Sokrates the study of what we call gnomologies for the improvement of himself and his friends.[88] Just enough is known about these *hupothêkai* to show that they were in fact compilations, even if they go under the name of a known poet: the same material could be found in collections attributed to different sources. The other practice is the adaptation of passages of poetry for use at symposia. Aristophanes' *Wasps* provides a good illustration in Philokleon's preparations for dining with Kleon and his friends (1222–48), where Philokleon proposes to sing some verses of Alkaios (1234).[89] There is no reason to think that this sympotic reuse of the poets began with Philokleon. Both practices, be it noted, entail repetition with variation.

The Theognidea reflects both these practices, but whether it is a sympotic handbook that incorporates a gnomology or vice versa is impossible to say. In either case, however, its formation can be assumed to be at least as early as the fifth century, whatever the date of its stabilization in the form in which we have it. The simplest, most prudent hypothesis is that some part—it is impossible to say how large a part—goes back beyond Hellenistic and Byzantine editing to the practices described in the preceding paragraph. From this point of view, West's eight pages of parallels between lines 255–1022 and lines 1023–1220 could reflect an early generation of variants on similar themes, whether or not they also reflect "two compilers . . . working over the same portions of a larger anthology."[90] It is notable how many of these parallels are not verbal or formulaic but only thematic; and where they are verbal or formulaic, they can just as well be explained as going back to an oral phase of composition.[91]

For the foreseeable future, the central point of contention in the study of the Theognidea will be the existence of a quantum of "identifiable Theognis," to use West's term. If there is such a thing, then the sympotic handbook and the gnomology are built on a collection of poems originally issuing in one way or another from the hand of a historical poet. If, on the other hand, the Theognidea belongs to the genre of *hupothêkai*, then the poet Theognis is a mirage.[92]

APPENDIX

The admirable brief discussion of the seal of Theognis by Mark Griffith, "Personality in Hesiod," *CA* 2 (1983) 42–44, argues that Theognis's relation with Kyrnos is the basis of the seal. Theognis's primary purpose is not to name himself or assert a claim for his published work but to command the loyalty of Kyrnos. Griffith states that "the poet's main concern is not authenticity or the publication of his name . . . but his relation to his addressee and to his wider audience, who are to benefit from his special kind of wisdom." This interpretation of the seal is easily reconciled with the political interpretation that I offer, because the loyalty of Kyrnos is not simply erotic but is homologized (e.g., 1311–16) with *philia*, the most fundamental institution of aristocratic Megarean society. When Kyrnos betrays Theognis, he not only takes a new lover but also goes over to another group, another aristocratic faction. See Lowell Edmunds, "Theognis and Foucault," *Classical and Modern Literature* 8 (1988) 83.

An episode in Alec Le Vernoy, *Without Drums or Trumpets*, trans. C. P. Le Vernoy and Joyce Bailey (London: Sphere Books Ltd., 1990; first published by Michael Joseph Ltd., 1988), provides a remarkable parallel to the betrayal of Theognis by Kyrnos. Le Vernoy, a Gaullist officer in the Infanterie Coloniale, was captured on the beach at Algiers as he and two companions were about to sail for Gibraltar in a small boat, with the ultimate goal of joining the Free French in London. He was sent to Tunis Central Prison, in May 1942. He was placed in a ward holding about 150 men. He learned that the men were subdivided into groups and that everyone in the ward belonged to a "family" ruled by a chief. Each family had a clearly defined territory, where the members slept and shared their meals. One family would sometimes entertain another. There were also parties, with prescribed preparations and rituals, for the smoking of marijuana. The members of a family were bound to each other by the obligation of sharing and mutual support. The episode:

One morning, a young boy, the beloved concubine of my powerful Family Chief, was found to be missing. He had been kidnapped and had literally disappeared into the bosom of another family. Had he gone willingly or had he been torn away from the arms of his lover? The answer itself was irrelevant as the forsaken family was *ipso facto* dishonoured and each of its members felt personally cuckolded. It was a very grave matter. The priest spent his entire day in ineffective secret negotiations, but everyone held fast. During the day bargaining continued as secret deals were made by chiefs of the different families, forming and reforming alliances invisible to the guards, and most of the prisoners had no concept of what was going on. As night fell, the tension mounted; the men, absorbed in their thoughts, became dangerously quiet. When the lights were switched off the ward was engulfed in a deadly silence. Here and there an oil lamp gave a puddle of light and lit men's faces with a wan glimmer. The men stood at opposite ends of the room, according to the alliances concluded during the afternoon. Between them lay a black stretch of no man's land; neutrality was out of the question!

The offended Chief stepped out of the ranks and advanced like a Homeric figure to take his stance in front of the assembled enemy. He hurled abuse and threats at them and in the same breath demanded the return of his beloved. I suddenly became aware that everyone was armed and ready to fight. (72–73)

In the ensuing brawl, twenty were wounded and three killed—the betrayed chief, the boy in question, and the priest. The Theognidea does not contain a description of such a brawl, but the political organization of the prisoners and the role of pederasty in this organization may remind readers of the institutions of archaic Megara.

Prose Genres for the Performance of Traditional Wisdom in Ancient Greece: Proverb, Maxim, Apothegm

Joseph Russo

MY INVESTIGATION into "poet, public, and performance" takes an approach that I should explain and justify at the start. I am deliberately stretching the sense of *poet* to mean anyone who employs speech in an artistic or creative manner;[1] by *public* I mean the audience or receiver(s) of such speech; and *performance* has a double sense, being both the moment of utterance, a "speech event" shared by all present, and the specific artistic and authoritative "speech act" of someone who utters wisdom in a traditional verbal genre.[2]

Since our study of such speech in ancient cultures is limited to what has been recorded in writing, it is self-evident that the only performances we can study are those deemed worthy of preservation for their illustrative or anecdotal value by historians, biographers, and essayists, who offer them as "true," and those invented by playwrights, poets, and writers of literary dialogues like Plato, Xenophon, and Lucian, who offer them as fictitious in varying degree. (Of course, this dichotomy collapses along its line of demarcation between truth and fiction, since all these writers are to some extent fictionalizing social practice.) I am leaving aside representations of wisdom speech in metrical poetic form—for example, gnomic expression in Pindar, the tragedians, or Menander —for several reasons. First, their sheer bulk entitles them to monograph treatment in their own right (see, e.g., Lardinois's recently completed study of *gnômai* in archaic Greek poetry, note 6 below). Second, the force of poetic meter and diction may interfere with the verbal texture of the utterance. Third and most important, these formal poetic genres invoke a totally different concept of performance from that which I am using. They were performed in the traditional sense of that word, involving rehearsal and formal, expected recitation, whereas I am concerned with a poetics of prose performance that is radically different.

In concentrating on the creative use of prose rather than verse, I am following the way opened by some recent performance-oriented studies by American linguistic anthropologists and folklorists.[3] The artistry I am concerned with involves not only the careful choice and arrangement of words and sounds—virtues regularly attributed to poetry—but also the skillful matching of words, and often of metaphor, to a specific social moment, virtues found in only some poetic genres but in all interactive prose performances. For the wisdom genres that form my topic—proverb, maxim, and apothegm—it is precisely the aptness of this match of speech to situation and its compelling effect upon the audience that are the essential poetic-performative virtues, creating a speech event the Greeks found worth preserving in memory for its embodiment of some key cultural value.

WISDOM SPEECH

The creative and spontaneous prose performances I choose to call *wisdom speech* belong to the oral tradition that expresses communal beliefs and norms for behavior through commonly understood, formally specific verbal forms. These forms were most commonly recognized in ancient Greece under the names *paroimia*, *gnômê*, and *apophthegma*.[4] The first two correspond closely to the modern genres of proverb and maxim; the third, as I hope to demonstrate, begins with a meaning close to the modern sense of apothegm and evolves toward that of "anecdote," an elusive but documentable oral genre most often characterized by dialogic content and memorable concluding utterance.[5]

The widespread use of distinct but related genres for wisdom speech in prose has drawn little interest from Hellenists.[6] What is particularly lacking, from the perspective of my present argument, is attention to the project of encompassing all these forms of folk speech within a single category of wisdom speech, demarcating their boundaries and their overlap with one another, and understanding their utterance as essentially emergent and responsive to specific contexts. It seems that those whose interests are primarily philological, historical, or philosophical find little in them that is significant. But to the Hellenist with a folkloric or ethnographic vision, the identification of the formal features of these genres and the analysis of their poetics of performance offer an attractive opening to the discovery of an almost invisible realm of folk literature that permeates ancient Greek culture at a relatively modest level of performance. I say "modest" because the poetics of this literature requires a relatively minor artistry compared to that of the oral tradition behind the *Iliad* and the *Odyssey*. Nevertheless, once we recognize it as another characteristic product of the Greek genius for artful verbal and dramatic forging of social wisdom, we should agree that its forms deserve an important place in any canon of oral genres of ancient Greek folk literature—a canon which we Hellenists have not yet constructed in adequate detail.[7] A first task in determining the range and limits of such a canon must be to establish adequate definitions of the three genres in question and significant distinctions between them, as well as to note possible zones of overlapping reference.

PERFORMANCE

The wisdom-speech genres are, like most other Greek literature, performance genres, but not in the sense we attribute to the word *performance* when we think of literary genres like drama or epic or lyric poetry. For these, performance constitutes an elaborately framed and scheduled event, taking place before formally invited audiences in habitual settings, and involving some degree of rehearsal and memorization. But the "performance" enacted in the oral genres I am examining is not so much the province of the scholar trained as philologist or literary historian as it is of the linguist, anthropologist, or folklorist. I define this performance as *the optional and impromptu creative response to an important social and psychological situation*, the kind of performance that sociolinguists and folklorists characterize as "emergent."[8] In the words of the noted sociolinguist Dell Hymes, it is essential to understand "the performance as situated in a context, the performance as emergent, as unfolding or arising within that context . . . as something creative, realized, achieved, even transcendent of the ordinary course of events."[9] And yet their improvised and emergent character does not mean that the verbal utterances lack formal, structured artistry. In fact it is a characteristic of such performance that its verbal and dramatic artistry be subject to audience evaluation because it is based on recognized conventions. In a recent study of the "Seven Sages," Richard Martin has taken a similar ethnographic approach and offers the following definition of performance: "a public enactment, about important matters, in word or gesture, employing conventions and open to scrutiny and criticism, especially criticism of style."[10] While a definable act of audience evaluation is only occasionally present in our written records, we may take the very fact of the speech's preservation as a mark of admiration on the part of the widest conceivable audience—the culture as a collective whole—for a successful performance.

Let me now turn to the task of identifying some distinctive formal, aesthetic, contextual, and functional qualities of the proverb, maxim, and apothegm.

PROVERB

The proverb differs from the other two genres in that its author is always anonymous and its truth is most often metaphorically expressed. Thus, in English, "the pot calling the kettle black" and "a stitch in time saves nine" are typical metaphorical proverbs, using familiar household imagery to comment on human behavior, whereas "honesty is the best policy" or "time is money" represent the less common type that states truth literally in the form of abstract principles. Most modern paroemiologists are willing to count both types as genuine proverbs, although some scholars like to identify the nonmetaphorical statements as aphorisms or maxims,[11] a distinction that goes back to Aristotle (his criteria for distinguishing *gnômai* from *paroimiai* are discussed below under "Maxim"). But aside from the question of a fuzzy boundary between proverb and maxim in both English and Greek, defining the proverb presents still more serious problems. It seems that no brief definition can capture both proverb form and proverb function in a way that matches the amazing versatility of this tiny oral genre.[12]

The earliest definition in Western thought is that of Aristotle, who wrote a whole treatise (no longer extant) on proverbs. But a fragment from another lost treatise ("On Philosophy") is preserved in a quotation by Synesius (*Encom. calv.* 22 = fr. 13 Rose):

Ἀριστοτέλης φησίν, ὅτι παλαιᾶς εἰσι φιλοσοφίας ἐν ταῖς μεγίσταις ἀνθρώπων φθοραῖς ἀπολομένης ἐγκαταλείμματα, περισωθέντα διὰ συντομίαν καὶ δεξιότητα.

Aristotle says that they are remains of an ancient philosophy that was lost in major human disasters, [remains] preserved because of their concision and adroitness.

This definition stresses their value as wisdom and some aspects of their form, but omits any consideration of the dynamics of their use in social context, their important "performative" dimension. A fairly comprehensive modern definition may be achieved by combining two descriptive passages from Abrahams:[13]

Proverbs are short and witty traditional expressions that arise as part of everyday discourse . . . nearly always stated in the form of a single sentence. They are among the shortest forms of traditional expression that call attention to themselves as formal artistic entities. . . . Proverbs are descriptions that propose an attitude or a mode of action in relation to a recurrent social situation. They attempt to persuade by clarifying the situation, by giving it a name, thus indicating that the problem has arisen before and that past practice has come up with a workable solution.

As the common linguistic property of all speakers constituting any linguistic community, proverbs have no known author. Thus when any speaker, ancient or modern, uses a proverb, he or she is invoking the authority of cultural norms as embodied in inherited verbal formulas that were invented by no one but are known to everyone.[14] The speaker momentarily ceases to use a personal voice in the here and now and instead uses the voice of the shared cultural tradition. Modern linguistics scholars have noted a variety of "framing" devices to mark such departures, ranging from the simple "(as) they say" to the more subtle use of a different intonation from that of ordinary speech.

In ancient Greek texts we lack the elusive intonational dimension, but can find the more overt markers preserved by our authors. Thus, Greek speakers usually indicated that a proverb was being uttered by prefacing it with a formula like the simple τὸ λεγόμενον, or occasionally with a more elaborate version like that used by Gyges to Kandaules in Herodotus 1.7: "Many good things were discovered by our ancestors, among which is 'every one should mind his own affairs,'" σκοπέειν τινὰ τὰ ἑωυτοῦ.

Platonic dialogues and Aristophanic comedy, which both simulate everyday discourse, sometimes represent a speaker using a proverb to impress the validity of his viewpoint upon his addressee. The strategy behind such usage is usually fairly obvious and does not call for special analysis.[15] Other cases, however, become more complex. We may, for example, find a speaker using a proverb (or maxim) whose verbal texture subtly evokes themes or images already implicit in the dramatic situation; therefore full appreciation of the layers of meaning and the polysemy of the text demands some degree of analysis. Let us consider Herodotus's story (1.7–13) of how King Kandaules of Lydia, obsessed by his wife's beauty and the unnatural desire that his loyal officer Gyges be compelled to admire that beauty, forces Gyges to spy on her nakedness and ends up losing his throne and his life to Gyges through the contrivance of the outraged queen. This unusual story also has an unusual concentration of proverbs, with Gyges and Kandaules resorting to three proverbs within a few paragraphs. The first proverb, σκοπέειν τινὰ τὰ ἑωυτοῦ spoken by Gyges to Kandaules, carries a double meaning in σκοπέειν. In the proverb by itself, without context, the verb σκοπέειν would mean "pay attention to." But in the context in which it is applied the more literal and visual sense of σκοπέειν, "look at," comes through clearly, prepared for by the dense vocabulary of vision that immediately precedes it (εἶδος, εἴδεος, ὀφθαλμῶν, θεήσεαι γυμνήν, θεήσασθαι γυμνήν), and reinforced by Kandaules' sharply pointed proverb, "people's ears happen to be less reliable than their eyes," ὦτα γὰρ τυγχάνει ἀνθρώποισι ἐόντα ἀπιστότερα ὀφθαλμῶν.[16] Thus, a strongly voyeuristic motif animates the entire action.

In Gyges' second proverb, "a woman when she takes off her chiton takes off also her *aidôs*," ἅμα δὲ κιθῶνι ἐκδυομένῳ συνεκδύεται καὶ τὴν αἰδῶ γυνή, the meaning of *aidôs*—"sense of shame, modesty, decent respect"—is rendered ambivalent, or indeed polyvalent, as its meaning continually shifts with the unfolding of the story. First the queen, because she was seen naked, may be considered, following the proverb, as a woman stripped of simple *aidôs* in the sense that she has lost her personal "modesty" or "decency," which was violated through indecent exposure to an outsider's gaze. But next we are shown the reverse side: she is presented as a woman possessed of a supreme sense of personal shame because she feels so driven to avenge the outrage and restore her proper respect. And then again she may be seen as a woman indeed without *aidôs* (in the sense of decent respect for humane or community values), because she can so easily have her husband murdered through deceit and take another man into her bed! Some of this polyvalence is, to be sure, inherent in the semantics of the very word *aidôs*; but the shifting meanings, the play of ambiguity within the proverbial truth itself, are best highlighted through dramatic embodiment in continually unfolding narrative form, as Herodotus, ever the consummate storyteller, cleverly exploits the ambiguity of ethical choices faced by his characters.

Within this narrative artistry we should not overlook the purely verbal artistry of Herodotus's proverbial play. Kandaules' ὦτα γὰρ τυγχάνει ἀνθρώποισι ἐόντα ἀπιστότερα ὀφθαλμῶν is characterized throughout by strong repetition of t-consonants (τ, θ) and alphas. In addition the key word *anthrôpoisi*, the human focus of the general observation, is placed at the exact center, and introduces -nt- and -op- combinations that will reappear in *eonta* and *ophthalmôn*, as well as echoing the long omega that opened the proverb in its first syllable and will close it in the last. In Gyges' second proverb, word order is again artfully arranged so as to place the key action of "stripping" at the exact center, with the ironic movement from physical stripping of a garment to metaphorical stripping of virtue almost iconically rendered in the two long middle-voice verb forms that, lying adjacent to one another, flaunt their formal parallelism even as they refer to different realms of being.

Another example of the play of proverbial polysemy is in Herodotus 7.162, the dramatic moment when the Sicilian tyrant Gelon receives a delegation from the Greek alliance asking him, in the spirit of Panhellenism, to join in the battle against the Persian invader. Gelon, himself protected by geography from the threat of Persian incursions and untouched by any sense of obligation to defend mainland Greece (he has his own barbarians, the Carthaginians, to deal with), refuses to contribute any forces unless he is given chief military command of the entire coalition. When this vainglorious request is rejected by the Spartan and Athenian delegates, Gelon sums up the situation with wisdom speech in the form of a powerful metaphor: tell the Greeks, he says, that "her spring is taken from the year," ἐκ τοῦ ἐνιαυτοῦ τὸ ἔαρ ἐξαραίρηται, an utterance that is clearly a proverbial expression based on a folk metaphor.[17] Again there is subtle sound play at work within brief compass: *exarairêtai* seems phonetically to repeat and include, and so in iconic manner to swallow up, *ear*; the opening *ek* seems momentarily canceled by the initial *en-* of *eniautou*, but then reaffirmed by the initial *ex-* of *exarairêtai*; and so there may be subliminal punning on whether the Greek springtime of hope is "in" or "out." Even the exact echo of the article *tou* in the closing *-tou* of *eniautou* may contribute, in the realm of Jakobson's "sound shape of language," to the tension between affirmation and contradiction that subtly informs this entire utterance.

Herodotus as narrator feels immediately obliged to explain the metaphor and says simply that the loss of the finest season refers to the loss of the finest army, that of Gelon. But effective symbolism is polyvalent and open; it succeeds by tempting us to see widening circles of significance. In the statement "the spring is taken from the year," the reference to seasons of the year evokes the idea of cyclic recurrence. Thus the first implicit meaning is that this springtime of opportunity, once lost, will not be at hand again for some time. A deeper implication is that it cannot in fact return until the other seasons have been experienced, a cycle that must include winter, the harshest season. Hence Gelon's proverb speaks with two voices: a first voice simply pointing out opportunity lost, and a second, more subtle, voice conveying a warning of hardship to come.

MAXIM

A challenging, but ultimately not very rewarding, question is how to distinguish the proverb from the maxim. Most modern paroemiologists, as noted above, accept that proverbs come in both metaphorical and nonmetaphorical varieties and say that the second type are synonymous with maxims. Others prefer to see two distinct genres and follow more strictly the distinction made by Aristotle in his *Rhetoric*: "proverbs also are metaphors from one species to another" (καὶ αἱ παροιμίαι μεταφοραὶ ἀπ' εἴδους εἰς εἶδος εἰσίν, 3.11, 1413a15), whereas "a maxim is a statement not about a particular fact, such as the character of Iphicrates, but of a general nature . . . about such things as concern conduct and should be chosen or avoided in conduct" (ἐστὶ δ' ἡ γνώμη ἀπόφανσις, οὐ μέντοι οὔτε περὶ τῶν καθ' ἕκαστον, οἷον ποῖός τις Ἰφικράτης, ἀλλὰ καθόλου . . . περὶ ὅσων αἱ πράξεις εἰσί, καὶ αἱρετὰ ἢ φευκτά ἐστι πρὸς τὸ πράττειν, 2.21, 1394a22–26).[18] The difference amounts to very little, since the degree of metaphor may be ambiguous and both types of wisdom statement have the same "performance" function. Proverbs instruct or comment by using one topic or activity metaphorically to represent another (English, "all that glitters is not gold"; Greek, "the elephant doesn't catch a mouse," *CPG* 1.74), whereas maxims do the same by using a truism to imply coverage of all particular instances that may fall under the general heading (English "everything comes to him who waits"; Greek, "nothing to excess"). Aristotle was aware of the impossibility of clearly separating the two and allows for borderline cases, saying that "some proverbs are also maxims" and citing as an example the cryptically understated "an Attic neighbor" (ἔτι ἔνιαι τῶν παροιμιῶν καὶ γνῶμαί εἰσιν, οἷον παροιμία, Ἀττικὸς πάροικος, 2.21.12, 1395a19–20).[19] He presumably means that this can be taken either (maxim-wise) as a literal truism, or extended (proverb-wise) in metaphorical application to situations in which neither neighbors nor people of Attica literally figure.[20]

Among the main features of maxims, according to Aristotle (*Rhet.* 2.21), are that they can be the final part of the logical structure called the enthymeme; that they are more appropriate for the arguments of older men than younger ones; and that rustics are especially prone to using them, and are among the people who apply maxims to areas where they lack experience. Thus he seems to view their proper use as characteristic of sophisticated and philosophical expression, to be used by those who have a right to be authoritative. Demetrius (*On Style* 232) would seem to be continuing Aristotle's view when he contrasts the "demotic and common" wisdom of the proverb with the more "ex cathedra" quality of the man who speaks in maxims and exhortations. It might appear that Demetrius diverges from Aristotle by assuming that proverbs characterize common people's speech, whereas Aristotle said that rustics characteristically used maxims. But their comments may be reconciled by noting that both authors share the judgment that rustics (and young people) lack the knowledge to use maxims properly and so are prone to inappropriate *gnômologia*.[21]

However we may view the sometimes blurred line dividing maxims from proverbs, it is important to emphasize that although *formally* often distinct, both proverbs and maxims were put to the same *functional* use: to persuade the listener and move him to correct action by utterance of familiar, unassailable wisdom. This is clear from the examples quoted by Aristotle, typically from speeches in epic or drama. These maxims are of course versified,[22] and thus represent a phenomenon quite distinct from the "emergent" utterance of the prose maxim according to the ethnographic criteria for performance that I have been applying. Such spontaneous emergence of maxims in fact seems less easy to identify with certainty in the kinds of prose texts I have been examining. It is likely that many maxims escape our notice because they are simply general statements that do not "call attention to themselves as formal artistic entities," to use Abraham's language, as do proverbs and apothegms. This is because they exhibit less poetic artistry than proverbs and less contextually framed dramatic force than apothegms. Thus the identification of maxims in an author like Herodotus, who is normally a good source of verbal and nonverbal[23] folk behavior, can be highly problematic, despite a recent study that attempts to show that he used them frequently.[24] Although it would take a lengthy investigation to establish the facts, it may be that maxims are less characteristic of the interactional prose discourse represented by authors like Herodotus, Xenophon, Plato, and Plutarch, and more common in poets like Pindar, Bacchylides, and the tragedians, in the didactic sections of biographical accounts like those of Diogenes Laertius, and in oratory. Because Aristotle continually exhorts his reader to employ maxims for effective and persuasive oratory, we may assume that they were widely used, but I suspect that their use was less spontaneous and more calculated than that of proverbs and apothegms, hence more characteristic (at least in the fourth century) of written style than of spontaneous oral discourse.

If their instructive and manipulative purpose makes proverbs and maxims similar, it sets them apart in some crucial respects from the third and most complicated of the wisdom genres, the apothegm.

APOTHEGM

The apothegm, unlike the proverb and maxim, is not so much tribal or traditional wisdom that the addressee in some sense already shares with the speaker, as the clever and inspired creation of an important individual at a critical moment, which has entered the social memory. The Greeks developed an extensive tradition of preserving the opinions and sayings of famous individuals, a preservation that would have been oral and anecdotal for centuries before attaining formal documentation in the highly literate postclassical era.[25]

We find extensive citation of apothegms in writers like Plutarch and Diogenes Laertius, and the apparent antecedents of this tradition are seen in Herodotus and Xenophon.

The authority of the apothegm is based on what I conceive as an underlying Greek ideology concerning verbal performance, namely that there is a special value and force inherent in the wise and pithy saying uttered by a distinguished individual at the opportune or critical moment, a point in time for which the Greeks have a special word, *kairos*. Such a belief in authoritative *muthos* or *logos* was so generally shared and accepted that no overt declaration or defense of its principles would have been necessary. Yet a brief but revealing defense of one aspect may be found in the introduction (172b–e) to the possibly spurious treatise of Plutarch on the "Sayings [Apophthegmata] of Kings and Commanders." In putting forth an argument for the usefulness of his treatise, the author offers a curious theory about words versus deeds. He explains that the best understanding of the ethos and policy of history's leading figures is to be found not in their deeds but in their words. The reason for this, he continues, is that men's actions are subject to the influence of chance, whereas their words, being free of such influence, are under their full control and therefore offer the best index of their minds and characters.

In light of the sociolinguistic vision I have sought to develop here, this Plutarchean statement fails to grasp the social, contextual, and interactive nature of speech events, conceiving the entire activity as that of the speaker. Indeed (pseudo-)Plutarch writes as if there existed only speech acts and no such thing as speech events! Or, invoking modern Bakhtinian theory, we may say that Plutarch fails to grasp the essentially dialogic character of any and every utterance, even that to which no response is given.[26] Every genre constitutes speech in reaction to earlier speech in that genre, and all the more so if the genre is oral. Therefore, insofar as it is a reaction, speech is never fully determined and controlled by the speaker. Plutarch, however, needs to imagine the speaker's full control of speech as a defense against the power of chance, Tyche. Such an optimistic vision (or fantasy) of human control includes the power to recognize the *kairos* and make the best social strategic use of it.

This is why so many stories of Plutarch and Diogenes aim at perpetuating the memory of how a wise or authoritative person delivered a wise and pithy utterance, perfectly matched to its "kairotic" moment. We are witnessing the recording of an oral tradition that preserves the nearer past just as epic recitations and their eventual recording preserved the more remote heroic past. While that earlier past, with its legacy of myth and heroic legend, may have enjoyed greater ultimate prestige, the more recent past offered paradigmatic examples of more immediate and practical worth for modeling daily behavior.

Of course, once tradition has made an apothegm familiar, it may be subject to quotation and reuse and may eventually approximate the maxim and proverb in function, as seems to have happened with some of the philosophers' apothegms quoted by Diogenes Laertius. But there is good evidence for arguing that the original nature of the apothegm remains quite distinct from that of the other two wisdom genres.

Although apothegms were liberally quoted by Greek writers, it turns out to be extremely difficult to define the limits of this popular form of speech. The etymology of *apophthegma* (the preposition ἀπο- plus the verb φθέγγομαι) suggests either the meaning "utterance, declaration," or the different sense "retort." "Retort" would be the most accurate translation if we allow the Greek preposition ἀπο- to have the particular force appropriate to verbs denoting speech: the sense of giving back an utterance particularly called forth by the social context operating upon the speakers, as in the verb ἀποκρίνομαι. In many cases the apothegms cited by ancient authors fit this category precisely. There are, however, abundant examples of apothegms cited as merely clever sayings, in effect bon mots, where context is *not* a factor. Here the meaning must be "utterance" rather than "retort" and the *apo-* would seem to denote simply the act of putting *forth* a statement, much like the *de-* in Latin *declamare*, "declaim," or the *aus-* in German *Ausspruch*.

A survey of the uses of the term over several centuries suggests that in ancient Greece the meaning of *apophthegma* retained a certain ambiguity while gradually shifting its semantic focus. Originally it most likely designated the "retort," whose significance came from a strict relation to the context in which the "saying" was said. Then it came to be understood in the more general sense of "saying," a virtual synonym of the maxim or *gnômê*. And finally there is the emergence of a meaning no longer connected with the root sense of speaking (*phtheng-*), the apothegm as merely an "anecdote."[27]

An argument for this sequence can be made from the fact that the earliest (fourth-century) uses of the word, first in Xenophon and then in Aristotle, clearly conceive the apothegm as a clever saying whose cleverness consists in its high degree of *responsiveness*, as a retort or summation, to a specific *context*. By the second century A.D., in Plutarch's four books of sayings called *Apophthegmata*, his understanding of the term is still close to "retort," since most of his quoted apothegms are statements whose significance derives from their context. But we also find a few cases where an *action* or *decision* has taken the place of an utterance: Plutarch reports not what the person *spoke* but merely what he or she *decided* (e.g., nos. 6, 7, 18, and 19 of the 31 *apophthegmata* attributed to Lycurgus). For Plutarch, then, we see that the meaning of apothegm no longer requires a response to context, but may now be stretched to include an anecdote, *apomnêmoneuma*, without any clever and quotable closing remark. By the third century A.D., in Diogenes Laertius's *Lives and Opinions* (Gnômai) *of Eminent Philosophers*, we find "apothegms" of famous persons preserved as clever sayings worth quoting in their own right, without context, and in effect identical to the maxims or *gnômai* of Diogenes' title. In his *Thales* (1.35), for example, Diogenes simply lists seven *apophthegmata* (which are in fact philosophical precepts) after several pages quoting clever and wise opinions that are actually *responses* to questions and situations but are *never* called apothegms. For Diogenes also, the word *apophthegma* has lost any sense of "response" or "retort," but for him it has become synonymous with *gnômê*.[28]

The evidence of the earlier Greek prose writers seems to suggest an intrinsic connection between apothegm and anecdote, which would follow from the fact that apothegms are inherently embedded in a brief story. Herodotus, the earliest surviving prose author, although he seems not to have the word apothegm in his vocabulary, nonetheless offers several good examples of anecdotes culminating in the characteristic apothegmatic response.[29] Some responses, indeed, are so memorable that we have only to quote them and the entire preceding scene or anecdotal moment springs instantly to the mind of any reader familiar with the *Histories*: "My men have become women, and my women men" (8.88); "Of all these many thousands, not one will be alive a hundred years from now" (7.46); "It is true that I would not have received such honors from the Spartans had I been a Belbinian, but neither would you although you are an Athenian" (8.125); and the almost untranslatable Οὐ φροντὶς Ἱπποκλείδῃ (6.129). Perhaps the cleverest specimen of anecdotal retort is in the scene on the eve of the Battle of Salamis, as Themistocles tries to convince the reluctant council of generals to make the decisive naval engagement at Salamis rather than the Peloponnese. The Corinthian commander attempts to win the point with the pithy saying "in contests those who start prematurely are whipped"; but Themistocles wins the duel of sayings by "capping" his adversary with a better retort: "Yes, and those who get left behind are never crowned" (8.59).

The earliest recorded use of statements specifically identified as *apophthegmata* is in the closing scene of book 2 of Xenophon's *Hellenica* (2.3.56). The context is tightly structured, and the specific sense of a "retort" that is cleverly responsive to context seems already well established.

Xenophon is describing the death of the Athenian politician Theramenes in

404 B.C. at the hands of the oligarchic, pro-Spartan faction called the Thirty, led by the arch-conservative Critias. The historian's report (2.3.15–56) is detailed and vivid, as he dramatizes the deterioration of these two men's friendship through a series of political arguments between them, culminating in a set of opposing speeches they make before the Athenian Boule. The story closes in a striking manner as book 2 ends with the recounting of two apothegms delivered by the victim just before his death. Since these are the first apothegms identified as such in Greek literature, it is worth looking closely at their context, form, and content. We shall see that these three aspects are perfectly interwoven to present an artistic finale to the tale of Theramenes' death: the narration is capped, in its closure, with a well-performed genre of verbal art.

Theramenes is charged by Critias before the Athenian Boule of 500 with disloyalty to the oligarchic movement and with chameleon-like shifts in his political allegiance; but he defends himself well, so that the Boule seems predisposed to acquit him. Critias cleverly counters by declaring him officially removed from the Boule's jurisdiction and subject solely to the power of the Thirty. He then orders the group in charge of political executions to remove Theramenes from the meeting. Theramenes, as he is being dragged through the marketplace by armed guards, keeps protesting loudly about the injustice being done him, calling on gods and men to witness it. Finally Critias's chief henchmen, a certain Satyrus, is so annoyed by Theramenes' noisy outbursts that he threatens him, in a succinct Greek sentence. He tells him "he would suffer [lit., "lament"], should he not keep quiet," οἰμώξοιτο, εἰ μὴ σιωπήσειεν. "And one utterance [ῥῆμα] of his is reported as this," says Xenophon: Theramenes' retort "And if I do keep quiet, don't I then suffer?" ἂν δὲ σιωπῶ, οὐκ ἄρ' οἰμώξομαι; Xenophon's narrative from this point is worth quoting in full:

> And then when he was being compelled to die and drank the hemlock, they said he tossed out the remaining dregs following the custom of *kottabos* and said: "Let this be for the handsome Critias!" [Κριτίᾳ τοῦτ' ἔστω τῷ καλῷ]. Now I am not unaware of the fact that these apothegms are not noteworthy, yet I judge that quality admirable in the man, that when death was before him neither intelligence nor playfulness deserted his spirit. (2.3.56)

The historian felt obliged to interrupt his narrative and insert an apology for including two apothegms that readers may think "not noteworthy," οὐκ ἀξιό-λογα. Yet his storyteller's instinct led him to use them, and to use them most effectively as capstones to the dramatic end of Theramenes' life and as significant manifestations of the man's intelligence and wit. His first apothegm plays successfully on Satyros's threatening statement by reversing the order of the verbs "lament" and "keep silent," and moving the verb σιωπάω from second clause to first clause in the conditional sentence. Theramenes' rhetorical transformation plays cleverly with the reality underlying the situation: the hopelessness of Theramenes' position renders Satyros's threats gratuitous and therefore meaningless. Both statements point to the inescapable fact that Theramenes will end up suffering (meaning dead) no matter whether he laments aloud or not. Thus his retort uses verbal play to epitomize this irony, creating a pair of conditional statements whose mirrorlike reverse symmetry serves as a verbal icon for the "heads I win, tails you lose" situation facing the speaker.

The concluding apothegm is the concentrated expression of anger of an unfairly condemned man. The custom of *kottabos* was ritually performed in banquet or symposiac contexts as a public affirmation of love. The loved one (normally a male friend) was "toasted," as it were, with an implied wish for good health in the public gesture of tossing the dregs of one's wine goblet accurately over a distance to land in a bowl. The success of the toss was in effect a "love oracle" demonstrating the success of the romantic liaison (much like the modern ritual of plucking daisy petals saying "she loves me, she loves me not"). In his final gesture and apothegmatic accompanying statement, "to the handsome Critias," Theramenes manages to use the conventional love formula in a context that totally reverses its meaning: since the former friend (and perhaps, lover?) has become, most literally, a deadly enemy, so the customary wine has been replaced by deadly poison. His use of apothegm as his final act in life wittily distills the speaker's political and biographical reality to an essence that is simultaneously verbal and gestural. The final unity of language and action in the *kottabos* gives an excellent demonstration of how the apothegm's full meaning is inextricably connected to a dramatic social context. Speech that is usually action only metaphorically (as in the term "speech act") becomes indissolubly fused with real, physical action when a social ritual is performed. And the impact is magnified when the ritual is parodied.

This pair of apothegmatic utterances were already well established in oral tradition: one is "reported," λέγεται, the other "they said," ἔφασαν. Thus Xenophon's rhetorical disclaimer that these apothegms are "not noteworthy," contrasting with his emphatic and dramatic use of them, suggests that he shared his culture's evaluation of them as extremely successful performances.

When we move to later centuries, however, the meaning of apothegm, as we have noted, seems to lose its clear dimension of verbal performance. Surveying Plutarch's four books of apothegms, *Sayings of Kings and Commanders*, *Sayings of Spartans*, *Sayings of Romans*, and *Sayings of Spartan Women*, it is impossible to limit the apothegm to verbal utterance alone. Several of the citations would be more accurately called anecdotes, *apomnêmoneumata*, since they contain no quoted memorable *saying* but rather a memorable *incident* that has become a good *story*. Plutarch sometimes uses the phrase λόγος ἀπομνημονεύεται to introduce an apothegm, and in this phrase we may discern the potential for emphasis to shift from what was once said to what is now recounted.

The evidence suggests that we posit an evolutionary semantic model in which the meaning of apothegm was extended from "retort" to "utterance" and then loosened even further to include "report," "reminiscence," or "anecdote." In the third meaning the term ceases to refer internally to what the character said and is now conceived from an external perspective, as the "story" told by the narrator about his character.

But the task of defining the full semantic parameters of the Greek *apophthegma* may still be incomplete. Inasmuch as the statement made in an apothegm often comments on a present situation by metaphoric comparison, an apothegm could be equivalent to an *allêgoria* (not modern "allegory" but more narrowly a "speaking in other terms"). Demetrius twice describes the kind of statement he calls *allêgoria* (*On Style* 99, 151; translated by Grube as "hidden/veiled meaning")[30] and illustrates it with the very same quotation that Aristotle uses in *Rhetoric* 2.20 to illustrate an *apophthegma*: "Be careful lest the cicadas sing for you from the ground" (meaning "you are in danger of having your trees devastated by the enemy"). Aristotle also characterizes this apothegm as similar to Laconic and "riddle-like" (*ainigmatodê*) sayings. We should then perhaps subdivide apothegms into two classes, the direct and the "allegorical" or "riddling."[31]

If the verbal performance of wisdom is in fact a central phenomenon in Greek culture,[32] it seems inevitable that Greek speakers over time should develop multiple terminology with overlapping meanings, as well as multiple meanings for a single term. We do the same thing when in English we use the four terms *adage, proverb, maxim*, and *saying* loosely to denote more or less the same form of traditional speech; the French are similarly redundant with *dicton, proverbe, sentence*, and *maxime*, and the Italians with *proverbio, detto, motto, sentenza*, and *massima*. In the case of ancient Greek terminology, multiple labels seem to have gone hand in hand with some widening of the definition of the form, beginning with the overlap between *paroimia* and *gnômê* and continuing through the constantly widening sense of *apophthegma*, including its eventual overlap with *gnômê*.

I conclude by reaffirming the larger issue that emerges from my specific examples. The pervasive presence of several closely related, distinct, but sometimes overlapping genres for the performance of wisdom through authoritative speech, perfectly matched to occasion and sometimes to action, and appreciated as such by its audience, deserves to be studied in its full range and complexity within the conceptual framework of an oral poetics of prose discourse. Any adequate pursuit of this investigation must necessarily rely on methodologies drawn from recent work in key areas of the social sciences dealing with the emergent and contextual significance of certain kinds of speech, where, as in the better-known area of oral poetry, convention and creativity join to produce verbal art.

Chorus and Community
in Euripides' Bacchae

Charles Segal

THIS ESSAY explores the implications of the remoteness of the chorus from the city and the values of the city in Euripides' *Bacchae*. There is, I suggest, a strong connection between the attack on the city from outside by a foreign band and its collapse from within in the devastation of the Theban royal house. This situation results from and reflects the ambiguous status of Dionysus, who is both a native of Thebes and a foreign invader and thus has the status of both insider and outsider. My concern, however, is not so much the nature of Dionysus as the role of the maenad chorus.

The city reflected in the *Bacchae* has no communal center because there is no chorus of citizens who can speak as a community of involved fellow citizens. Instead, the dominant collective voice is that of the barbarian followers of a beautiful but dangerous god who is even more unpitying than they. Even when the chorus does sympathize with the common woes of mortality in gnomic generalities, the contexts make its utterances problematical. The mortal sufferers at the end are driven out of their city, and this collapse of the civic authority has been prefigured in the ruin of the king's palace and in Dionysus's figurative breeching of the walls of Thebes (585–603, 653–54). The survivors, in the closing moments of the play, can only comfort one another as private individuals, alone, defeated, and on the verge of exile.

Because the chorus of the *Bacchae* stands in an adversarial relation to the human protagonists, it has less interaction on the stage with the members of the polis than does the chorus in most tragedies; and even that interaction is narrowly focused on the conflict between Dionysus and Thebes. The effect is to create a sharp division between the chorus's world, defined by the cult of the god and the imagery of animal energy and a landscape of mountains, rivers, and forests, and the world of the city, defined by its walls, prison, and the palace of the authoritarian king.[1]

Aside from the royal palace and the walls, there is little depiction of a landscape of a polis such as occurs elsewhere in Euripides and Sophocles.[2] The city itself receives very weak representation. The maenads' cry, "To the mountain, to the mountain" (116), resonates throughout the play, and the two dazzling messenger speeches, which describe the spectacular and horrible events on that mountain, draw attention away from the city to the remote places of the god's revels. The city's symbolic center, the palace of the king, is mocked and destroyed in the first part of the play (576–659) and adorned with the grisly trophy of the god's power over his worshipers near the end (1200–1207). The representative of the city who advises the misguided attack on the maenads embodies the worst features of urban life: he is a "wanderer around the town and a man well versed in words" (τις πλάνης κατ' ἄστυ καὶ τρίβων λόγων, 717), a hint at the demagogic atmosphere of late fifth-century Athens.[3] In the prologue Dionysus himself, appearing in his divine form, warns of his possible opposition to the polis and his readiness to enter into direct conflict with "the Thebans' city" (Θηβαίων πόλις, 50).[4]

Whenever any character speaks of the polis as a whole, the context undermines the image of a strong, healthy civic life. When Teiresias, for example, urges Cadmus to entreat the god "for the sake of the polis" (362), he is accompanying the aged ex-king to the mountain in bacchic dress, a spectacle whose comic associations have often been pointed out. When the disguised Dionysus tells Pentheus that he alone "toils in behalf of the city" (963), he has the king entirely in his power and is leading him to his sacrificial death in his rite. When Cadmus speaks of "the whole city," he is describing its total subjection to the madness sent by the god: ἐμάνητε, πᾶσά τε ἐξεβακχεύθη πόλις ("You went mad, and the whole city was driven into bacchic frenzy," 1295). And the god's power over the city has just been enacted on the stage as Agave asked to have the walls of the royal palace adorned with the spoils of her hunt, that is, the decapitated head of the city's king (1212–15). In making this request, her first speech in iambic trimeters, she opened the scene by reminding us of the vulnerability of the city's walls as she addresses the citizens of Thebes as "dwellers in the lovely towered town of the Theban earth" (ὦ καλλίπυργον ἄστυ Θηβαίας χθονὸς / ναίοντες, 1202).

Each of the three human protagonists suffers a loss of the polis. Pentheus is separated from the city's warriors and paraded "alone" (963) through the wild places outside where he meets his death. Agave is "deprived" (στερεῖσα) of her father, of the strength of family support at a time of grief (1364–67), and of house and city (1368–70). In her last lines she views the scene of her former revels as accursed with pollution (1383–85), and her "corevelers" (1172) become her "coexiles" (1381–87). Cadmus is not only deprived of his city and his human form but also becomes a destroyer of Greek tombs and altars (1354–62). This ruler who had been willing to accept Dionysus for the sake of the family's glory (334–36) now sees the destruction of his male line and then leaves Thebes, doomed to lead a horde of barbarians against other Greek cities.[5]

Aristotle, in a celebrated passage, remarks that the chorus should function as an integral part of the action, an actor among actors, as in Sophocles (*Poet.* 1456a25–27). But this is only one of the chorus's many functions in Greek tragedy. It can provide necessary background material, suggest mythical parallels to the main action, or offer gnomic reflections that universalize the implications of the specific events. Although the chorus is never merely the mouthpiece of the dramatist, it can introduce a perspective wider than that of any single character. It can say or imply more than it actually knows as an involved participant in the action and thus can enlarge the resonances of the action. Its language, set off from the iambic dialogue by dialect, meter, denser syntax, richer and more figurative poetry, often evokes images that prove to be significant for the meaning of the play as a whole.

The collective voice of the chorus is its most fundamental quality. It complements and often contrasts with the individual voices and perspectives of the single actors. In the majority of Greek tragedies this collective voice belongs to members of the city or the household whose fortunes are closely identified with those of the protagonist. In Euripides' *Bacchae*, however, the choral persona is sharply antagonistic not only to the protagonist but also to the traditional values of the polis.[6] The closest parallels are the chorus of Furies in Aeschylus's *Eumenides* and the Danaid chorus in his *Suppliants*. In both cases, however, these outsiders' threat to the city is averted. In the case of the Danaid women a reconciliation of some sort is effected in the second play, even though the final outcome is disastrous for their own household. The Erinyes, moreover, are dread goddesses, not human worshipers of a god, and (more to the point) they are converted to a civic role at the end of the play. Their songs in the exodos accompany a procession (*pompê*) that celebrates this conversion.[7]

The exodos of the *Bacchae* is almost the exact opposite of that of the *Eumenides*. The chorus has a brief moment of sympathy for Cadmus, but for the most part it stands aside in silence as Dionysus announces the sufferings that await the aged king, sufferings that will end only when Ares will eventually transport him and his wife Harmonia to the Islands of the Blest (1337–39). The chorus is on stage, of course, but has no response other than to sing the closing tag, used in four other plays: "Many the shapes of things divine; many the surprises that the gods accomplish. The things expected are not accomplished, and of the things unexpected the god has found a way. So did this event come to pass." This chorus expresses none of the communal commiseration and compassion that end so many other tragedies, including a number of Euripidean tragedies. At the end of *Hippolytus*, for example, the chorus of Troezenian women connects the private suffering in the house of Theseus with the "common grief for all the citizens" in the closing lines (1462–66): "This woe came without expectation as a common grief to all the citizens. There will be an oarbeat of many tears; for the tales of the great prevail as meriting greater grieving." The chorus thus incorporates the present suffering of the royal house into a communal emotion that extends to "all the citizens" (κοινὸν τόδ' ἄχος πᾶσι πολίταις); and, as I have suggested elsewhere, it figuratively and emotionally affirms the solidarity of the citizen-spectators as a community within the theater.[8] The *Heracles* ends with the chorus's statement of sorrow and loss. As Heracles exits with his friend Theseus to Athens, it sings (1427–28), "We depart, full of pity, much lamenting, having lost the greatest of what is dear" (στείχομεν οἰκτροὶ καὶ πολύκλαυτοι, τὰ μέγιστα φίλων ὀλέσαντες). The chorus's silence at the end of the *Bacchae*, however, only intensifies the isolation of the two survivors of the disaster present on the stage, Cadmus and Agave.[9]

Even plays that do not end with so strong an expression of communal sympathy allow the chorus a greater role as a voice of commiseration. In the *Oedipus Tyrannus*, for example, the chorus moves toward an increasing intensification of sympathy after Oedipus's self-blinding and acknowledgment of his misery. Although there are tense moments, such as when Oedipus sharply defends his self-blinding (1369–90), the chorus expresses pity for him at length in the preceding ode, calling him *philos* (1321, for the first time in the play) and "poor man" (*tlamôn*, 1299; *deilaios*, 1347). In response to his litany of the horrors of his life, it agrees that he would be happier dead than alive in his blindness (1368–69). In its last address to him (not counting the problematical trochaics that end the play), it is responsive to his changed position. Oedipus's emotional meeting with his two daughters then takes place in its sympathetic presence, while Creon stands by as the new ruler of Thebes (1471–74). Even in the exodos of *Antigone*, where the chorus of Theban elders is not particularly compassionate (see 1270), it nevertheless affirms the place of Creon's suffering within the limits of the human condition. To his repeated request for death, for example, it replies, "Pray for nothing else now, for mortals do not have escape from misfortune that is fated" (*Antig.* 1337–38). This statement may seem harsh to us, but the chorus is still speaking as a mortal to a fellow mortal, implicitly recognizing the place of Creon's sufferings in the generality of the woes that afflict all men.

The closure that perhaps offers the closest parallel to the end of the *Bacchae* in Euripides' work is the *Medea*, and comparison is illuminating. The magical power and supernatural atmosphere of Medea's chariot (however the scene was staged) seem to cut the protagonists off from the rest of the city. Yet even here there is a strong and sympathetic choral presence. The choral song just preceding Jason's entrance registers horror at Medea's filicide; and Jason's first words are addressed to the chorus, which commiserates with him for the suffering of which he is still ignorant (1306–7). As at the end of the *Bacchae*, however, the chorus is silent during the ensuing dialogue, in which Medea demonstrates her ruthless power and leaves Jason crushed and helpless, begging in vain for the bodies of his sons. The refusal of full ritual closure in this denial of the bodies for normal human burial creates a bleakness and a suspension of social and moral order that are analogous to the frustration of Cadmus's demand for justice.

In the *Bacchae*, to be sure, Cadmus and Agave can comfort one another; but this consolation, unlike that at the close of *Hippolytus*, is presented as an entirely private matter, dominated by the impending exile. And even that comfort is severely diminished by the destruction of the royal house.[10] The protagonists of Greek tragedy are regularly threatened with the loss of community, but rarely is that threat fulfilled with so total a devastation of the community itself. Although Thebes will survive and is in fact more nearly intact than the Troy of the *Hecuba* or *Trojan Women*, its ruin seems in some ways even more total and unrelieved because there is no choral voice to represent city or family at the end.

One could argue, of course, that Dionysus's arrival only transforms Thebes into a future home for his cult; but the end of the play has nothing positive to say about Thebes's future, nor does Dionysus himself (at least in the extant text) place any emphasis on his future worship in Thebes or indeed on his Theban origins. In fact, he identifies himself only as the son of Zeus (1340–41, 1349), not as the son of Theban Semele, even though this latter relation motivated his choice of Thebes as the first Greek city to receive his cult (23–36; also 3–13).[11] If one looks beyond the frame of the play, of course, the result of the action is the establishment of Dionysus's worship at Thebes; and one might envisage the play as a *fabula sacra*, dramatizing Dionysus's coming as an ultimate blessing for the city, if not for the royal house.[12] That, however, is not our play. There is nothing celebratory in the ending. Euripides concentrates on the bleakness of the final moment; and the absence of a sympathetic civic chorus deepens this tone of unrelieved sorrow.

From the moment of its entrance, the chorus's foreign dress visually sets it apart from the Theban characters.[13] At the end of his prologue Dionysus introduces the chorus emphatically in terms of its Phrygian origin and instruments (55–62). That foreignness is essential to the depiction of the nature of Dionysus and his cult throughout the play; and at the end it intensifies the absence of a civic or familial voice that often provides a stable point of reference even for the most disorienting catastrophes, as we have observed for the endings of *Medea*, *Hippolytus*, *Antigone*, and *Oedipus Tyrannus*.[14]

Throughout Greek tragedy, as in much of Pindar or Bacchylides, the chorus's gnomic pronouncements embody the anonymous voice of traditional wisdom.[15] The chorus's gnomic utterances in the *Bacchae*, however, are problematical because this chorus has such a distinctively alien presence as it enters singing of Asia, Tmolus, Cybele, the Phrygian flute and drums and continues with the bacchantic cries and the details of the *ômophagia* (64–65, 78–82, 105–16, 126–40, 152–65). Throughout the play it maintains its distinctive Dionysiac identity in both its visual appearance and its actions. Thus the cries for bloody vengeance in the fourth stasimon (977–1000) contrast sharply with the gnomic generalizations on wisdom and happiness in the preceding ode and indeed with the similar language within the fourth stasimon itself (cf. 902–11, 1004–17).[16] The conflicting functions of this chorus probably cannot be fully resolved, for the contradictions express the paradoxes of Dionysus as a god of the polis and as a god whose presence threatens the polis.

This contrast between bacchic celebration and gnomic generalizations reflects the chorus's vacillation between its conventional role as a tragic chorus and its role as the chorus of a cult devoted to a specific god whom it celebrates in dithyramb, paean, or hymn. As a tragic chorus, it is a vehicle of the gnomic wisdom that it speaks in the first and third stasima and in part of the fourth. As the vehicle of the cult worship of a god, it sings the specifically Dionysiac cult song of the parode. In its cultic role, this chorus has an allegiance neither to city nor to family but to a god who, though born in Thebes, comes from remote places in the eastern barbarian lands and is bent on extending his sway over all of mankind. In the majority of extant tragic choruses, on the other hand, the chorus generally has a specific identity as citizens of a polis or sharers in a household within the polis.

The two choral roles come together and clash most sharply in the fourth stasimon, the last full stasimon that the chorus sings. The chorus affirms its cultic identity as it cries out for bloody death to the enemy of its cult. It then moves to a general statement on the gods and human happiness such as is appropriate to the "normal" civic role of a tragic chorus (1002–10). The ode ends, however, with the chorus's full cultic role as it prays for its god's epiphany in his bestial forms of bull, snake, and lion and calls for the release of his vengeful, destructive power against the intruder (1011–23)—a violence that will, in Dionysiac fashion, still wear the face of the smiling god (γελῶντι προσώπῳ, 1021). From this point on, the chorus's gnomic, civic voice almost totally disappears and is not heard in the closing movement of the play (or at least in as much of it as our text allows us to see), except for the concluding tag. The absence of this civic voice is felt especially in the ambiguity of its sympathy for Agave in her murderous Dionysiac madness in the commos (lyrical dialogue) when she enters with the head of Pentheus.

Most interpretations of the *Bacchae* concentrate, quite rightly, on the radical threat to the polis-ethos posed by the invading force of a foreign, ecstatic religion. Yet the play also explores the paradoxes of the presence of Dionysus and the Dionysiac within the established religion of the community and potentially within every human community. It examines the delicate balances within the polis that would be necessary for a healthy acceptance of the Dionysiac.[17] The beauty and happy fusion with nature promised in the first three odes and in the scene reported by the First Messenger are among the beneficent gifts of a god whose cult in Athens and other cities is associated with joyful celebrations in open air, festive release from work, pleasure, theater, and life energies of all sorts.[18] In Sophocles' *Antigone* and in Aristophanes' *Frogs* Dionysus is a god of the city, and these civic associations are vital to his cult.[19] But the Dionysus whom Euripides shows us in the *Bacchae* is primarily the ecstatic god of maenads. The play clearly distinguishes between the Asian and the Theban maenads, between those who have accepted the god's gifts and those who resist them or try to use them for their own ends.[20] Even so, the god's uninhibited release of our animal nature is shown to be a dangerous power; and it is the meeting and interchange between the two sides of the god that the play explores with that mixture of beauty and horror, appeal and repulsion, that continues to challenge interpreters.

There is something inherently unstable, unpredictable, and therefore frightening in this area of experience. Both the Theban maenads on the mountain and the Lydian maenads can change abruptly from beauty to bloodthirsty rage (695–768, 862–76, 977–96). Even in the parode the Lydian maenads' beatific vision of vegetative exuberance changes quickly to the *ômophagia*, the rending and eating of the raw flesh of wild animals (135–40). Euripides may have been influenced by the wilder and freer Dionysiac cult at what was still the fringes of the civilized (e.g., Hellenic) world and so was particularly sensitized to the contradictions that were involved in such a god's presence among mankind and in the cities of Greece.[21] The threat to the polis-ethos is particularly sharp in the persona of a god whose retributive justice (*dikê*), like that of Medea, destroys not only an individual but a house and by implication an entire city.[22] This polis-ethos is what Protagoras, in Plato's myth of the development of civilization, calls the *desmoi philias synagôgoi*, the unifying bonds of loyalty, affection, and intimacy. And these bonds are not only personal but also sacred, for they involve the ties of blood, the obligations to house and family, and the respect commanded by gods of the household like Hestia.

The intense solidarity and vehement commitment of these Asian maenads leave little if any room for reaching out to those who do not accept their god. In the first two thirds of the play the chorus has only two short, nonlyric exchanges with a mortal character, and both of these are statements of devotion to its god. It replies to Pentheus's harsh denunciation of Dionysus's cult in his first speech with a criticism of his "impiety" and lack of reverence for the gods and accuses him of "shaming his race" (264–66). It addresses him not as "lord" or "king," but merely as "stranger," *xene*, which emphasizes the gulf between the ruler of a Greek city and a band of worshipers of Dionysus. The chorus reserves the title "lord," *anax*, for the figure who has all its allegiance, Dionysus. After Teiresias defends the god's cult in a counterspeech (267–327), it replies with two lines of praise: "Aged sir, you do not shame Phoebus Apollo in your words, and you show good sense in honoring Bromios, great god" (328–29). Its approbation of Teiresias's "not shaming Phoebus" is symmetrical with its disapprobation of Pentheus's "shaming his race" (Φοῖβόν τ' οὐ καταισχύνεις λόγοις, 328; καταισχύνεις γένος, 265). The symmetry conveys the narrow range of the chorus's sympathies.

The chorus's only other exchanges in this section of the play are with Dionysus himself, disguised as a Lydian follower of the god. In the scene of the "palace miracle" it has an intense, lyrical dialogue with the Lydian Stranger, who leads it in what effectively is an enactment of the god's epiphany to his worshipers (576–603) as it summons him to its holy band or thiasos (582–84). The Stranger/god urges his followers to kindle their torches and burn the palace; and the scene ends with the chorus's statement that the god has in fact come, overturning the palace of its enemy, King Pentheus (601–3). The following scene (604–41) contains the chorus's longest remarks outside of the odes before the entrance of Agave; but even these are in trochaic tetrameters, consist of short exchanges with the Stranger, and are entirely focused on its loyalty to the god as it expresses joy and relief at seeing its leader safe.

That same narrow focus appears in the chorus's only other iambic trimeters in the middle section of the play, namely the three verses praising Dionysus after the Messenger reports the miracles on Cithaeron (775–77): "I fear to speak free words to the ruler, but it shall be spoken: Dionysus is inferior to none of the gods." In the entire preserved portion of the play, in fact, the maenad chorus speaks only thirteen lines of iambic trimeter. This meagerness of its dialogue also contributes to the gulf between itself and the Theban characters, who (with the exception of Agave in her bacchantic madness and Cadmus and Agave in the closing lines) speak in iambic trimeters. Chorus and protagonists virtually speak different languages.

The separateness of the chorus from Thebes is further emphasized in Pentheus's exit, now under the spell of the god, at the end of this scene. The Stranger, predicting the king's doom, takes the chorus into his confidence. He addresses it as "women" and prefigures the destruction of Pentheus's manhood as he announces, "Women, the man takes his place in the net, and he will come to the bacchants, where he will pay the penalty with death" (848–49). He then apostrophizes the god: "Dionysus, now the deed is yours" (849). By treating the chorus with special insider's status and making it privy to the god's plan of revenge, the Stranger detaches it even more fully from the mortal inhabitants of Thebes. The effect reverses the usual situation in tragedies of divine vengeance, where the chorus is closely attached to the human protagonists and shares its fear and uncertainty of what the gods may bring (e.g., *Ajax*, *Oedipus Tyrannus*, *Hippolytus*, *Heracles*).

Feeling its cult vindicated and its freedom assured, the chorus begins with the bacchic gestures of tossing the hair freely into the air in its nocturnal revels and compares itself to a fawn leaping joyfully in thickets and beside streams in the forest, having escaped the hunter (862–76). The ode then changes abruptly to a more heavily moralizing mood with reflections on the gods' punishment of impiety (882–96). The last stanza contains traditional gnomic wisdom in traditional choral language and the familiar form of the *makarismos* (902–12):

> Fortunate he who has escaped the storm from the sea and has reached harbor. Fortunate he who is above toils. One man surpasses another in different ways in power and wealth. Myriad men have myriad hopes; some come to fulfillment with wealth for mortals, others go astray. He whose life is fortunate from day to day I consider happy.[23]

The chorus here comes as close as it ever does in the play to functioning as a voice of communal wisdom. Yet, given the context, the maxims are surprising and have troubled commentators. The imagery of the first strophe remains strongly Dionysiac in its close identification with the energies of nature and the aggressive polarity (soon to be reversed) between hunter and hunted. The chorus makes no reference to the city or to civic life, but it does at least comment on the common fate of mortals, and for the first time it articulates a point of view that extends beyond its intense engagement with its cult and its god. The opening strophe frames the ode's concern with happiness in Dionysiac terms, that is, the joy and pleasure in the Dionysiac cult (e.g., ἡδομένα, "taking pleasure," in 874).[24] But, as the ode continues, the chorus seems to view happiness not just as the spontaneous gift of its bounteous god, as in the previous odes, but as a fleeting and precarious possession clouded by all the uncertainties of mortal "hopes."

Each of the odes contains some elements of a "normal" tragic chorus alongside elements specific to a cult hymn to the god, but the nature of this god introduces ambiguities. In the first stasimon the chorus offers admonitions about staying within the limits of mortality and the dangers of lawlessness and folly (387–402), but it dwells on the bliss that came from Dionysus (403–23). The third stasimon shows broader and more humane sympathies (especially 903–11); but even here (if the text is right), the chorus is still narrow and partisan: "Among mortals there is no more lovely honor from the god," it sings, "than to hold one's hand in superior strength above the head of one's enemy" (877–80).[25] In the fourth stasimon, the chorus utters warnings about injustice and divine punishment (977–1023); but it also dehumanizes Pentheus as a monster, and calls upon a justice that carries a sword and slits throats (977–96, 1011–1123).[26] The following antistrophe, to be sure, returns to traditional gnomic reflections on pursuing "wisdom" and achieving a "life without pain" by behaving in a moral way, acting piously, and honoring the gods (1002–10); but this moment of calm quickly disappears in the repeated cry for blood and the call for Dionysus's bestial epiphany with a "deadly noose" for his enemy (1017–23). This punitive emphasis prepares for the Second Messenger's news of the retribution visited upon Pentheus in the following scene.

The third stasimon ended with the theme of happiness "day by day" (τὸ κατ' ἦμαρ, 910) and so implied the uncertainties of the life of mortals, defined as *ephêmeroi*, creatures subject to and defined by the changes of a single day. But in the fourth stasimon the motif of "day" changes to the perspective of the gods' demands, namely to "practice piety by day and by night" (ἦμαρ ἐς νύκτα τε εὐαγοῦντ' εὐσεβεῖν) in accordance with what is lawful and just (*nomima* and *dikê*, 1008–10).[27] Although the sentiments taken by themselves are unexceptionable, there is a disturbing shift from the more tolerant mood of the previous ode. The justice (*dikê*) of line 1010 has an ominous ring in the context of the bloody justice in the refrain before and after (1013–14 = 991–92): ἴτω δίκα φανερός, ἴτω ξιφηφόρος φονεύουσα λαιμῶν διαμπάξ ("Let it go forth, justice manifest, forth, sword-bearing, slaughtering with a stroke through the throat").

The voice of the chorus is here at its most ambivalent. Even the gnomic generalities do little to bring it closer to the Theban participants. The small hint of compassion for the human condition in the third stasimon, as we shall see, will have a limited development later in the scene with Agave. But now, immediately before the news of Pentheus's punishment, the chorus has the remoteness and ambiguity of its god. Even the Dionysus of the chorus's last lines is both a murderous hunter who traps and kills his enemy and a god who comes with "smiling face" (1017–23).

This ode, with its call for a bloody, throat-slitting justice, calls into question the chorus's humane generalizations in the previous ode. At a number of points the play implies that the gods' moral standards may be no higher than those of mortals (see 321, 1348);[28] but these mortals, the Lydian maenads, not socialized by a polis, place loyalty to their god above the bonds of a common humanity. More specifically, the intensity of their religious devotion obscures and destroys the broad sympathy for the human condition that they articulate in the third stasimon. At its best, the emotional expressiveness released by the Dionysiac cult produces paradisiacal visions of joy and abandon in a green world of abundance and beauty. When the god is resisted, the maenads respond with a narrow, unpitying fanaticism. The pitch of violence and hatred rises from the third stasimon through the fourth's evocation of murderous justice by the sword at the throat (cf. 877–81 = 897–901, with Dodds's text, and 991–96 = 1011–16); and its climaxes here in the chorus's delight in the horrible vengeance described by the Second Messenger.

The radical, antipolis spirit of this chorus emerges most powerfully in this scene with the Second Messenger.[29] At the first news, the chorus cries, "Lord Bromios you are revealed a great god" (1031). Taken aback, the Messenger answers, "How are you speaking? What have you said? Do you then rejoice at the misfortunes of my lord?" And the chorus answers in the same terms as before: "A stranger, I cry the bacchantic *euoi* in barbarian songs, for I no longer cringe in fear of chains" (1032–35). The Messenger sympathizes with the praise of the god but, in his last words before his full narration, still criticizes this delight in others' woe: "To rejoice at sufferings that have been accomplished, women, is not decent" (*ou kalon*, 1039–40). The chorus, however, has a different standard of what is *kalon* (noble, lovely, decent). In the third stasimon it declared that no honor from the gods was "lovelier" (*kallion*) than power over one's enemies (877–81 = 897–901). Its next song praises Agave's killing of her son as "a *lovely* contest" (καλὸς ἀγών, 1163–64). In its dialogue with the Messenger it takes no notice and sees no other point of view than its own: "Come tell me," it asks, "explain by what doom perished that unjust man who did unjust deeds" (1041–42). Neither here nor elsewhere does this chorus have a word of pity for the death of the city's ruler. In fact, except for a very few hints of compassion for Agave after her rending of Pentheus and for Cadmus at the very end, most of its utterances in the play are hallelujahs of praise for Dionysus's triumphs over his enemies.

As the Second Messenger completes his account of the death of Pentheus, the chorus of maenads sings a brief ode of triumph in which it calls out exultantly to Dionysus and once more dehumanizes its enemy (1155). It echoes the Messenger's account of how Agave came to the city calling on the god as her "fellow tracker, fellow worker in the hunt, the victorious one, for whom she gains tears as her prize of victory" (1145–47); but it makes the paradoxical conjunction of tears and triumph part of its direct address to the Theban women: "Cadmean bacchants, glorious is the hymn of victory that you have fulfilled—into lamentation, into tears" (τὸν καλλίνικον κλεινὸν ἐξεπράξατε ἐς γόον, ἐς δάκρυα, 1161–63).[30] It ends with the gruesome image of a mother "plunging a dripping hand in the life's blood of her child" (1163–64).[31] At this point it hails Agave, who arrives, the sign of madness in her eyes, for the *kômos* or procession of the bacchantic god ("Receive the *kômos* of the god to whom one cries *euoi*," 1167).

The following commatic exchange between the maenads and Agave is the longest sustained dialogue of the chorus with a human protagonist. In form and substance the scene parallels the lyrical dialogue with the Stranger at the Palace Miracle (576–603), but now the enemy's destruction is total and has reached from the palace to the body of the king. Although the chorus speaks of "lamentation and tears" (1161–63), its task is to exult in, not sympathize with, the suffering. Indeed, it uses the characteristic Dionysiac compounds in *syn-* to express Agave's fusion with its sacred band (thiasos). It now addresses to her the reception into the Dionysiac processional revel that the chorus leader has just addressed to the chorus as a whole: "I receive you as my fellow reveler" (σε δέξομαι σύγκωμον, 1172; cf. δέχεσθε κῶμον εὐίου θεοῦ, 1167). The generalizations about human happiness in the previous choral odes now change to congratulations of the maddened infanticidal mother for her "blessedness" as a Dionysiac huntress. At this climax of the horror, the chorus rings the changes on all the terms for human happiness that it had generalized about in the previous odes.[32]

The form of the chorus's response in short phrases and echoing word-for-word replies has still another register of meaning. It corresponds to the intense antiphonal cries between women in funerary lamentation. There are numerous examples of this kind of responsive lament in all of Greek tragedy, from Aeschylus's *Persians* through Sophocles' *Oedipus at Colonus*.[33] A typical scene is the exchange between Hecuba and the chorus in Euripides' *Trojan Women* as they both give utterance to their misery and contemplate the life of slavery ahead as they are about to be led off on the Greek ships (1303–11):

Εκ. ἰὼ γᾶ τρόφιμε τῶν ἐμῶν τέκνων.
Χο. ἒ ἔ.
Εκ. ὦ τέκνα κλύετε, μάθετε ματρὸς αὐδάν.
Χο. ἰαλέμῳ τοὺς θανόντας ἀπύεις.
Εκ. γεραιά γ' ἐς πέδον τιθεῖσα μέλεα καὶ
    χερσὶ γαῖαν κτυποῦσα δισσαῖς.
Χο. διάδοχά σοι γόνυ τίθημι γαίᾳ
    τοὺς ἐμοὺς καλοῦσα νέρθεν
    ἀθλίους ἀκοίτας.
Εκ. ἀγόμεθα φερόμεθ' . . . Χο. ἄλγος ἄλγος βοᾷς.
Εκ. δούλειον ὑπὸ μέλαθρον.   Χο. ἐκ πάτρας γ' ἐμᾶς.

Hecuba: O land that nurtured my children.
Chorus: Alas, Alas.
Hecuba: O my children, hear me, recognize your mother's voice.
Chorus: It is the dead you shout to in your dirge.
Hecuba: Throwing my old limbs on the earth and beating the earth with
   my two hands.
Chorus: Following you I throw my knee to the earth calling on my dead
   below, my poor husband.
Hecuba: We are being led off, being carried off . . .
Chorus: Pain, pain you are crying forth.
Hecuba: To a house of enslavement.
Chorus: Yes, from my native land.

The intense commatic exchange between Agave and the chorus in the *Bacchae* comes just at the point where one would expect a scene of formal lamentation at the death of the king, which has been described at length. But Euripides obtains a shocking *coup de théâtre* by replacing what might have been a lyrical lament shared between the mother and a chorus of women with a scene of maenadic exultation in hunting and bloodshed. The substitution is part of the gender reversals that run throughout the play (exhibited most strikingly in the Theban women's victories as hunters and warriors and the dressing of the king as a maenad);[34] but it also enables the play to register the distance between the familiar practices of city and house and the Dionysiac cult that has entered the polis so violently from the barbarian world. The play brings into the theater, at the center of the city, the wild rites of women that belong on the mountain or in barbarian lands. Corresponding formally to the traditional antiphonal lament of choral song, Dionysiac exultation juxtaposes the outlandish with the familiar. The shock effect not only jolts our formal expectations but also brings home to us the otherness of this Dionysiac world. The displacement of funerary lament by Dionysiac rejoicing also shows how successful has been that Dionysiac invasion of the polis.

To understand better this formal resemblance between maenadic celebration and intense antiphonal lament, we need to recall the chorus's gratuitous mention of lament in its song of triumph (1160–62):

Βάκχαι Καδμεῖαι,
τὸν καλλίνικον κλεινὸν ἐξεπράξατε
ἐς γόον [γόνον, P], ἐς δάκρυα.

Cadmean bacchants, glorious is the hymn of victory that you have fulfilled—into lamentation, into tears.

Soon after comes the chorus's exchange with Agave (1184):

Αγ. μέτεχέ νυν θοίνας.   Χο. τί; μετέχω, τλᾶμον;

Agave: Now take your share in the feast.
Chorus: What? Shall I take a share, wretched woman?"

The chorus's evocation of "lamentation and tears" in 1160–62 (ἐς γόον, ἐς δάκρυα), even in the midst of its exultant triumph of the hunt, further suggests that *tlamon* in 1184 expresses pity, and calls attention to the appropriateness of choral lament at this moment.[35]

The substitution of maenadic violence for intense female lament, moreover, draws on the special relationship between these two forms of female emotional expression. Several passages in tragedy characterize paroxysms of female grief as "bacchantic." Hecuba begins "a bacchic tune" when she finds her last surviving son, Polydorus, washed up on the shore dead (*Hec.* 684–87). In Euripides' *Suppliants* Evadne rushes out in bacchantic fury when she first learns of her husband's death (1038–39; cf. 1065). In the *Phoenissae* Antigone, mourning over her dead brother and mother, calls herself "a bacchant of Hades" (1489–90).[36] In the passage from the *Suppliants* Euripides may even have in mind the famous scene in *Iliad* 22 when Andromache is "like a bacchant" in the first access of her grief over Hector's death (μαινάδι ἴση, *Il.* 22.460).[37] The chorus in the *Heracles* compares its song of sorrow for the approaching catastrophe to a destructive

Dionysiac song: in this ruined house Lyssa, goddess of madness, will rage as a bacchant (*HF* 889–97).[38]

The valuable studies of Richard Seaford and Renate Schlesier have shown how tragedy uses such Dionysiac language as the model of disorder and destruction in the house.[39] The passages cited above, taken together with the fifth stasimon and its following commos in the *Bacchae*, extend this model to a more specific area of female emotionality, autonomy, and potential disorder, namely female lament and particularly funerary lament. These texts develop an equivalence between the intense emotionality of women in funerary lamentation and the emotions released in maenadic celebration. Both the maenadic revel on the mountain (the *oreibasia*) and funeral lamentation are the special activity of women and are conducted wholly or partly away from male supervision. In both cases, this release of female emotion is perceived as threatening to the male-dominated civic order of city and household. From the time of Solon Athens attempted to restrict female lamenting; and in the second half of the fifth century the issue was still very much alive as the official civic lament, the *epitaphios logos* (exemplified in Pericles' Funeral Speech reported in Thucydides), attempted to appropriate for the male civic voice the place of the traditional lamentation by women.[40]

For understanding the affinities between the extreme emotionality of female lamentation and the release of violent emotions by maenads the work of C. Nadia Serematakis on the ritual laments of the Mani is particularly suggestive. Women's laments show remarkable similarities across different cultures, and these in themselves would make Serematakis's material of interest for classical Greece.[41] As Margaret Alexiou has demonstrated at length, moreover, there are also strong continuities in the lament tradition in Greece from antiquity to the present day.[42] Serematakis describes in detail the kind of line-by-line or word-by-word responsion exemplified in the tragic texts cited above. These ritual laments include

> singing refrains, such as doubling the last word of the verse or the last verse of the lament, and stylized sobbing that occurs simultaneously with, and in counterpoint to, the singing of the *koriféa* [leader of the lament]. This acoustic interplay between soloist and chorus is accompanied by a physical interplay of gestures that also serve as validating responses to the solo improvisation. Antiphonic interplay also occurs in the successive alternation between soloists as they "take" the lament from each other. The gender dichotomies of the lament session, in which women are vocal, emotionally demonstrative in public, and the men are silent, inhib-

ited, and spatially separate, can also be understood as a further anti-phonic dynamic. (Se, 100)

The fusion of the women engaged in this lamentation produces an intense feeling of community that, like the maenadic celebration, is essential to the meaning of the ritual:

> "Screaming the dead" counters the isolation of death. It separates the mourner from residual social contexts, yet registers her entry into a social relation with the dead and the rest of the mourners. "Screaming" both demarcates and encloses a collectivity of subjects in exile. Of course, those in exile are united in pain. Rooted in shared substance, emotional ethics, and memories of reciprocity, "screaming" is witnessing pain. (Ibid., 101)

This antiphonal, collective lament is characteristic of an oral culture, such as that of early Greece, and indeed of some outlying areas of modern Greece. The respondents echo the last word to fix the lament in their minds and also to take the other speaker's words into their own mouths, making her words part of their utterance as the fullest possible sharing in the overpowering emotion of the group. Seremetakis describes the response of her Maniote informants when she played back to them tape recordings of their laments:

> They did not begin to mourn, but they became musically engaged. At first I noticed that they repeated the last word or phrase of each verse sung on tape. I realized this was a form of oral writing, a technique of memorization, of record keeping that I had also witnessed in the actual *kláma*. I soon noticed that they did not only echo the last words or phrases of the verse sung, but often anticipated them, as if they already knew where the singer's poetics were directed, thus sounding as if they were singing simultaneously with the improviser. This was a technique for printing the lament in their minds, for touching it, for taking it in their mouths as shared substance. (Ibid., 105)

It is also characteristic of an oral culture that it expresses its most intense emotions in interactive and interpersonal contexts—a situation exactly the opposite of North American and North European industrial societies that reserve such emotions for private moments. Seremetakis describes a chance meeting with a woman of the area expert in mourning songs. The woman discovers that Seremetakis is a relative and invites her inside:

> She started by alternating between prose and poetry to give me a *moiróloi* and its context. As she continued mourning quietly, she stared at me with

piercing eyes till my lips moved. I was humming along, at first with each verse's last syllable, then the whole verse as her head and body movements encouraged me to follow. The more I entered her rhythm, her mourning intensified. With pain in her face and eyes, she turned at key moments of her *moirolói* to seek my nodding, my voice, leading me to taste her pain till I burst into tears. (Ibid., 106)

This description illustrates how closely the sympathetic transfer of violent emotion between women caught up in the collective furor of the lament can approximate the ecstasy of the bacchic thiasos. She continues:

One scream, coming from the elder sister, rose above all others. It retained its peak without subsiding till the woman passed out. A little old lady passed out quietly right behind her. A male voice emerged, "Take her out!" (The young woman's husband had attempted to bring her out of her deep mourning by calling her name a couple of times during the ceremony, mentioning something about her health.) Women were standing and screaming, pulling their hair out. It was the peak. It was impossible to be fully conscious, to be an observer. (Ibid., 110)

At these events there is a sharp separation of the men and women, and the men's role is defined as that of outsiders and guardians of rationality and health. Serematakis describes the men's fear and their readiness to intervene:

The men, aware of the power of the emotions in that room, were alarmed and frightened. *A woman can actually impose death on herself. This is the female challenge of Death* [Serematakis's emphasis]. People are alert in ceremonies for this type of catharsis, and they are ready to catch the collapsing body of the overwhelmed mourner. The men took the women out of the room to bring them back to consciousness. They pulled them out "to give them coffee and fresh air." For men—especially young men— these acts were a "medical intervention" in a ritual process that eluded their understanding; they reduced it to physiological disorder and issues of personal health. (Ibid., 110–11)

The scene is of interest to show the anxiety that such female emotionality can arouse in the men, even in a society that is, after all, in touch with the modern world, and also to indicate their role in reviving the women who are overcome by their participation. This is, of course, the role of Cadmus in the next scene of the *Bacchae* (1264–96).[43]

In the *Bacchae*, then, the displacement of funerary by bacchic ritual raises the inversions of the scene to a second degree. A bacchant-like lament of a bereaved mother over her son is shared by a chorus of emotionally engaged women of the city and the household. In an ecstatic celebration the mother rejoices in the bloody hunting down and dismemberment of her son and is joined and urged on in the collective intensity of the bacchantic *kômos*. Funerary ritual thus becomes another area in which the antiworld of Dionysiac emotionality engulfs the structures and boundaries of the city and its forms. And as Agave's bacchantic madness jars the expected forms of ritual structure from their usual paths, so her iambic description of her joy and success in the hunt comes at the point where the mother's funeral speech might have stood. Displaced by the bloody maenadic ecstasy, the scenes of proper lamentation will have to wait for Agave's return to sanity.

As Agave's speech in iambic trimeters moves to this quieter phase of her excitement in the hunt, the chorus, also moving back to trimeters, asks her to display her trophy and again addresses her with compassion (1200–1201):

δεῖξόν νυν, ὦ τάλαινα, σὴν νικηφόρον
ἀστοῖσιν ἄγραν ἣν φέρουσ' ἐλήλυθας.

Show the citizens now, O wretched one, the victorious prey with which you have come.

The lines recall the chorus's eagerness to learn the news of Pentheus's death from the Second Messenger (1041–42; cf. also 1039–40, 1199–1200). But the eagerness is now tempered by the sympathy of its address to Agave (ὦ τάλαινα), which in turn echoes and reinforces the commiseration in its τλᾶμον of 1184. That phrase of commiseration, ὦ τάλαινα, will also be addressed to her later by her father (1306). Here, however, in asking her to show her prize "to the citizens" (ἀστοῖσι, 1201), the chorus is also demonstrating how the terrible power of its god and his vengeance becomes a public, theatrical spectacle for the city. The chorus's form of address, ὦ τάλαινα, seems to hold in balance both a sense of her suffering and an exultation in the power of the god which that suffering makes manifest. Yet, even at the moment when it might seem most to resemble a civic chorus, its behavior points in exactly the opposite direction: delight in the sufferings of the city and its rulers.

The chorus seems to identify more closely with Agave than with any of the other Theban characters, and this identification may have something to do with a bonding between women in a community of female suffering that the chorus, despite its role as a band of Asian maenads, cannot fully escape. Unfortunately the lacuna near the end of the play prevents our seeing whether Euripides allowed the chorus any greater sympathy for Agave in her lament over Pentheus in the *compositio membrorum*.

The chorus has only one further exchange (aside from the closing tag), and again it is an expression of sympathy for the mortal sufferers, indeed its strongest in the play. As Cadmus finishes his funerary eulogy for Pentheus and ends with a statement about the power of the gods (1325–26), the chorus replies (1327–28):

τὸ μὲν σὸν ἀλγῶ, Κάδμε· σὸς δ' ἔχει δίκην
παῖς παιδὸς ἀξίαν μὲν, ἀλγεινὴν δὲ σοί.

As for your part, Cadmus, I feel pain; and yet the son of your son has the retribution that he deserves, painful as that is to you.

The chorus here behaves a little more like a civic chorus, although even the commiseration is balanced by the insistence on retribution (note the μέν . . . δέ construction). It is, however, more compassionate than its god, whose remoteness and indifference stand out all the more sharply against the chorus's momentary softening (1344–51). In any case, its words comfort neither Agave nor Cadmus. Agave seems to disregard the chorus completely as she addresses Cadmus and speaks of the overturning of her happiness (1329). Unfortunately the lacuna after this verse makes further conclusions impossible.

Dionysus's cool assertion of Zeus's decree increases the loneliness of the two mortal survivors. Even their ability to comfort one another is pitifully small, but it is all they have (1363–67). Their final farewell, sung in lyrics, now gives full emotional expression to the glimmers of pity from the maenad chorus. The chorus's touches of sympathy in the previous scene assure us that it is, after all, human; and, as I noted above, its lyrical exchange with Agave in the commos after the fifth stasimon offers a hint of the common bond that women can feel for one another. Yet its gestures of compassion only show how far it stands from a normal civic chorus and how isolated are the survivors of Thebes's royal house.

The suggestion of a "procession" at the end (cf. *pompoi* 'followers', 1381) underlines the movement into exile. We have come very far from the victorious revel-procession of Agave's entrance; now she will have a bitter *pompê* into exile and misery.[44] Her companions are not fellow maenads who "share the revel" (1172), but her own flesh and blood whom she now recognizes as such, the "sisters" (1381) of her ruined house over whom her father sheds tears (καὶ σὰς ἐδάκρυσα κασιγνήτας, "and I wept for your sisters," 1373). The communal life of both house and city is shattered, and for Agave so is the ecstatic collectivity of the maenad band. "Let these things be a concern to other bacchants" are her last words (1387). The closing tag, "Many the shapes of things divine" may seem mechanical, but these words about the power of the gods, however familiar, are not completely without effect. After the collapse of the social world of the play, they reinforce the isolation of the human survivors in a world of unpitying divinities. The chorus here at the end resumes its hieratic voice, and its small moments of pity seem both remote and insignificant.

The rulers and women of Thebes come to experience the dark side of the god they have worshiped. Agave is punished by entering fully into the destructive aspect of what the god embodies. Her experience enacts the Athenians' worst fears about female emotionality; but its performance on the stage also implies another area of female threatening activity, namely the unchecked expression of grief and mourning. In the play, as I have argued, female lament makes its first appearance in a shocking reversal of sorrow and joy. This nightmarish inversion of female lament is then completed in an even more grisly form in the *compositio membrorum* later in the play. Elsewhere in tragedy and in epic the funeral creates a quiet moment of resolution in which a mother or wife can have a last, intimate contact with the body of a son or husband, as in *Iliad* 24 or the finale of Euripides' *Trojan Women*. Here, however, the funeral is itself a continuation of the Dionysiac inversion of traditional rituals, for in this case it consists of the actual handling of the parts of a horribly mutilated body.

After these scenes Cadmus speaks over the recomposed body of Pentheus in the equivalent of an *epitaphios logos*, a funeral speech by male leader of the city praising the virtues of king and son (1308–22).[45] Yet this speech is pallid beside the spectacular mode of female lament in the *compositio membrorum* just preceding and seems almost completely overshadowed by it. The virtues of Pentheus that Cadmus praises, furthermore, have not been exhibited to the spectators; and the praise of the grandson for upholding the house (*melathra*, 1309) has been undercut by Dionysus's toppling of this house in the Palace Miracle (*melathra*, 589, 603; cf. 392).[46] The authority of Cadmus's speech is further qualified by his recognition of the power of the god that has destroyed his house (1303–4) and his own impotence (1323–26). It is an *epitaphios* from which all the force and authority of civic leadership and civic power have been drained.

These inversions of funerary rituals at the end are mirrors of the larger collapse of community in the city. This collapse, to recapitulate, has taken three interrelated forms: the lack of a civic voice of communal lament; the transformation of female lament into its most emotional and threatening form; and the overshadowing of an *epitaphios logos* from the remaining male authority in the city by the *compositio membrorum*. This last focuses on the mother's grief, on her intimate relation with the body of her son, and of course on her terrible bacchantic madness that has reduced the king's body to this condition. The mortal inhabitants of Thebes come to experience in their own lives what it means to resist Dionysus, but also what it means to worship him without the restraints of city, family, or king.[47] The community embodied in the maenads of the chorus is not of a kind that is usable for the civic life of a Greek polis.

When Euripides composed the *Bacchae* in exile, at the court of King Archelaus in Macedonia, he presumably still had in mind its eventual performance at the dramatic festivals of his native Athens, where he had presented so many plays. Yet many elements in the *Bacchae* point to a wider world. In the prologue the god describes how a barbarian, non-Greek cult makes its way from Bactria, Arabia, Persia, and Lydia to Greece (13–17, 64–65, 85–88), how this cult mingles Greeks and "barbarians" in the cities of Asia Minor (18), and by implication how universal is the power of the new god as he now reaches the first of the Greek cities on the mainland.[48] These wide geographical horizons self-consciously juxtapose Greek and barbarian, European and Asian (cf. 482–84), and emphasize the Dionysiac chorus's repeated gnomic claims to wisdom that applies to "all mortals" (e.g., 387–402, 876–81 = 897–901, 902–11; cf. 861). But the other side of these universalizing tendencies is a dissolution of the communal voice and civic consciousness that is manifested especially in the role of the chorus.

The *Bacchae*, among its many other aspects, is also a reflection on tragedy and the tragic chorus. I would like to push my observations on the chorus a little further and suggest that the dissolution of the civic center that the play enacts also implies a statement about tragedy. Euripides anticipates a form of tragedy that is no longer primarily a civic or communal experience for the members of its audience, but speaks primarily to them as individuals who suffer a private grief, not the "common woe" commemorated by the chorus at the end of the *Hippolytus*. The communal sharing takes place *outside* the city, in the wild intensity on the mountain where the maenads rage.

The negative side of this situation is the city's loss of the elasticity that can take in the Other embodied in Dionysus and his Asian worshipers. The calm, beatific visions and the ecstasy that appear in the first four odes of the play belong only to the Lydian maenads and are not accessible to the Thebans, who experience Dionysus only through his punitive violence and bloodshed. The positive side, however, lies beyond Thebes itself, namely in the play's evocation of a world of experience that extends beyond the polis and belongs to a wider frame of reference in which the distinction between Greek and barbarian is blurred. This is the aspect of Dionysus that appealed to the world of Alexander's conquests—a cosmopolitan deity whose power extends far beyond the walls of any single Greek polis. This cosmopolitan Dionysus, as I noted above, is already present in Sophocles' *Antigone*. For Euripides, perhaps because of his distance from Greece when he wrote the *Bacchae*, the Dionysus who moves between Greeks and barbarians is far more vivid. He could not, of course, have guessed that his Macedonian hosts would eventually bring Dionysus to the limits of the Greek *oikoumene*; but he seems to have captured a facet of the god that was to have a remarkable life in the imagery of the Hellenistic and Greco-Roman world.[49]

The Ion of Euripides
and Its Audience(s)

A. Thomas Cole

T HE *Ion* is easily read—up to line 1553—as a proto–New Comedy.[1] Except for two episodes incorporating the kind of action (narrowly averted murder of a close kinsman) that Aristotle (*Poet.* 1454a4–15) deems most suitable for evoking the "tragic" emotions of pity and fear, it is a medley of motifs encountered time and again in the works of Menander and his followers, both ancient and modern: the child abandoned at birth, the foundling with unsuspected noble parentage, the sanctuary-providing altar, the *anagnorisis*-enabling nurse, and—lest the intricacies of Fortune's or Providence's plan for a happy ending fail to be properly understood or its ironies properly appreciated—the explanatory prologue (here delivered by Hermes). Conspicuous among such intricacies and ironies—in Euripides as in comedy—are those stemming from potentially disastrous but ultimately harmless or even beneficial mistakings of identity (the foundling Ion, son of Apollo and the Athenian princess Creusa, taken for the son of Creusa's foreign husband, Xuthus). At line 1553 however, all of this changes. Athena appears as a dea ex machina, proclaiming to everyone present that "la commedia è finita," and inviting them to consider—if they have not done so already—the consequences and implications of what has happened thus far. Ion is to accompany his stepfather, Xuthus, to Athens, where he will become, through the birth of four sons, progenitor of the Ionian race, and where his mother, Creusa, will bear to Xuthus the eponymous ancestors of the Dorians and Achaeans.

The wide-ranging character of these implications will be evident to anyone who compares the genealogy they presuppose with the traditional family tree of Ionians, Dorians, and Achaeans—a genealogy already present in Hesiod (fr. 9 Merkelbach-West), Herodotus, and probably Thucydides:[2]

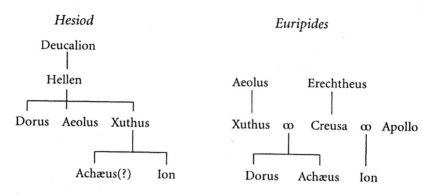

Hesiod

Deucalion
|
Hellen
|
Dorus   Aeolus   Xuthus
|
Achæus(?)   Ion

Euripides

Aeolus   Erechtheus
| |
Xuthus   ∞   Creusa   ∞   Apollo
| |
Dorus   Achæus   Ion

What is involved here is nothing less than the dislodging of Deucalion's son Hellen from his central position as eponymous ancestor of all those who call themselves Hellenes and his replacement by the Athenian king Erechtheus. Dorians and Ionians no longer trace their origin to the sons of Hellen, but to the daughter of Erechtheus and one or the other of her two consorts; and the human member of that pair, by virtue of the fact that he belongs to a branch of the genealogical tree—the Aeolic—that is largely absent from the rival military lineups of the late fifth century,[3] has to be considered a person of minor importance.

Up until now scholarship has concerned itself primarily with the "when" and "why" of this ambitious project of remythicization. What were the particular political considerations that made it advisable and how can a satisfactory answer to this question contribute to a probable dating of the play? Some argue for placing it between the Peace of Nicias and the Battle of Mantinea, a three-year period during which Alcibiades' ambitious schemes in the Peloponnesus might have been seen as an effort on the part of Athens to recover the patrimony of the Dorian, Ionian, and Achaean descendants of Erechtheus;[4] others prefer the years immediately following the defeat in Sicily, when the danger of rule by foreigners referred to several times in the play must have seemed more imminent,[5] and when the only part of the empire that had a chance of being retained—a few Ionian islands and coastal cities—was that inhabited by the descendants of the only grandson of Erechtheus who, in the Euripidean version, had no admixture of non-Athenian blood.

The second hypothesis strikes me as considerably more probable than the first:[6] but it is not the intention of the present essay to argue for one or the other. Both belong to what may be called a "pre-Gentilian" phase of our discipline. What will be offered here is a distinctly "post-Gentilian" speculation having to do with probable audience reaction when the play was represented for the first—and, presumably, last—time on an Athenian stage. Was it a simple matter to create a performance that attributed to Ion a place in Athenian history strikingly or totally different from that with which the spectators were familiar? Or did the poet have to expect a certain amount of resistance and unwillingness to believe? And if so, what measures has he taken to cope with the difficulty?

Not surprisingly, previous scholarship has chosen, by and large, to avoid such problems of performance and the relation of poet to public—by positing in the pre-Euripidean history of the Ion legend a version, obscure but not altogether unknown, identical to his.[7] Euripides' own role will thus have been that of an Alexandrian *poeta doctus* bringing to the attention of readers a tradition of which few of them were aware but of which he could have said— also in the manner of his Alexandrian successors—ἀμάρτυρον οὐδὲν ἀείδω.

Yet the *argumentum ex silentio* against this view is fairly strong. In Herodotus and Hesiod, Ion's father is Xuthus; Creusa is not even mentioned; and her very existence is problematic if one accepts the tradition, followed by Euripides himself in his *Erechtheus* (fr. 476.65–70 Mette), that in the war which resulted in the death of their father the virgin daughters of Erechtheus were sacrificed, or sacrificed themselves, to ensure the survival of their city. For Creusa to have avoided the fate of her sisters, her marriage would have had to occur before, not, as in the *Ion*, after the war in which they perished.[8]

Besides failing to include any mention of Ion's mother, the earliest version of the myth fairly well excludes the possibility that she was an Athenian. Ion owes his position in the city to services performed during a war in which his future subjects "sent away for him" (μετεπέμψαντο [Arist. *Ath. Pol.* 3.2]) to come to their aid, and after which we find him associated (Philochorus 328 fr. 13 Jacoby) with a festival in honor of Apollo "Run-to-the-Rescue" (*Boêdromios*) held in Athens, as well as established in the city with his followers in the capacity of "fellow settlers" (συνοικησάντων [*Ath. Pol.* 44.2]).[9] The point of departure for Ion's run to the rescue was the northern coast of the Peloponnesus, where his father was living as a Thessalian émigré.[10] In some post-Hellenistic attestations of the myth Ion is provided with an Athenian mother by the insertion of an Attic sojourn into the family's voyage southward from Thessaly. The sojourn ends when either the family's descendants (Strabo 8.7.1) or Ion himself in the company of his father (Paus. 8.1–2, Apollod. 1.49) proceeds on to the Peloponnese, only to return later for the purpose of participating in the Ionian migration or the war against Eleusis.[11]

This "return" of the family of Xuthus to Attica recalls the more famous "return" of the family of Heracles to the Peloponnese, and serves the same purpose of making an invasion (or immigration) seem like a restoration. It is possible that Euripides has some such version of the myth in mind when in the *Melanippê Sophê* (prologue 7–9) he makes Ion the son of Xuthus and "a daughter" (unnamed) "of Erechtheus."[12] But the earliest parallel to the more radical and exclusive assertion of Athenian origin found in the *Ion* is Plato *Euthydemus* 302c, where Socrates says that among Ionians Apollo receives the epithet " 'ancestral' on account of his engendering of Ion" (πατρῷος διὰ τὴν Ἴωνος γένεσιν). And here, obviously, one must reckon with the possibility—or probability—of direct Euripidean influence.[13] The cult of Apollo *patrôios* was an ancient one at Athens, but there is no clear trace of it in Ionia,[14] as one would expect if it had anything to do with Ion—just as one would expect some reference to the cult in the play itself, where, however, even the word *patrôios* fails to appear.[15]

Arguments from silence are never, of course, decisive, but in this case they can be supported by strong evidence from Euripides' own text. No one, except for the characters present on the stage during the final recognition scene between Ion and Creusa, is to know the truth about the young man's father. Athena's instructions to Creusa (1601–03) are quite clear on this point:

> νῦν οὖν σιώπα παῖς ὅδ' ὡς πέφυκε σός,
> ἵν' ἡ δόκησις Ξοῦθον ἡδέως ἔχῃ,
> σύ τ' αὖ τὰ σαυτῆς ἀγάθ' ἔχουσ' ἴῃς, γύναι.

> So be silent, now, as to how you are the one who bore this child;
> that way Xuthus is kept happy by the thought that it is his,
> and you, lady, can depart with the blessings that are yours.

Equally clear are the narratological considerations that make Athena speak as she does. If an author tells us that the facts of the historical episode he is recounting were only known to its protagonists and that these protagonists were committed to concealing them from everybody else, he can only be inviting us—whether we are an audience of readers, listeners, or spectators—to ask ourselves when and how the truth of the matter came to light. And if the text itself provides no other answer, as the text of the *Ion* does not, the only alternative is to assume that the author himself is the one responsible. The true history of Ion has remained concealed up to the point of its oral publication—by Euripides—during the course of the performance in progress as Athena delivers her speech.[16]

New and amazing light on the origin and history of the Ionian race—this is what the author claims to be offering in his play. For twentieth-century readers like ourselves, new light on a subject as remote and poorly documented as the semilegendary kings of Attica can hardly be anything but new theorizing or new fabrication. But for Euripides' audience—hearers and spectators in the fifth century B.C.—the division between legend and history was far less sharp and clear. Whatever doubts might attach to certain episodes from the "legendary" past as reported in poetic or popular tradition, the frequency with which the precedents supplied by those traditions were appealed to in advancing territorial claims, contracting political alliances, or settling political disputes shows that there was no barrier on principle to treating legend as if it were history. And Euripides' play contains just such an appeal to past precedent. Its call for heightened awareness of the ties linking Athens and Ionia would have failed of its effect had any significant portion of the audience taken its plot as a piece of poetic fabrication.[17] Viewing the *Ion* as an attempt to give the appearance of truth to a version of the past that lacked any support in earlier tradition provides, I believe, an important clue for understanding the workings of the poet-audience relationship during the play's premiere—not the only clue certainly, but a hitherto neglected one that it is worthwhile to pursue.

Seen in this light, Athena's command to remain silent is not simply a way of calling attention to the fact that truths hitherto hidden are being revealed during the course of the performance. It serves to explain why they have remained hidden for so long. The course of action recommended, like most of those suggested or required by Athena in literary contexts, is also the one demanded by simple prudence. The only way to legitimize Ion's presence in Athens is to conceal the truth about his birth and pass him off as the son of Xuthus. Otherwise he will be a bastard without a father—not a citizen fully entitled to the political career that, as everyone knew, he was destined to follow.[18] In the heroic world in which the action represented originally took place, divine parentage on the father's side and royal parentage on the mother's would doubtless have opened any and all doors to power, but the *Ion* was written for performance before citizens, not warriors or courtiers. Their reaction to its characters and plot could not help but be influenced by the standards of the world with which they were familiar, and in that world illegitimate birth was a stain hard to wash away—even with divine or royal blood.[19] Similar considerations would operate in Creusa's case. It was only by pretending to be Ion's stepmother that she could hope to recover her child without ceasing to meet the fifth-century requirement that a proper lady be someone of whom nothing is heard—either for good or for ill—outside her own home.

Counsels of prudence would be all the more welcome, given Ion's own reservations, expressed in an earlier scene (lines 582–675),[20] about what awaits him in a city such as Athens, where talent, he fears—echoing criticisms with which a fifth-century audience would be familiar—is always suspect, and doubts about purity of lineage can be an obstacle or even a danger to aspiring politicians. And after barely averted attempts to encompass each other's destruction, both he and Creusa would have been well aware, even without Athena's admonition, of what can result from pressing one's claim to a throne openly or at all costs—no matter how valid the claim may be.

In following the only sensible course of action, given Creusa's present situation and Ion's future prospects, mother and son are, of course, falling in line with a plan devised by Apollo from the start. The plan is also one for which—once its outlines finally become clear—they praise and thank the god (lines 1606–12), taking back the criticisms and doubts they had expressed earlier. Modern critics have often set themselves the task of deciding whether Euripides himself would have gone along with this change of opinion—whether he would have considered the eventual happiness of Ion and Creusa a sufficient compensation for everything that the god had made them suffer earlier.[21] But all speculation of this sort is largely pointless if, as the present argument would suggest, the sufferings of Ion and Creusa are to be laid at the door of the poet rather than the god. Euripides has simply sought out and come up with the plot best calculated to prevent his version of events from seeming less probable than the official one(s). It was inconceivable—or, at any rate, unattested elsewhere in the corpus of Greek myth—that anyone could be the son of a god and still grow up in the house of his mother without the fact being recognized. There was no choice but to have the divine child disappear from home in the simplest and most economical way. And since infants who disappear in this fashion do not ordinarily return until they are fully grown, mother and child had to be subjected to a separation of many years.

It is also the poet, not the god, who has inflicted on Creusa an obsessive need to recall, at every possible moment during the course of the drama, the story of her rape by Apollo and the subsequent exposure of the child born of the union. She tells the story no less than four times—first in describing to Ion her own experiences as if they were those of a friend, then in conversation with the old retainer who offers her his services in the plan to poison Ion, then in the aria that follows on this conversation, and finally in the scene of reconciliation and recognition. Those inclined to psychological interpretations will doubtless see all this as a faithful reflection of the anguished mental state of the protagonist. I am inclined to see it as something rather different: an elementary illustration of the principle that a lie repeated often enough eventually comes to be taken as the truth. All the members of the poet's audience knew—or thought they knew—that Ion was the son of Xuthus; but many of them might begin to have their doubts after hearing the contrary on four separate occasions (or six if we add the speeches of Hermes in the prologue and Athena in the epilogue). And their doubts would have been increased by the fact that the six birth narratives are richly supplied with identical or nearly identical complements of detail, as well as located in a spot with which some of the audience were doubtless familiar (the grotto of Pan and the nymphs on the slope of the Acropolis just opposite the one where the play was being performed). The exact knowledge of Attic topography demonstrated in these narratives,[22] as well as the apparent exactness of their references to events and monuments dating back to the earliest years of Athenian and Delphic history,[23] could easily suggest an equal exactness in setting forth the details of Erechtheid genealogy.

Naturally, what seems true to one spectator may appear false to another—hence, I suggest, the decision on the part of the poet to create at least two types of verisimilitude and, as a result, the existence of a certain disparity, noted by many scholars, between the play's treatment of Creusa and that accorded to the other protagonists. Tragedy is usually replaced by comedy or tragicomedy whenever the focus shifts from the suffering woman forced to relive her past to the lover, husband, or son attempting to investigate or atone for it. Some would attribute this to a deliberate effort—possibly part of an anti-Delphic polemic—to trivialize Apollo and his oracle.[24] But it is hard to reconcile such an interpretation with the dramatist's obvious eagerness to compliment and flatter the Ionian race by tracing its origin to that same Apollo. Downgrading the god—or appearing to do so—was, at most, a minor consequence of his desire to create a version of the past that could be interpreted as either rational reconstruction or reverent "remythicization." Keeping both interpretations in mind one might offer the following summary of the play's "message(s)":

Ion, the eponymous ancestor of the Ionians, is usually thought to have been the son of an Aeolic condottiere named Xuthus and a woman whose name and nationality are variously reported in the tradition. In fact, however, it is the father's identity not the mother's that is open to question. Ion was not Xuthus's son, but his stepson, an illegitimate child born to Creusa, the Athenian princess who was later to become Xuthus's wife, in the period before her marriage. Exposed by his mother in a cave on the Acropolis, Ion was somehow transported while still a baby to Apollo's shrine at Delphi, where the Pythia adopted him and where, many years later, his identity became known to his mother through the recognition tokens she had left in his cradle when she abandoned him. The circumstances under which this recognition occurred—during the course of a visit of Creusa and Xuthus to discover how to end the childlessness of their marriage, and immediately after an oracular response proclaiming to Xuthus that Ion was the child he was seeking—contributed to the spread of the false belief, later encouraged, for obvious reasons, by Ion hi· ıself, that he was the son of Xuthus rather than of Creusa. The identity oı the real father cannot be known for certain. Creusa, however, had always insisted that it was Apollo, and it is possible that the oracle proclaiming Ion to be the son of Xuthus was, like the original transportation of the newborn infant to Delphi, part of a plan devised by the god to rescue his son and reunite him with his mother without compromising either her reputation or his own.

Conceived in this fashion, the series of events represented in the play was open to whichever interpretation a given spectator found the more likely. Many—perhaps most—of the audience would have seen in prologue and epilogue a decisive confirmation of the truth of Creusa's convictions. The tradition involved was one of great antiquity, and antiquity's time-honored prerogative— ut miscendo humana divinis primordia urbium augustiora faciat [25]—was something acknowledged by Greeks as well as Romans, and in connection with the primordia of gentes as well as those of urbes. The more skeptically inclined, however, might have seen the embarrassing situation in which Apollo eventually finds himself—unable to appear in person before those who have been criticizing his conduct—as a reflection of the author's own embarrassment when confronted by the absurdities of Delphic religion, or even enjoyed the truly comic mess in which the machinations of the Delphic god have landed the hapless Xuthus by the end of the play. His role henceforth is to be that of the perfect cuckold, condemned by the terms of the denouement to bringing up his wife's bastard in his own house, while thinking all the time that he rather than she is the one who should bear the blame for whatever suffering the child's birth has caused.

As if to ensure that the choice between these two interpretations [26] continued to remain open, Euripides has devised—here and here only, if I am not mistaken, in what survives of his work—a plot that has no need whatsoever of the divine "apparatus" that serves the ostensible purpose of setting it in motion. [27] The foundling's arrival at Delphi, the visit to consult the oracle, the oracle's false (or misunderstood) response, the accident that saves Ion's life, and the revelations of the priestess that save Creusa's could all have occurred without the intervention of any god. Moreover, as was pointed out earlier (above, at n. 18), the decision on the part of Ion and Creusa to conceal rather than reveal what has occurred follows the commands of common sense as much as it does those of Athena; and an Athenian audience did not require the prophetic revelations of a goddess to be made aware of the historical importance of Ion and his descendants.[28] Like his Menandrean counterparts—Tychê, Agnoia, and the like—the Hermes of Euripides' prologue does not direct in any way the development of the action; he merely informs the audience of the things it must know to appreciate fully the salient ironies and foreshadowings in the scenes that are to follow. This system of double motivation is similar to one used by Euripides' contemporary Gorgias when he argues that in eloping with Paris Helen was either the passive instrument of divine will or the helpless victim of human violence, passion, and persuasion (*Encomium Helenae* 6–20), and which can also be documented, half a century later, in Gorgias's pupil Isocrates. Athens, Isocrates tells us, is the cradle of all the arts—either because the arts are an invention of men and the Athenians are, of all men, the most inventive, or because the arts are a gift of the gods and the Athenians are the nation whose piety makes it most entitled to be a recipient of divine largesse (*Paneg.* 22–23); and monarchy should be considered the best form of government, either because it is the form chosen by the gods for themselves, or because it is the form that men, realizing its superiority, have always assumed to be the one chosen by the gods for themselves (*Nic.* 26). One could offer the same double justification of Euripides' revisionist approach to Greek genealogy. The human progenitors of the Ionian race are not to be sought outside the royal house of the Erechtheids—either because Ion was the son of Creusa and the god Apollo, or because the circumstances of his birth and recognition as Creusa's son were such as to exclude the paternity of a foreigner such as Xuthus.[29]

The discussion has sought thus far to explain both the basic architecture of Euripides' plot, as well as certain emphases and dissonances in the details of its construction by reference to the poet's desire to insert—or imprison—Ion within the genealogy of the Erechtheids in such a way that his recasting of the past would have seemed plausible to a late fifth-century audience. Obviously, however, the importance of the "truths" to be revealed in this true-seeming tale was far too great for its quest of verisimilitude to be anything but part of a larger design. The basic, ultimately political character of this design has already been indicated in the opening pages of this essay. But the design had, I believe, an important ritual or quasi-ritual dimension as well, of which a few words should be said in conclusion.

Whether we think of it in mythological or rationalistic terms, the recognition which brought Creusa and Ion together was a kind of epiphany, but only a partial one. In order to become complete it had to wait until the first performance of the *Ion* before its first audience. And there is a kind of parallelism and confusion—intentionally created, it seems to me, by the author—between the two phases of the process. Phase One begins with Hermes' original entry into Athens to take charge of the newborn child and transport it to Delphi; it ends when the child, now grown to maturity and recognized, though only by its mother, finally returns to Athens. Phase Two begins with the entry of the actor playing Hermes onto an Athenian stage to take charge of the audience and transport it to the imagined Delphic site where the action of the play takes place; it ends when the audience—following as always in the steps of the play's protagonist—finally returns from an imagined Delphi to a real Athens, but to an Athens where now, thanks to the revelations of the poet, all recognize the son of Apollo and Creusa for who he really is. Self-referential to a degree unparalleled anywhere else in Euripides, the *Ion* is at once a ritual representation—infinitely repeatable—of the disappearance and return of a hero, and, at the same time, the act of return itself—unique and unrepeatable. The representation takes place in dramatic space, the actual return in theatrical space[30]—before an Athenian audience, which is literally present at the creation and naming of the new hero in the play's prologue[31] and which, in the epilogue, receives him into its pantheon, both as a symbol of the common ancestry that had always linked Athenians and Ionians and as a guarantor of the common policy and purpose which at the particular moment of performance must have been longed for with an intensity that had never been encountered before in the history of the city and would never be encountered there again.[32]

Poet, Public, and "Theatrocracy": Audience Performance in Classical Athens

Robert W. Wallace

I N A well-known passage in *Laws* 700a–701b, Plato attributes the Athenians' "progress in extravagant freedom of living" under the democracy to their progressive violations of the laws of music. In earlier days, he says, different types of music were clearly distinguished, and musicians were not permitted to use one type of music instead of another or to mix the different types. Furthermore,

> the competence to take cognizance of these rules, to pass verdicts in accord with them, and in case of need, to penalize their infraction was not left, as it is today, to the catcalls and discordant outcries of the crowd, nor yet to the clapping of those giving praise. The educated made it their rule to hear the performances through in silence; for the boys, their attendants, and the rabble at large, there was the discipline of the order-ing rod [*rhabdos kosmousê*] to enforce order. Thus the mass of the citi-zens was willing to submit to this strict control in such matters without venturing to pronounce judgment by uproar [*thorubos*].

But afterward, Plato continues, an unmusical license set in, with the appearance of poets (700d) who, though "by nature *poiêtikoi*," were "possessed by a raving and excessive lust for pleasure," and "in ignorance of what is just and legiti-mate," mixed up the various types of music.

> Their folly led them unintentionally to slander their profession by the assumption that in music there is no such thing as right and wrong, the right standard of judgment being the pleasure given to the hearer, be he high or low. By compositions of such a kind and discourse to the same effect, they naturally inspired the crowd with contempt of musical law,

and a conceit of their own competence as judges. Thus our once silent audiences have found a voice, in the persuasion that they understand what is good and bad in art; the old "sovereignty of the best" in that sphere has given way to an evil "theatrocracy."

This contempt for musical laws, Plato claims, led to a general conceit of universal knowledge and contempt for laws generally, and liberty followed in train.[1]

In *Gorgias* 502b, Plato makes his view explicit that contemporary tragedy was similarly debased.

> *Sokrates:* And what is the aim of that stately and marvelous creature, tragic drama? Is it tragedy's endeavor and ambition, in your opinion, merely to gratify the spectators; or, if there is anything pleasant and charming, but evil, to struggle against uttering it, but to declaim and sing anything that is unwelcome but beneficial, whether they like it or not? For which of these two aims do you think tragic poetry is equipped?
>
> *Kallikles:* It is indeed quite evident, Sokrates, that its impulse is rather toward pleasure and the gratification of spectators.

Earlier, in *Gorgias* 501e, Sokrates asks Kallikles, "Do you imagine that Kinesias son of Meles is in the slightest concerned with saying anything likely to improve his hearers, or merely what will gratify the mob of spectators?" Kallikles responds, "That is quite obvious, Sokrates, at least in the case of Kinesias."

Finally, in *Laws* 659b–c Plato introduces a second theme concerning theater and the demos, that popular audiences had a marked but adverse effect on the dramas and music performed before them. "The present custom . . . leaves things to the mass of the spectators and decides the victory by their votes, a practice that has corrupted the poets themselves—since their standard in composition is the common taste of their judges, with the result that it is actually the audience who educates them—and equally corrupted the tastes of the audience."[2]

The themes of these and other passages in Plato,[3] against the value of popular judgment, proved influential in later antiquity, in both theatrical and other public contexts. According to Plutarch, when once the advice of the fourth-century rhetor and general Phokion, formerly a student in the Academy, received cheers and applause from the demos, he turned to his friends and asked "if he had inadvertently said something foolish."[4] The late fourth-century Peripatetic music theoretician Aristoxenos condemned the *harmonikoi* if, in "aiming to please the general public," they think that "the layman should be set up as a judge of the sciences."[5] Lucian recommends to musicians that, although many of the crowd know how to clap (*krotein*) and hiss (*surisai*), musicians should seek praise only from "those who know" (*Harmonid.* 1–3). In his sixty-seventh oration, on popular opinion, Dio Chrysostom states that the philosopher is superior to others in his knowledge of the truth and so will regard popular opinion as nothing but a shadow.[6] As for the effect of audience approval on writers and composers, in *Poetics* 1453a Aristotle observes that the common use of a particular type of dramatic structure in the fourth century is "due to the weakness of the audiences; for the poets follow along, catering to their wishes" (trans. Else).[7] In *Politics* 1341b he remarks that in theatrical performances the "listener is a common person and usually influences the music accordingly, so that he has an effect both on the personality of the professionals themselves who perform for him, and because of the motions which they make, on their bodies too" (trans. Sinclair, rev. Saunders).

The immediate source of Plato's two theses on performance and the public was of course his elitist, antidemocratic sensibilities: in his view the demos was incapable of discerning the truth. In a general sense Plato's contention that the purpose of theater should be not to give pleasure but to serve a higher goal was anticipated both by Thucydides and by Euripides' *Medea*, as Gentili and Cerri have noted.[8] The nurse in *Medea* (190–201) condemns "the poets of old" who wrote songs for pleasant social gatherings, because "none of them has discovered how to put an end to grief with their singing or musical instruments. . . . Why raise a voice at a banquet to no purpose?" (trans. Warner, adapted). In a similar venue (the public Assembly), Kleon calls the Athenians victims of their own pleasure in listening to speeches, "by praising a good point even before it is made, and by being as quick at seeing how an argument is going to be developed as [they] are slow at understanding what in the end it will lead to. . . . Simply overcome by the pleasure of listening," the Athenians "are more like an audience sitting at the feet of sophists than people who are deliberating about the polis" (Thuc. 3.38.6–7, trans. Warner, adapted).

In the current context, Plato's comments in *Laws* raise two related questions. First, is his description of the greater significance of applause in the theater in fourth-century Athens historically accurate, or merely a fantasy of *patrios-politeia* idealizing, of the "Golden Age" variety? The conception informing that description has often been accepted by modern scholars, who, following Plato, comment on the growing influence of the demos in theatrical productions during the fourth century. Isobel Henderson's assertion (although it partly misunderstands Plato) is only an extreme version of this: "that [the poorer citizens] had to be kept quiet with sticks [in the fifth century] is only one instance of the well-known fact that Periclean ideals of enlightenment failed to penetrate the lower strata of society."[9] Though probably few other scholars would accept Plato's claim that fifth-century audiences sat quietly in theaters watched over by officials ready to strike any noisemaker,[10] it is common to accept his general point of increased audience involvement in the theater during the fourth century, and to represent this as something bad. For example, in the *Cambridge History of Greek Literature* Charles Segal writes that during the fourth century, "as Plato charges in the *Laws*, taste formed by aristocratic values has given way to taste formed by the mob and the 'theatocracy' (3.700c, 701a, cf. *Gorgias* 501e)."[11] In an essay entitled "The Theater Crisis in the Greek World in the Fourth Century B.C.," Pauline Ghiron-Bistagne states that Athenian audiences had now "become moody, and their reactions were often unpredictable," symptoms of Athens's social malaise (*einer inneren Unruhe*). "The actors, governed purely by the search for success and money, promoted the *theatrokratia*, that tyranny of the spectators which according to Plato was as destructive as political tyranny."[12] These judgments in essence accept both the historical reality of increased audience participation as described by Plato, and his interpretation and negative valuation of it. However, each of these different aspects of Plato's report needs to be carefully evaluated, and also evaluated separately—not least because Plato was a hostile witness.

Plato's historical statement about rod bearers, although at best misleading, raises the question of if and how the *role* of Athenian audiences—their "performance" in the theater—evolved during the fifth and fourth centuries. In this essay I shall argue that during the fifth and fourth centuries the audience's performance may well have evolved in the direction that Plato so despised. Thus, in part I agree with Plato, Charles Segal, and others. However, despite modern scholars' insistence on the "unruly mob," Plato has also rightly divined one explanation for this development, which in the first instance he attributes not to the demos of Athens but to its dramatists and composers. In the fourth century some dramatists, musicians, and other artists grew increasingly skilled at eliciting responses from the audience, and some of these may well have regarded the applause of the demos as their principal goal. Our evaluation of this development must depend in part on our assessment of popular tastes in the fourth century. Surely now only a few harmless eccentrics would claim that everything that the demos liked or that Plato condemns was ipso facto unworthy. Finally, from yet another perspective, Plato has ignored a major development that began in the later fifth century, in the increased importance of writers (such as Plato himself) who worked principally for themselves without any regard for popular approval. New modes of communication had given them this freedom. These wider developments help put into context the increase in the demos's participation in the public theater during the fourth century.

Before we turn to these questions, one preliminary issue must briefly be addressed. Plato and his modern followers have distinguished an earlier period when audiences behaved properly, from a later period when they did not. What periods are meant? In *Laws* 698a–700d, just before his discussion of musical license, Plato praises Athens at the time of the Persian Wars and states that its degeneration began "afterward, in the course of time" (*meta tauta, proiontos tou chronou,* 700d). In the passage from *Laws* first quoted in this essay, Plato regards the degeneration of contemporary Athens as a consequence of the city's musical revolutionaries. Quite helpfully the comic poet Pherekrates, roughly contemporary with Aristophanes, ridicules these "new-wave" composers in chronological order (ap. [Plut.] *De mus.* 1141d–1142a). The first was Melanippides; he is followed by Kinesias, then by Phrynis, and then by Timotheos. Melanippides' floruit cannot be fixed more narrowly than 480–430. The others belong to the years of the Peloponnesian War and after.[13] A standard view is that for Plato the cultural degeneration he describes began after the Persian Wars.[14] Hence, despite the vagueness of Plato's chronological indications in *Laws* 700d, the period he refers to could well have included a significant part of the fifth century. However, few modern scholars who are sympathetic to Plato's criticisms of the fourth-century theater have marked the start of Athens's literary and political degeneration before the late fifth century. Ghiron-Bistagne dates the break circa 420; she also refers more generally to the later period (in Plato) as "the fourth century." Others speak more straightforwardly of the cultural break represented by Athens's defeat in 404. For most, it is the fourth century that is problematic.[15] For our purposes, therefore, the question of a cultural division between the fifth and fourth centuries is central. However, we must also consider whether important aspects of fourth-century culture may well have begun substantially earlier, in a transitional period during the second half of the fifth century.[16]

. . .

BY VIRTUALLY all accounts except Plato's, from our earliest records the Athenian theater audience was both vocal and even physically active during theater performances.[17] In the sources, this appears to apply nearly as much in tragedy and musical recitals as in comedy, where the playwright sometimes directly provoked the audience through unmediated verbal and even physical approaches, as we shall see.[18] Unfortunately, the evidence to document audience activity in any period is often problematic, largely because the behavior of the public was of no great interest to ancient writers except as it illustrated the reception accorded famous artists. For fifth-century audience behavior, much of the evidence is anecdotal and hence of questionable value. A number of these anecdotes pertain to Euripides, especially because of his plays' sometimes scandalous content. Thus, according to Plutarch (*Mor.* 33c), after the audience of Euripides' *Aiolos* made a *thorubos* when it heard the line "what's shameful if the users think it not so?" Antisthenes responded in matching iambic trimeter, "shameful is shame whether it seems so or not." Also according to Plutarch (*Mor.* 756c, and see Lucian *Iov. trag.* 41), a *thorubos* erupted in the audience when Euripides' *Mela-nippê* opened with the line, "Zeus, whoever Zeus is, for I do not know except in logos." The playwright later changed the line and restaged the play (frs. 480–81 N). According to Seneca (*Ep.* 105.15), after a character in one of Euripides' plays uttered a scandalous speech praising money above all else, "the whole audience rose up with one accord to drive out both the actor and the play. But Euripides jumped to his feet and asked them to wait and see what end this grasper after gold would meet." According to Cicero (*Tusc. Disp.* 4.29.63) at least one member of the audience—Sokrates—was so pleased by the opening of Euripides' *Orestes* (which asserted the power of human endurance) that he called for a triple encore.[19] Finally, in a story told by Plutarch (*An seni resp. ger.* 795d), when the audience hissed (*surittein*) a musical performance by Timotheos for its new-fangledness (*kainotomia*), Euripides encouraged him by saying he would soon have the applause of every audience. Most of these anecdotes are almost certainly unhistorical.[20] However, even if themselves fictitious—and even if Euripides' notorious provocations might imply that the Athenians' response to his plays was not typical—these anecdotes might well reflect generally a transitional period in audience response during the later fifth century.

Except for the Sophilos vase from the second quarter of the sixth century, which shows an energetic audience gesticulating from the bleachers at Patroklos's funeral games,[21] our earliest reasonably credible report of audience activity in the theater pertains to Aeschylus.[22] According to the early Peripatetic Herakleides Pontikos (fr. 170 W = *Comm. in Arist. Gr.* 20.145), during a dramatic performance in which he made revelations about the Eleusinian mysteries, Aeschylus was forced to flee to the altar of Dionysos to avoid being killed by the crowd. His subsequent defense, of ignorance that what he said was secret, was known to Aristotle (*EN* 1111a10). In the later fifth century Aristophanes says that the spectators might "cry oh!" (*ôzein*) at daring dramatic dancing (*Vesp.* 1525). Aristotle also records (*Poet.* 1456a17 = Ag. 39 T 17 Snell) that the tragedian Agathon (f. 416–ca. 401) was hissed off the stage[23] because he included too much material in a dramatic plot. In Aristophanes' *Frogs* (405 B.C.) the contest between Aeschylus and Euripides was accompanied by great *thorubos*, *boê*, and *loidorêsmos* (lines 757–58).[24] Another source that may be fourth-century ([Andokides] *In Alcib.* 20–21) tells of an episode in which as a choregos of boys Alkibiades drove off the competing choregos Taureas with his fists. The spectators "showed their sympathy with Taureas and their hatred of Alkibiades by praising the one chorus and refusing to listen at all to the other one." However, "partly from fear, partly from wishing to gratify him," the judges gave the prize to Alkibiades. This surely was not what Plato had in mind when he wrote of the theater judges' independence from the spectators in earlier Athens.[25] But much of this must again be apocryphal.

As for the public use of projectiles, evidence for the fifth century is limited to a single quite doubtful example, though again our source record is inadequate. According to the early Peripatetic Chamaileon,[26] the later fifth-century comic poet Hegemon of Thasos himself brought stones into the theater, threw them into the orchestra, and said—in verse—"throw if you want!" since his play would be good. Pelting could certainly occur in reverse. According to Aristophanes' *Wasps* (56–59), in some comedies servants scattered nuts from the stage among the audience. In *Peace* 960–63, Aristophanes has slaves throw what is called sacrificial grain to the audience, thereby introducing an indecent pun (κριθή = barley or penis). In *Wealth* 797–801, Wealth says that with a poet like ours, we don't need to shower the audience with *ischadia* (dried figs?) and *trogalia* (figs and nuts and other tidbits).[27]

As for evidence specifically documenting applause (*krotos*),[28] in the fifth century, Aristophanes attests applause in the Boulê (*Eq.* 650–51) and by symposiasts (*Vesp.* 1313–14). Although he does not specifically mention it, the audience in the theater must also have applauded. Vociferous shouting in support is certainly attested during the fifth century, and some of the terms for this, notably *thorubos*, may have included applause. In *Knights* 546–48, the poet asks the audience to raise a great loud shout (*pothion*) for him, "a noble Lenaian *thorobos*, so that he depart rejoicing." (In Plut. *Alcib.* 10, *thorubos* appears to be equated with *krotos* and *boê* in an anecdote about Alkibiades in the assembly; in Dem. 21.14, the orator mentions "both *thorubos* and *krotos*.")[29] As a general point, applause in the theater *can* certainly occur without simultaneous shouts of approval, as often in modern performances. The reverse is perhaps less common. There is no evidence that fifth-century theater audiences merely clapped—though that again may reflect the state of our evidence. In the passage from Thucydides already discussed, Kleon describes the Athenian Assembly as just like an audience at a sophist's lecture, listening with pleasure and praising clever points. Other fifth-century evidence is again anecdotal. So, for example, according to Plutarch (*Mor.* 785b), after reciting a chorus from *Oedipus at Colonus* in a suit brought against him by his son, Sophokles was "escorted from the court *as if from a theater*, with the *krotos* and *boê* of those present." However, in the manner of ancient biography (which often reconstructed poets' lives from details in their written works), the story of the aged Sophokles' dispute with his son Iophon may have been derived from the story of the aged Oedipus's dispute with his son Polyneikes, as Lowell Edmunds has argued. "In order to make the point crystal clear, the biographical tradition has Sophocles read the tragedy aloud in the courtroom in which he successfully defends himself against his son. In some of the testimonia, it is of course the stasimon in praise of Colonus that the tragedian recites, as would be expected of Sophocles the native of Colonus."[30]

In the fourth century, audience performance was similar in type, although several new kinds of expressions are attested. Applause (*krotos*) is frequently mentioned. As we shall see, in a number of plays Menander asks the audience to applaud his work. Theophrastos describes the obnoxious man as one who claps (*krotein*) in the theater when the others have stopped (*Char.* 11). Clapping was sometimes accompanied by *poppusmos*,[31] which LSJ defines as smacking the lips or clucking, and Gow as "an explosive hiss" like English *pst*.[32] Both definitions clearly interpret the word as onomatopoetic. Xenophon (*Eq.* 9.10) says that one could calm (or, alternatively, stimulate) a horse with this noise (the Loeb here curiously translates "chirp"),[33] and Plutarch reports that the same was true of a cow (*Mor.* 713b). According to the *Palatine Anthology* (5.245 and 5.285), *poppusmos* was a kissing sound: in both passages lips are specified (and hence the first of LSJ's meanings). By contrast, Theokritos (5.7) uses the verb *poppusdo* to describe bad playing on an aulos; this would appear to account for Gow's interpretation. None of these sounds is instantly easy to imagine in the context of applause. My research on *poppusmos* continues.

Clapping (we have seen) could also be accompanied by *thorubos*, which (as in Aristophanes' *Knights*) might be a positive rather than negative noise.[34] In later writers we even find the term *krotothorubos*.[35] In the *Republic* (492b–c) Plato complains about the praise or blame of *hoi polloi* when they are gathered together in assembly, courts, theaters, or camps, *kai ekboontes kai krotountes*. In addition to applause, *thorubos* and *poppusmos*, Eratosthenes (ap. *Schol. Eur. Hec.* 574) and much later the *Souda* (s.v. *periageiromenoi*) attest the practice of *phyllobolia*, pelting with flowers or leaves, unfortunately without chronological details. (The *Souda* remarks that in its day, also, people threw hats and *zônai* [belts?] and chitons!) The symposiasts at Xenophon's *Symposium* 9.4 shout αὖθις—*bis!*—with much *krotos* at the performance of a pantomime. Other exclamations, such as θαυμαστῶς and οὐά, οὐά, are attested first in the Roman period.[36] Among gestures, so are flapping a corner of one's cloak,[37] and thumbs-up or -down.[38]

Negative responses by the theater public included above all hissing, *surittein*. In an example of literary judgment by the theater audience, Aristotle says that the character Amphiaraos was actually hissed off the stage because the audience noticed an entrance whose effect the playwright Karkinos had not properly calculated (*Poet.* 1455a27 = Kark. 70 F 1c). Demosthenes says that "those of you who were spectators at the Dionysia hissed [*esurittete*] and hooted [*eklôzete*] Meidias when he entered the theater" (21.226). In Theophrastos's *Characters* 11, the obnoxious man hisses the actors when the others are enjoying the show. According to Demosthenes (18.265), the actor Aischines was hissed off the stage, with Demosthenes himself contributing to the noise. Elsewhere (19.337) Demosthenes says that when Aischines played tragic parts, "you [Athenians] drove him and hissed him from the theaters, and almost pelted him with stones [*kataleuô*]."[39] In the earlier passage where he describes Meidias, Demosthenes refers to a hostile noise called *klôzmos* or *klôgmos*, a sound which Pollux (5.89) says was that of crows, but others of chickens.[40] This was surely analogous to our booing, though whether the sound was similar is uncertain. The conjunction *klôzein* and *surittein* occurs elsewhere,[41] as in English "hiss and boo." As for throwing stones, Lynkeus of Samos (*RE* no. 6), Menander's contemporary, wrote that the kitharode Polyktor, drinking greedily some lentil soup, hit his tooth on a stone. "You poor thing," the parasite Lark said, "even the lentil soup pelts you" (Athen. 245d). Athenaios there suggests that the same kitharode was referred to by Machon, the third-century Alexandrian: "a very bad kitharode" asked for some stones to repair his house, remarking that he would "pay them back in much greater numbers after the performance." It is not perhaps altogether credible that Athenian audiences actually threw stones at the players.[42] By contrast, however, Demosthenes says that when Aischines was performing on stage, he "picked up figs and grapes and olives, like an orchard-robbing fruitmonger, and made a better living from these missiles than by all the battles that [he] fought for dear life. For there was no truce or armistice in the warfare between [him] and [his] audiences, and [his] casualties were so heavy, that no wonder [he] taunts with cowardice those of us who have no experience of such engagements" (18.262).[43] According to Athenaios (583f), the people carried the comic poet Diphilos out of the theater because "he had greatly disgraced himself." Finally, according to Pollux (4.122; cf. 2.197), "striking the seats with the heels is called *pternokopein*; they did this whenever they wanted to drive somebody off." It is unclear, however, whether this passage refers to Athens, and whether a wooden theater is presupposed.[44] Making the sign of ass's ears, putting fingers behind the ears and flapping, and sticking out the tongue are also not attested before the Roman period.[45]

Thus, to judge from the sources, the public itself performed quite vigorously in the theater during both the fifth and the fourth centuries, sometimes even interrupting the drama. These performances were enhanced by the much lower barrier, both literally and figuratively, between stage and public that exists in the modern theater. Physically, the audience was not separated from the performers but surrounded them, with nothing between the orchestra and the lower banks of seats. The stage was also minimally elevated.[46] Comic writers frequently erased the boundary of theatrical illusion altogether by speaking directly to the public, notably but not only in the *parabasis*.[47]

Was there an increase in the public's "performance" in the theater during the fourth century, as Plato says? I note that, according to Aischines (3.232), in the fourth century the demos actually levied fines on the judges of (at any rate) the cyclic choruses, "if they do not judge correctly" (*dikaiôs*). This is at least not attested earlier. It is also worth remembering that Plato, born in 429, was himself present at the productions of some fifth-century music and drama and could have witnessed one part of the transition he describes—although all of his experiences would obviously have occurred toward the end of the century.

The answer to this question, however, need not depend on such details, but may emerge from the history of fourth-century drama, particularly in the light of our second question, of the extent to which the approval of the audience affected dramatists and musicians.

According to the elite of Athens, we have seen, some fourth-century artists *focused* on winning applause: this was the main purpose of their work, which they fashioned in order to receive it. Later, in Lucian's *Harmonides* (1–3), Harmonides asks his aulos teacher how he can become famous, because, he says, fame is the reason why he took up the aulos. Was the approval of the audience the principal goal of many fourth-century dramatists and musicians?[48] Approval was, of course, always important in Greece, as the rather unusual phenomenon of competitive cultural events attests.[49] When in the early fifth century Lasos of Hermione apparently lost a poetry contest with Simonides and remarked *oligon moi melei*,[50] that seemingly dismissive remark surely shows how much Lasos cared about winning. Aristophanes often claims that he is writing not to flatter the Athenians, but to educate them. As the chorus says of him in the *parabasis* of *Acharnians* (lines 656–58, trans. Sommerstein),

He'll carry on impeaching
Every abuse he sees, and give much valuable teaching,
Making you wiser, happier men. There won't be any diddling
Or flattery or bribes, or any other kind of fiddling,
Nor will you drown in fulsome praises, such as all the rest
Bestow on you: he thinks his job's to teach you what is best.

However, in the *parabasis* of *Clouds* (lines 518–62), Aristophanes reproaches the Athenians for not liking the first version of his play, and hopes very much they will like the second.

While fifth-century playwrights tried hard to please the demos, they also sought to write on serious themes of contemporary intellectual and political importance: they were still (in Detienne's phrase) *maîtres de vérité*.[51] According to Aristophanes (*Ran.* 1054–55), "boys have a schoolteacher to instruct them, grown-ups have poets." As a generalization, most fifth-century dramas surely had two goals, to please and also to educate the audience, and at times these goals collided, as frequently with Euripides. There can be no doubt that the Athenians found Euripides fascinating—the tradition that he left Athens for Macedonia in 408 because he was unappreciated is unjustified. Still, Euripides' plays took first prize in only four years, compared with Sophokles' twenty-four. An analogy may be made with the Ekklêsia, where speakers tried openly both to win the approval of the public and to bring the demos over to their point of view. Conversely, starting with Thucydides 2.65.8–12, elite Athenians began to criticize those orators who (they claimed) sought only to please the people.[52]

This is not the place in detail to defend the view that during the fourth century serious tragedies and serious comedies continued to be produced for performance at Athens, works that aimed both to please and to enlighten the demos.[53] Serious music was certainly produced; despite Plato's criticisms, the fourth century saw the high point of Athenian musical composition.[54] Although as a general trend fourth-century dramatists turned away from theology, intellectual exposition, and (to a lesser extent) politics, in favor of personal drama and theatrical spectacle, such dramatic innovations should not automatically be condemned as degenerate, in accordance with the opinions of antidemocratic cultural reactionaries such as Plato. Webster thus summarizes the central innovations of this type of fourth-century drama: "excitement of story, scenic effects, good speeches for the actors, and what today we call 'theatre.' "[55] Lesky writes of "a strong preference for the suspenseful and the gruesome, and . . . a significant heightening of pathos" in these plays.[56] Hence, a primary aspect of this new work was its effect on the audience. The fourth century also saw the staging of more purely popular entertainment, which in the Theater of Dionysos at any rate may have been something of an innovation. In large part the raison d'être of this kind of drama was its appeal to the demos. A central purpose was to stir the public's emotions. This will therefore support the hypothesis (and to this extent Plato) that during the fourth century there was an increase in popular response in the theater. A second argument in support of the theater's increased preoccupation with audience enthusiasm is the spread of theatrical interpolations in dramatic texts.[57] The extent of such interpolations is indicated by Lykourgos's statute that the tragedies of Aeschylus, Sophokles, and Euripides "be written out and kept in a public depository and that the secretary of the city read them to the actors for comparison, and that it be unlawful to depart from the official text in acting" ([Plut.] *Vit. X Orat.* 841f). As with nineteenth-century Italian opera, which often provided to the diva a great aria during the first act lest she insert one from a different work(!), actors in Athens inserted famous lines or set speeches into stage dramas to win the cheers of the public. A third useful indication of the development of popular response in the theater is the appearance of the star.[58] As Polyainos wrote (*Strateg.* 6.10), at least some of the audience attended the theater to see these stars: the content of the drama was not critical. According to Aristotle (*Rhet.* 1403b33), in the fourth century actors had more power than playwrights. Aristotle also reports that people who brought food to the theater snacked especially when the actors were bad (*EN* 1175b12–13); he does not say they ate when the plays were bad. According to Xenophon (*Symp.* 3.11), the actor Kallipides, "who had a name and fame among the Greeks and was eagerly courted by all" (Plut. *Ages.* 21.4), took great pride in his ability to reduce audiences to tears. The Athenian Theodoros, the great actor of female parts, who insisted on appearing first on the stage (Arist. *Pol.* 1336b28) and who was buried on the Sacred Way (Paus. 1.37.3), was (we are told) nearly killed by Alexander the tyrant of Pherae for having brought him to tears.[59] According to Plutarch (*Mor.* 674b–c), several rivals of the fourth-century comic actor Parmenon, who prided himself on his imitation of a pig's squeal, tried unsuccessfully to outdo him. Finally, they brought a live pig on stage, concealed under a jacket. "The audience, even when they heard the genuine squeal, murmured 'What is this compared with Parmenon's pig?'" whereupon the pig was released into the crowd. Some of this would surely not have amused Plato.

If therefore audiences were more involved with theatrical productions during the fourth century, this reflected in part an evolving attitude in some artists to produce works of immediate popular appeal. Aristotle notes that even good poets "stretch out" a plot beyond its capacity and dislocate its sequence in order to compose set pieces for the actors (*Poet.* 1451b34–38). It is abundantly clear that early fifth-century audiences could also be stirred to great passion—and even direct action—by theatrical productions. The essential difference is not so much that in the fourth century a now corrupted demos was more emotional than in the fifth, though shifts in what was accepted as proper behavior by a theater audience could also have had an effect. (The lack of adequate sources precludes any demonstration of this.) Rather, partly in their search for popular acclaim and partly to create something new, some artists deliberately played to the emotional side of the theater audience. They created new types of drama and music that were characterized by direct emotional appeal. Plato describes this development in the passage from *Laws* that began this essay. The negative aspects of this phenomenon may be linked with one aspect of the rise of individualism during the later fifth and fourth centuries, with the appearance of individuals (such as Alkibiades) who sought success regardless of principles or policies.

A similar process of reducing elitist or high-brow elements (or from another perspective, lowering standards) in drama to achieve a broader appeal has probably characterized the history of television and, more generally, the history of capitalism of which the media are a part. Hence, as Plato laments (but we may not), the tastes of popular audiences probably did have an effect on some types of drama and music. As we have seen, it has proved easy to phrase the issue of audience response in a pejorative or elitist way. However, there can be no doubt that much of what fourth-century dramatists and composers achieved was genuinely innovative—and therefore attracted conservatives' scorn. Finally, the greater participation by theater audiences may also have reflected, not simply a more popular treatment of dramatic materials, but also the demos's greater sense of self-confidence in expressing its judgment, something we also see in politics. The standard opinion that in the Assembly the Athenians were more passive and apathetic during the fourth century than during the fifth can no longer be defended, as Mogens Hansen and others have shown.[60] I note the contradiction between standard scholarly conceptions of fourth-century Athenians as more passive in the Assembly than fifth-century Athenians, but more vocal in the theater. That image may be colored by the world of the Roman Empire, when a powerless populus had to content itself with public entertainments of a gross and vulgar nature.

Thus in the fourth century theatrical performance did in part evolve in the direction of public entertainment—entertainment for which popular approval was its raison d'être.[61] Popular musicians and dramatic artists of this type now understood better than their fifth-century predecessors how to appeal to ordinary theatergoers. Thus in essence one main point of their work was to win applause.[62] The first explicit requests for applause in a drama occur in Menander.[63] So far, then, Plato was right: the deepest thoughts of his age were no longer expressed in this type of work, or on the public stage. But in this development Plato failed to see a crucial counterbalancing factor. By contrast with fifth-century dramatists whose complex tasks included both entertainment and education through the complex medium of sung poetry, in fourth-century Athens, the deepest thinkers and finest teachers had moved into a different world, where they could think and write without considering the applause of the moment. In most cases, serious intellectuals during the fifth century were directly engaged with their community. The oral, public nature of communication meant that many works bearing the weight of society's deepest reflections were necessarily presented in public and to the demos. During the fourth century the position of Athenian intellectuals had shifted. The different manifestations of the new intellectual world included the written page, prose texts, and the philosophical school. Isolated intellectuals—philosophers who hated the crowd—could write in prose for a restricted, often international audience. As Thucydides expressly stated (1.22), "my work is not a piece of writing designed to meet the taste of an immediate public." Isokrates notes that he himself was too timid and had too weak a voice actually to speak in public. Accordingly he wrote, "to give advice to Athens and to the Greeks at large and to the most distinguished among men" (*Ad. Phil.* 5.81–82). Hence, public drama no longer had to carry the weight of society's reflections. In *Rhetoric* 1413b, Aristotle mentions the existence of "poets whose plays are meant to be read and circulated." In essence Plato ignores the positive side of the cultural phenomenon that he observed, which was the growing specialization of culture, most broadly here into popular culture and elite culture.[64] In the fourth century a popular theater developed, largely for entertainment, but so do important new genres such as rhetoric and philosophy, as with Plato himself. These genres took over part of the paideutic function that tragedy once possessed. Even in drama, Aristotle notes (*Pol.* 1342a16ff.), there were now two types of theater audience, one educated and the other common—mechanics, hired workers, and suchlike, for whom competitions and spectacles had to be provided. Artists are now effectively divided into two groups: popular artists, who sought fame by appealing to the demos, and artists who worked purely for their craft. Some of these, like Plato, were openly opposed to the demos, who henceforth would not listen to them. The artist who does not perform in public, and who scorns popular acclaim, reflects one aspect of the emergence of the individual during the fourth century.

Menander is in part symptomatic of what had occurred. His plays' themes are not perhaps so conventionally "serious" as those of Aristophanes (which included the political, intellectual, and literary salvation of Athens). Many of his plays make direct requests for applause from the audience, as we have seen. Yet these elegant dramas are in their way also serious, illuminating, and dealing poignantly with the daily lives of their audience. This represents a fresh development in literary history. The Athenians may not have altogether warmed to Menander, either. According to Gellius (17.4), he won first prize only eight times. As an indication of the theatrical disturbances that Plato complained of, Gellius also reports that Menander's rival Philemon won many victories over him with the help of his claque of supporters. Claques are also mentioned by Alkiphron (3.35.3) in the third century, as useful to prevent *klôzein* and *surittein*.

The antidemocratic elite objected to popular sentiment in part because a separate, elite intellectual world now existed that provided to them a vantage point from which to criticize the demos, and in part because it meant that the elite's authority over the people was less. On a more personal level, Plato's contempt for fourth-century theater may have been influenced by his own dislike of earthly pleasures. This is indicated not only by his elevation of the spiritual over the body, but also by suggestive details such as his scorn for good cooking—he compares many things he disapproves of to cooking or cooks.[65] I also note Aristotle's report that when Plato proposed to give a lecture on the good, many came expecting to hear about human good. When he spoke on mathematics and numbers, they fled.[66] This cannot have lessened Plato's dislike of public audiences.

Plato's attempt to erect an elitist barrier between poet and audience had no effect in his own day. He could not take drama away from the public and make it serve his authoritarian pedagogic goals. However, since the nineteenth century he has had more success.[67] Instead of once calm audiences becoming more raucous as Plato supposed, modern audiences that once were raucous have become more sedate and repressed. In good Platonic style, audiences now listen respectfully while the artist teaches. We may consider, for example, the public repression of the self that is evident in the customary silence of the crowd between musical movements. The public is controlled not so much by the architecture of the theater or the whips of beadles, as by the ethos inculcated by Plato and his heirs that drama is for respectful instruction, not irreverent amusement. When versions of this text were delivered at the American Academy on "Gentili-Day" and later in Florence, my audiences sat quietly, with little *krotos* or *boê*, but also without throwing stones, figs, olives—or tomatoes! For that I was grateful. Valete, et plaudite.[68]

All the (Greek) World's a Stage: Notes on (Not Just Dramatic) Greek Staging

Maria Grazia Bonanno

T HE FAMOUS monologue of Jaques in *As You Like It* (2.7), comparing the whole world to a stage where men are but actors, is an essay of the type based on the motto *Totus mundus agit histrionem* of the Globe Theater, into which Shakespeare's company had just moved (1599). It takes in its turn a central position in the essay that E. R. Curtius dedicated to the metaphor of the *theatrum mundi* that comes into medieval literature (and afterward in European literature) from both pagan and Christian sources.[1] It begins, as Curtius observes, in Plato. While in the *Philebus* Plato talks about the tragedy and comedy of life (50b3), in the *Laws* he refigures man as θαῦμα, a puppet in the playful hands of some god or other (644d7). In question is one of the same θαύματα evoked together with the θαυματοποιός, the puppeteer, in the myth of the cave (*Republ.* 514b7), which today we can see as an early metaphor for the cinema.

If we here misuse this Shakespearean motto, it is because the reification of the classic metaphor suits the Greek world better than any other. The Greek world really was theater in the sense that Greek culture was the culture of performance par excellence, at least until the end of the Hellenistic period. Even afterward, it survives in the fiction of certain "nostalgic" literary forms.

Greek performance was born—before theater as such—with the birth of poetry, epic and lyric, identical with its own execution (and sometimes also composition) before an audience of listeners-spectators. This view of archaic poetry, which now seems obvious, is however the latest synthesis of relatively recent studies. Among these the most influential perhaps is that by Havelock, which aims at measuring the effects of orality of communication above all on epic poetry—the exclusive and exhaustive property of Tradition (with a capital

"T"): a sort of "encyclopaedia of ethics, politics, history and technology."[2] "The originality of the argument," as Gentili notes, "lies in its having isolated in the very cultural structures represented in Homeric epic the underlying reasons for the harshness with which Plato attacks artists and poets for producing a re-elaboration of experience doubly removed from reality": a dangerous reelaboration because via the performance the author-executor, miming the story, did not leave the listener-spectator indifferent, but "through the psychosomatic pleasure inherent in the visual (gestural) and auditory (musico-rhythmical) aspects of the spectacle, he became involved to the point of being himself actor and participant in the mimetic action."[3]

Gentili deserves credit for noting the same effects in lyric poetry. "Seen simply as forms of oral communication, Homeric epic and archaic lyric are part of a continuous line of development. . . . What is involved is a mental attitude focused on performance—a 'performance psychology' aimed at giving public dimensions to what is personal and subjective and so setting up an emotional rapport between speaker and audience. Hence the frequent use of metaphors, images, and similes . . .—an esoteric coterie language, so to speak, evident above all in the allegories of Alcaeus."[4] Gentili refers to politically oriented groups such as that of Alcaeus (the same would hold for Archilochus, Solon, or Theognis), which were particularly accustomed to sympotic occasions. Neither should the occasion of the thiasos sacred to Aphrodite, the thiasos of the ἁγνά Sappho, nor the appearances of Ibycus and Anacreon as courtiers at the court of Polycrates be forgotten. And least of all the public occasions for the city festivals and for the athletic victories celebrated in the great choral lyric poetry from Alcman to Pindar: it is, above all, these exquisitely theatrical occasions that precede what is normally understood by "Greek theater": Attic tragedy and comedy.

On the continuity from Homer to Attic tragedy, Bérard had long ago affirmed: "Homère fut . . . un auteur de scène, récité et joué par les aèdes d'abord, par les rhapsodes ensuite," and "il faut donc lutter en nous-mêmes contre tous les enseignements et tous le préjougés de notre éducation littéraire pour apercevoir que, de l'épos homérique à la tragédie athénienne, il y eut continuité de développement et identité de nature: l'épos est un drame en hexamètres, à un seul récitant; la tragédie est un drame en mètres mélangés, à un, puis à deux, puis à trois, puis à plusieurs récitants." On the subject of poetry read and poetry heard, Manara Valgimigli had long ago observed: "we today have a criterion for, and a sentiment of, poetry completely different from the Greeks of the classical to the Hellenistic periods." Moreover, she continues, "everything in ancient Greece was as if it were recited and enacted," thus involving not only the history of Herodotus but also that of Thucydides, as well as philosophy, from that in hexameter by Empedocles (recited by ῥαψῳδοί as Athen. 14.12 informs us) to that in the form of dialogue-mime by Plato: all is drama, beginning with Homer, the "dramatic poet."[5] But one has the impression that intuition, ingenious in Bérard and highly refined in Valgimigli, expressed (though to unreceptive ears) instances of Aristotelian as well as of Platonic recollection in its founding of a direct connection between Homer and tragedy.[6]

Returning to the theme of our conference, indeed a contemporary theme, thanks to an ever growing number of contributions that are historically, anthropologically, and semiotically sensitive, it is becoming more usual to listen to and to see Greek poetry as an art based on performance (that is, as a performing art) with often very complicated histrionic, choreographic, and musical effects: a sort of "drama before drama," as Herington puts it.[7] With such a formula (which today is no longer provocative) we reaffirm that diachronic continuity that, as far as its communicative aspect is concerned, places tragedy in line with earlier poetry, executed as performance often in a context of competition on the occasions of the more important religious festivals. The performance of choral lyric poetry is, in particular, highlighted in terms of "song culture" and is based, as later the tragic drama was based, on dance and music as much as on the word.[8]

For performance, the phenomenon of δεῖξις in archaic lyric poetry was stressed by Rösler, who provoked a constructive debate that in Bühler's terms we can sum up in *demonstratio ad oculos* versus *deixis am phantasma*—real versus fictive *deixis*.[9] The theme is a complex one, implying the idea of reality and/or imagination, as well as the role of "I" and of "You" in choral lyric poetry. The complexity of such problems has given rise to a large array of hypotheses and solutions, some rather schematic and already obsolete.[10] Others are more flexible and may yield interesting results. It is sufficient here to cite—from the recent collection presented at Urbino in honor of Gentili—the research of Cingano on Stesichorus, and also Aloni's on Cynaethus, concerning the peculiar case of the *Hymn to Apollo*. Aloni pays special attention to pragmatics and context, to the relationship between "I" of the poet and the "You" of the chorus, and to the proemial function. This article immediately calls to mind situations and functions from a large part of archaic Greek lyric poetry, to which Aloni has also dedicated another recent essay with the programmatic intention of "a comprehensive analysis of poetic performance in ancient Greece."[11] He is right in lamenting our scarce knowledge of hieratic-ceremonial lyric poetry "in which the close bond between choral execution and rite opened greater chances of explicit interaction among the participants in the ritual action." He refers to Fantuzzi's work on the "prehistory" of the two so-called Doric hymns by Callimachus (5–6), from which an indirect recovery of means and forms of the ceremonial-religious lyric poetry of Alcman, Simonides, Pindar might be possible. The last-named is "disastrously lacunose" with respect to the epinician as much as to the partheneia, paeans, dithyrambs, and above all the prosodia, the genre presumably most capable of inspiring the two Callimachean hymns.[12] Critics are almost unanimous in accepting the hypothesis of Giorgio Pasquali, who attributed to Callimachus the invention of the so-called mimico-sacred poem, "or the description of religious festivals with strong realistic effect as is found in *Hymns* II, V, VI."[13] The use of deictic (sometimes also called "indexical") words, called up by Rösler in the field of constructive, or rather reconstructive, fantasy, returns here functionally if one considers that already in choral lyric poetry, in the case of the reuse of a composition, the change of function and of meaning of the deictic elements, through the loss of the original pragmatic picture, can be described as the passage from the manner of the *demonstratio ad oculos* to that of the *deixis am phantasma*. However, in the case of the repetition or, if you will, of the reperformance—that is, the reuse of a composition in an analogous situation—it was only possible to have a renewed *demonstratio ad oculos*.[14] And even in the Alexandrian era, almost by a principle of inertia, the nostalgic attempt at a mimetic effect is possible: by Callimachus, but also by Theocritus,[15] and if the *Mimiambi* of Herondas were not performed—as Pasquali held, with arguments, however, that are not completely convincing[16]—many apparent indications of a theatrical destination would have to be interpreted as allusions to a fictitious performance.

We are on the path—even if by a secondary route (that of mime)—toward the theater par excellence, that is, toward the triumph of performance. The most recent studies, in the field of classical philology, are at last sensitive to the text as written, or at least conceived of, for the stage, and sensitive also to a precise space-time dimension, in fact that of the mise-en-scène. Leafing through, for example, the new publication *DRAMA*, it is possible to deduce that a time of reckoning has arrived: "It is time to rethink performance criticism," as Slater explicitly notes.[17]

Yet above and beyond the ever increasing amount of research on the theatrical text, the fact remains that the scholar of performance must imagine the object of his studies and (re)see it with the eye of the mind. While the famous Aristotelian precept (to which we will return), δεῖ δὲ τοὺς μύθους συνιστάναι καὶ τῇ λέξει συναπεργάζεσθαι, ὅτι μάλιστα πρὸ ὀμμάτων τιθέμενον (*Poet.* 1455a22), is turned back onto the dramatic poet so that he knows how to (pre)see the scene and thus avoid the fiasco of Karkinos, it is also valid for the posthumous and thus inappropriate reader (even if he is critical and aware) of a text written for a scene already exhausted by others and by time. The λέξις (the verbal dimension of the complex scene writing) constitutes the surviving textual element, to which we can add all the extratextual data that the results of historical, antiquarian, sociological, and anthropological research are able to furnish for an idea of the scene imagined as far as possible πρὸ ὀμμάτων.

In any case, the line of inquiry that, with unbroken continuity, leads us from epic via lyric performance to dramatic theater remains theoretically significant. Here I will take as an example an "average" case, from choral lyric poetry, rightly preferred by scholars of performance: the partheneia of Alcman, for which Herington, again hitting the nail on the head, spoke of "lyric dramatization of lyrics": a formula with which I would like to experiment here, developing in the theatrical sense some of my previous philological observations, moving away from the λέξις.[18]

In the Louvre Partheneion (fr. 1 *PMG* = 3 C), Hagesichora, whose significant name indicates *choragos*, has chosen as her closest friend Agido, excluding the rest of the chorus for which only praising the couple remains. However, the δεύτερος scheme,[19] already tested by Homer for his own heroes, functions conventionally. Agido is to Hagesichora as Peisandros was to Achilles (cf. Alcm. 58–59; Hom. *Il.* 16.194–95). There is no competition between the two since, just as Peisandros, "second" after Patroklos, was already elevated above the other Myrmidons, so the "second" Agido is assimilated to Hagesichora and elevated above the other chorus members. Before the eyes of those present, the grace of Agido is asserted almost as much as the beauty of Hagesichora, as the simile of the Colaxaean horse shows: "she who is second in beauty after Agido will run as a Colaxaean against an Ibenian" (58–59). The encomiastic intention is announced by an earlier equestrian metaphor (46–49), dedicated to the praise of Hagesichora. It is worth observing the transformation (or rather the reperformance) of another epic precedent, *Iliad* 10.249–50, in which Odysseus asks Diomedes not to praise him, since each of his words would be superfluous in the presence of the Argives who already know (having seen it with their own eyes):

Τυδείδη, μήτ’ ἄρ με μάλ’ αἴνεε μήτε τί νείκει
εἰδόσι γάρ τοι ταῦτα μετ᾿ Ἀργείοις ἀγορεύεις.

In the same way, Hagesichora makes the praises of the coryphaeus unnecessary (cf. 43–45) because her beauty is obvious in front of an audience of real spectators, and in fact the chorus desists:

διαφάδαν τί τοι λέγω;
Ἁγησιχόρα μὲν αὕτα.
            (56–57)

It is not worth talking about because "this is Hagesichora" (here she is, you can look at her because she is here, before your very eyes). The strong deictic exalts her effective presence (cf. ἦ οὐχ ὁρῇς;) before the eyes of the entire city gathered at the festival. To pay respect to the Homeric *model*, but in virtue of the Alcmanian *reperformance*, we could also speak of the "lyrical dramatization of epic."

Turning to the Second Partheneion (fr. 3 *PMG* =26 C), the partheneion of Astymeloisa, we shall limit ourselves to recalling just a few verses. The chorus is fruitlessly consumed by love of the protagonist:

Ἀστυμέλοισα δὲ μ' οὐδὲν ἀμείβεται

. . . .

ὥτις αἰγλάεντος ἀστήρ
ὡρανῶ διαιπετής

. . . .
. . . .

]. διέβα ταναοῖς πο[σί].

(64–70)

Astymeloisa "does not respond." The chorus (and the audience) sees her pass "as if she were a meteorite in a glittering sky," they see her pass "with rapid steps": obviously through a space, and actually a theatrical space. The Alcmanian scene (straight from a textbook, one might say) is nothing but a poetic, and prophetic, performance of Brook's celebrated declaration: "I can take any empty space and call it a bare stage. A man walks across this empty space whilst someone else is watching him, and this is all that is needed for an act of theater to be engaged."[20] It is certainly insufficient to say, with Fischer-Lichte, that theater occurs when " 'A' represents or plays the role of 'X' while 'S' watches," for the first condition is a space:[21] a theatrical space or better still a performance, because in that moment space is created by a body or bodies. With regard to the space created by art, in this instance by sculpture (but "die plastischen Gebilde sind Körper"), Heidegger asks himself in what relationship artistic space stands to physical, objective space. And, asking himself "wovon spricht sie [i.e., die Sprache] im Wort Raum?" he answers "darin spricht das Räumen." The word "space" talks about "making space."[22]

Räumen: it is the key in every performing art, whose product necessarily consumes itself in the *hic et nunc*, where and when production and reception occur together.[23] Insisting on the space-time dimension of the performance, Slater reaffirms that "a play proceeds linearly through time" and "the audience of a play experiences the play in the time frame set by performance."[24] However, that for which we feel the need to theorize constituted a daily practice for the

Greeks of the archaic and classical periods, who, in carrying out performance with unbroken continuity from epic to lyric poetry to drama, in the diachronic sense indicated so far but also in a synchronic one, ignored the traumatic passage, obligatory in every *Buchkultur*, from an individual experience to a collective one. Artaud's aphorism, "le théâtre est le seul endroit au monde où un geste fait ne se recommence pas deux fois,"[25] would not have impressed the Greek spectator, archaic or classical, who was used to the tempo of performance, before it became normal for the (habitual) Alexandrian reader to return to the written text to reread it.

Let us turn to theatrical space. Edmunds makes use of a distinction already functionally tested in the modern French theater: "theater space, stage space, dramatic space."[26] The first type is determined by the architecture of the theater, which imposes precise and unalterable conditions. The second type concerns stage and set design in the material sense but also the costumes and the bodies of the actors; and to these various aspects further separate codes can correspond, for example, to the body of the actor, makeup, masks, hairstyle, with interrelational consequences between codes and speech. The third type, the so-called dramatic space, is the space created by that which we can call the "stage-word," which can be distinguished from diegetic space, when the word brings into focus the offstage, and from mimetic space, when the word brings into focus the visible space on the stage. Diegetic space can also be divided into the space seen by the characters but not by the audience and the space invisible to both.

Much has been written on the stage-word: a functional word for Shakespearean theater,[27] but already for Aeschylean or tragic theater, if, for example, when talking about the falling of the Oceanids together with Prometheus, Taplin rightly hypothesizes a virtual (i.e., verbal) staging of this fall.[28] It was also functional in the comic theater of Aristophanes. In a study allusively entitled "Scena e parola nelle 'Rane' di Aristofane," Del Corno reexamines with a new understanding the problem of the so-called stage directions—are they internal to or inserted in the theatrical text?[29] Taplin resolved the problem, showing convincingly how the thirteen cases in which such stage directions are found in tragedy all constitute interpolations made by readers and transcribers in later ages and are inspired by the text. It is plausible to extend this principle to comedy, in which Taplin examines various cases with positive results.[30]

The "didascalia," as belonging to the text as pronounced by the characters, are still a problem. An escape route, first taken by Taplin—that is, the directions would have originally been not for the reader but rather "to the audience in the theater"—is followed without hesitation by Del Corno.[31] However, about twenty years earlier, A. M. Dale, discussing "Seen and Unseen in the Greek Stage," acutely commented on the descriptive directions given verbally by the poets, pointing out that signs of this type must have been more often than not (as a sort of paradox) concerned with that which was invisible to the listeners-spectators, or visible in such a rudimentary form that the audience had to have help in order to interpret what it saw. Hence in this case the text clarifies and completes the performance.[32]

But already earlier, Aristotle had said that the dramatic author should

τοὺς μύθους συνιστάναι καὶ τῇ λέξει συναπεργάζεσθαι, ὅτι μάλιστα πρὸ ὀμμάτων τιθέμενον· οὕτω γὰρ ἂν ἐναργέστατα ὁ ὁρῶν, ὥσπερ παρ' αὐτοῖς γιγνόμενος τοῖς πραττομένοις εὑρίσκοι τὸ πρέπον καὶ ἥκιστα ἂν λανθάνοι τὰ ὑπεναντία. (*Poet.* 1455a22)

construct plots and work them out in words, placing them before his eyes as much as possible. For in this way the one seeing, as if present at the events taking place, would discover what is fitting and would least forget incongruities.

There is a necessity that the poet finish his work by *supplying words* and, at the same time, have as far as possible the development of the events in front of his eyes. Such visualization, as if he were in front of the very action of a scene, will help him find that which is worthwhile and avoid incongruities. Proof of this, Aristotle goes on to say, is found in the error of Karkinos: ὁ γὰρ ᾿Αμφιάραος ἐξ ἱεροῦ ἀνῄει· ὃ μὴ ὁρῶντα τὸν θεατὴν ἐλάνθανεν, ἐπὶ δὲ τῆς σκηνῆς ἐξέπεσεν δυσχερανάντων τοῦτο τῶν θεατῶν (Poet. 1455a27 ff.). Amphiaraos's exit from the temple (where he was hidden) would not have been perceived except by a spectator. The incongruity in question (τὰ ὑπεναντία), understood and booed by the audience, must have been (here Aristotle is prescribing an appropriate λέξις!) the lack of coordination between ὄψις and ἀκοή, and the insufficiency of the poet (here instructed not to disappoint the αἰσθήσεις of the audience) in adapting the audial to the visual dimension.[33] Karkinos has, then, completely omitted the verbal marking of what was either supposed to happen or was happening already in the stage space.

The expression πρὸ ὀμμάτων found just once in the *Poetics* is repeatedly used by Aristotle in the *Rhetoric* with reference to the figures often associated with metaphors and created with the ends of σημαίνειν ἐνέργειαν and ἄψυχα ἔμψυχα ποιεῖν (1411b4). This animation is due to "the eidetic capacity of the poet . . . , which some centuries later the Anonymous of the *Sublime* (15.1) will define as φαντασία in the strictest sense of the word: ὅταν ἃ λέγεις ὑπ' ἐνθουσιασμοῦ καὶ πάθους βλέπειν δοκῇς καὶ ὑπ' ὄψιν τίθῃς τοῖς ἀκούουσιν."[34] The roots, then, of the stage-word and (if you will) of "verbal scenography,"[35] are deep. The eidetic capacity of the poet and its effect on the spectator can be applied to the dramatic space, where the Greek stage-word was most trium-phant, engaging the "fantasy" of the spectator. So it is in the dramatic space that the "fantasy" (in the sublime sense of the Anonymous) of scholars, posthu-mous spectators (necessarily heedless of such *contradictio in adiecto*) of every classic performance, more readily comes into play. Thus one proceeds to the eminently symbolic space of Aristophanes.

The space of Aristophanic comedy is extemporaneously invented out of the πρωταγωνιστής who was able to create spaces (*Räumen*, as Heidegger puts it). Dikaiopolis for example is creator first of the opposing space of the Assembly, and afterward of the opposite space of his own house, and thus by progression, of each new stage space, defined by his movements but, *in primis*, by his words.[36] In this, nevertheless, the Aristophanic stage-word does not come across as more thaumaturgical than the Aeschylean or tragic stage-word, which is institution-ally creative, as has been already mentioned, and even of astounding stage de-signs. More stupefying rather is the freedom of the comic actor to exit from and reenter into his character for the frequent breaks in the dramatic illusion, the frequent addresses to the audience, to attract its attention with a centripetal force inside the stage space. This self-concentration and the reciprocal (centrifu-gal) movement of the entire comic action around its pivot, the πρωταγωνιστής, seems to follow "always the same principle, which could be defined as a principle of expansion."[37]

But the space, expandable theoretically to infinity, of the Aristophanic comic actor can symbolically identify itself, in the extreme or rather impossible limit, with the space of utopia. I refer not only to the aerial space traversed by Trygaeus (in a parody of Bellerophon), but also to the impossible space of Cloud-cuckoo-town reached by Peisthetaerus and Euelpides; as well as to the space of the hereafter in the *Frogs* on the particularly fortunate grounds of which "various suggestions can compete: the paradox of realizing that which is impossible in nature, the mixture of protagonists of different epochs, the over-turning of the real—the most drastic of utopias."[38] The nostalgic passion for Euripides that drives Dionysus to his absurd descent surprises Heracles: πότε-ρον εἰς ʺΑιδου κάτω; (69). Dionysus answers: καὶ νὴ Δί' εἴ τι γ' ἐστιν ἔτι κατωτέρω. This god is ready to go even further down if there exists some other place. It is confirmation of the principle of expansion (up to the heights of the sky and to the deepest depths of Hades), an expansion that takes us, with the only oxymoron admitted by the absurd comic, to the *topos* of utopia.

Δοκεῖ δὲ μέγα τι εἶναι καὶ χαλεπὸν ληφθῆναι ὁ τόπος (Arist. *Phys.* 212a7–8): to Aristotle's *Poetics* is attributed a complete lack of attention to—in reality a total theatrical lack of interest in—the space-time category.[39] However, nothing could be more normal, one would have to admit, for a theorist completely uninterested in performance, and for whom these two elements pose difficulties. But since his own poetic system is notably composed of μῦθος, ἤθη, διάνοια, λέξις, μελοποιία, and ὄψις, and the last of these, the visual dimension,[40] is the only one that is absolutely necessary (in that it is unavoidable) for every performing art, we want to understand why Aristotle downgrades ὄψις (and subsequently μελοποιία). To conclude, we turn to this question, which is perhaps closest to our heart.

Since recent readings favor a healthy ambiguity for Aristotle's words, if not for autonomy of the performance recognized *malgré lui*, once again it seems indispensable to return to that "storeroom of definitions" constituted by chapter 6 of the *Poetics*, where the six elements are listed more than once.[41]

The first definition (1449b33) necessarily begins with ὁ τῆς ὄψεως κόσμος, since drama is being treated. It then continues with μελοποιία and λέξις, and finishes with the series ἦθος, διάνοια, μῦθος. Immediately afterward (1450a9) there follows a second list, μῦθος, ἤθη, λέξις, διάνοια, ὄψις, μελοποιία, and then (1450a13) a third that begins with the expression notoriously, and inappropriately, daggered by Kassel: ὄψις ἔχει πᾶν. The visual dimension contains everything and in equal measure (ὡσαύτως), ἦθος, μῦθον, λέξιν, μέλος, διάνοιαν, but μέγιστον δὲ τούτων ἐστὶν ἡ τῶν πραγμάτων σύστασις (i.e., μῦθος). Aristotle's assertion of this sequence on its own would be enough to dispel any impression of ambiguity: unmistakably, if we look at the "scale of six elements" (1450a38),[42] the μῦθος is defined as the ἀρχή and, so to say, the ψυχή of the tragedy. There follow, in order, δεύτερον . . . ἤθη, . . . τρίτον . . . διάνοια, τέταρτον . . . λέξιν, . . . τῶν δὲ λοιπῶν ἡ μελοποιία, . . . ἡ δὲ ὄψις. Of the last two elements, the first is μέγιστον τῶν ἡδυσμάτων, most important of the external embellishments. This is an appreciation, though reductive, of an element that is certainly pleasant, but also "accessory, extrinsic";[43] the other (the more comprehensive: see ὄψις ἔχει πᾶν above) is ψυχαγωγικόν, but ἀτεχνότατον, as well as ἥκιστα οἰκεῖον τῆς ποιητικῆς, "very seductive, but, with regard to poetic art, the most extraneous and the least proper"; and as if that were not enough, there comes a final gibe: "the efficacy of tragedy exists in fact even without representation and without actors; furthermore, for the realization of the spectacle the art of the scenery designer is more important than that of the poets."[44]

It is difficult to accept a double reading of the *Poetics* like the following: from one point of view, it "lends itself to being read as a (contemptuous) assertion of the rule of the marginality of *opsis* in poetry, but from another . . . [it] contains, instead, in a nutshell, the precious recognition of the autonomy of an art of staging, which requires its own specific competences and rules."[45] It is a short step from this second point of view to the recognition of theatrical autonomy (beyond the obvious autonomy of the stage), and the blame of Karkinos is commonly cited as confirmation of the Aristotelian notion of the theatrical text as indeed a script.

In any case it is not my intention to simplify the text of the *Poetics* where we are "confronted by a real and proper system of theoretical tensions which must be taken note of as far as they constitute Aristotle's own thought,"[46] but rather, if possible, to put Aristotle's reasons into a historical context with a usefully posthumous sense.

On the occasion of the last conference at Syracuse (1993), "How to Stage Ancient Theater Today," I spoke about the cinematographic translation of the tragic μῦθος of the *Oresteia* by Pasolini, discussing this production in particular and, in general, filmatic compared with theatrical production, relying on the Pasolinian "heretical empiricism." The Pasolini of *Edipo*, of *Medea*, but perhaps more suggestively of the incomplete *Orestiade Africana* still in outline form, did not in any way make a "filmed theater" but reinvented the classic μῦθος for the expressive medium born in this century, if you like, for the latest ποιητικὴ τέχνη, the cinematographic one.

We have come full circle, and perhaps fatally, to the θαύματα quoted at the beginning of our discussion, and their shadowy projection on the "screen" of the Platonic cave. The shadows of the Erinyes-Eumenides are projected onto the Pasolinian screen in a doubly brilliant form, one arboreal (the giant and impressive trees of the African forest), the other humanized (the dancing choruses of the African tribe): two forms, however, completely "natural," even doubly natural because cinematographic and thus—for Pasolini the poet (before theorist) of the cinema—words of the "written language of reality."[47] Such intuitions are notoriously the result of that "empiricism" with which the "heretic" intellectual loved, more than to theorize, simply to provoke *en poète*. It was his conviction that "at the latest stage of reality as representation one finds the theater."[48] Having produced some time ago (and in the Syracusan theater) his own script of the Aeschylean trilogy, the only thing left for him was of course to go further, visualizing a real *Oresteia*. The medium, however, that he thought capable of expressing the extreme stage of "reality as representation," in the "written language of action," was the cinema, because in the cinema we would have the "written moment" of a "language both natural and complete that is action in reality."[49] I do not know if Pasolini had in mind the Aristotelian statement (I am sure he would have liked it) that the μῦθος is important as being the μίμησις of action, and that tragedy is the mimesis not of a man but of action; thus also in life happiness and unhappiness lie in action. In any case, if for Aristotle tragedy is really μίμησις πράξεως, able (with respect to epic and lyric poetry where the categories of action do not appear) to represent people who act (πράττοντες), from a "classical" point of view, the modern cinematographic outcome of ancient tragic performance might turn out to be more than orthodox. There might also be a consequence, both paradoxical and reassuring, for the passage from the theatrical performance to the viewing of the πράττοντες at the cinema: only the cinema is able to entrust the μῦθος to a determined ὄψις that contains it (ἔχει as Aristotle said) once and for all.

A posthumous proof also follows of the theoretical necessity for Aristotle to expunge ὄψις as the element ἀτεχνότατον and ἥκιστα οἰκεῖον τῆς ποιητικῆς. The Aristotelian ποιητικὴ τέχνη, precisely because philosophically linked to the καθόλου, could only find in ὄψις the showiest element and also the most extraneous one, because it is short-lived (together with the μελοποιία, the other seductive element, but this one, too, destined to consume itself in space-time), and thus linked to the καθ' ἕκαστον so as to live on the occasion of that and not another performance, irrepeatable as such and unreproduceable.[50]

Today, in the era of technical reproducibility—of a τέχνη that is cinematographic through ποιητική—the ποιητής filmmaker establishes an ὄψις, once and for all (together with the μελοποιία, the sound track, also forever), which contains the μῦθος, the syntax of the events, that belongs to editing (itself nothing more than the mechanical execution of the σύστασις τῶν πραγμάτων). But it also happens, inevitably, that the fixing of the two elements considered unrelated by Aristotle (with respect to the dramatic τέχνη) coincides with the end of performance: on the cinema screens, where the editing, perhaps not by chance, works as a metaphor for death. Moreover, the definition given by Aristotle of the tragic "form" coincided with its own historical decadence. Saving the savable, the verbal nucleus (but potentially useful for other and future performances!), was, to paraphrase the famous definition of the poetic universal in comparison with a historic particular, φιλοσοφώτατον καὶ σπουδαιότατον: the most logical and serious task, for the ancient philosopher, theoretically obliged to renounce μελοποιία and above all ὄψις.

Remarks at the American Academy in Rome, February 12, 1994

Bruno Gentili

T HE TWO meanings of Italian *giubilare* are perfectly suited to my current
situation, because I am now *giubilato*, "retired," from the University, and
also *giubilato*, "celebrated," by today's festivities. What more could I now desire? I am happy and profoundly grateful to the American Academy, to its
director, Professor Caroline Bruzelius, and to my American and Italian col-
leagues, for offering me the honor of this friendly encounter on a theme that
has marked my intellectual journey.

This theme was occupying more and more of my mind just in the years
when I had the good fortune to discover a book pointed out to me, if I remember correctly, by my friend Franco Munari, then a lecturer at the University of
Berlin and just back from the United States (1969). I asked him what new things
he brought with him from his academic travels. He answered that there had just
appeared a book by Eric Havelock, *Preface to Plato*, which had aroused great
interest and curiosity in America—one of those books destined to turn the
study of ancient Greece in a new direction. I immediately acquired a copy, but—
in part from the misleading title—put off reading it, for I was then immersed in
the problems of archaic Greece, and especially that of the relations between
poet and patron, the subject of my inaugural address at the University of
Urbino, where I was named Professor Ordinarius of Greek Literature. After
several days, however, at a break in my work, I felt impelled to read Havelock's
book. I was profoundly struck. This book at once opened perspectives for me
on a whole series of sociological and literary issues which I was reflecting on at
that time. I proposed an Italian translation to the publishing house Laterza,
which agreed to undertake the project. This initiative had an immediate effect
on the orientation of Italian research both within and outside of the study of
classics. It contributed to reawakening interest in oral epic poetry and, by

consequence, in lyric poetry as viewed from this perspective. The success of Havelock's book served to counter its lukewarm review in *Gnomon*. In Germany, as is well known, the book was not liked and fell into oblivion. It stimulated me to look with interest at developments in America. Bundy's work on Pindar dates back just to these same years—work that left me somewhat perplexed. His critical technique of explaining Pindar by Pindar, eliminating extratextual materials, recalled to my mind the ancient grammarian Aristarchos of Samothrace, who interpreted Homer through Homer, without regard for historical references, just as Bundy did in explicating Pindar.

The themes developed in today's papers all proceed from the perspective of performance, of the reception of the text, of its specific function of involving the public on particular occasions in the life of the community. A particular cultural characteristic of archaic, classical, and even in part Hellenistic Greece is the oral, aural, and visual nature of its poetry, and also of some of its types of prose. So it was a "culture of spectacle," bringing author and public together in a shared emotional relationship, when the public either applauded these communal performances or noisily dissented, hearing something that did not appeal to its taste. I prefer to use the term *spectacle* rather than *the theater, tout court*, adhering to Plato's distinction of three basic genres (*Republ.* 3.392d–394c): simple narrative in the third person (ἀπλῆ διήγησις); mimesis (διὰ μιμήσεως), as in tragedy and comedy; and mimesis within narrative, when the poet presents a character as speaking, as in Homer, so that the narrative is mixed (διὰ ἀμφοτέρων). In addition to epic, lyric poetry is implicitly included in the third of Plato's basic genres, the one combining mimesis and narrative (cf. *Republ.* 3.394c4–5). In fact, the grammarian Diomedes was to subdivide the mixed genre into "heroic" and "lyric," giving Archilochus and Horace as examples of the latter (*Gramm. Lat.*, vol. 1, p. 483 Keil).

Precisely on the level of the institutional difference between the language of the mixed (mimesis within narrative) and mimetic or dramatic genres must be located the problem of the greater conceptualization of theatrical language. While the notion of truth in lyric poetry is almost always unambiguous, as Charles Segal has observed,[1] that of tragedy is multifaceted, controversial, and contradictory. But these multiple, contradictory aspects of tragedy emerge insofar as they are expressions of the characters' multiplicity of viewpoints and conflicting interests, appearing on the stage in dramatic dialogue. It is the preeminent function of dialogue, not as narrated within a mythic story as in epic and choral song but active on the stage, that permits the confrontation between differing viewpoints, and here is the essential difference between the poetic genres of lyric and tragedy. Both share in ὄψις in that both are "spectacles," but the first describes as it were in deferred form the same actions which in the second are acted out directly upon the stage.

In the evolution of fourth-century theater, the public at large was seduced not so much by the contents of a drama as by ὄψις in the sense of all those elements that are inherent in scenic effect and the author's virtuosity. Here lies the importance of Aristotle's polemical statement (*Poet.* 1451b34–38) concerning the tendency of certain playwrights, even those with ability, to write plays according to the wants and needs of the actors. This phenomenon has occurred in other periods as well, for example, in the case of Gioacchino Rossini, who inserted in his operas virtuoso arias composed to suit the celebrated singers of his day. This theater of entertainment then becomes prominent in the third century, in the phenomenon of theatrical anthologies, where the role of the solo singer is paramount.

Already in the fifth century, Euripides' *Bacchae* anticipates a type of theater unshackled from the polis, focused on a universalizing perspective accessible more to the individual than to any specific group. However one may understand the idea of the universality of tragic poetry asserted by Aristotle in the *Poetics*, the central fact of the *Bacchae* is the separation of the chorus from the civic community, which could not identify with the ritual manifestations of a wild and primitive form of Dionysiac worship alien to the urban Dionysos, who by contrast was integrated into the sociability of the symposion and hence the shared social values of fifth-century Athens. The Athenian audience's normal experience of tragedy was different. In respect to its emotional participation, we cannot but recall the statement of Gorgias (82 B 23 D-K) on the illusion that poetry works upon the audience: "he who deceives is more just than he who does not deceive, and he who is deceived is wiser than he who is not deceived." The wisdom of those who let themselves be deceived, that is, of the theater public, lies in their capacity to put themselves on the same level as the author and emotionally to join in the situation proposed by the performance. This emotional relationship is evident also in a statement of Aristotle (*Poet.* 1453b11–13): "The tragic playwright must procure by means of mimesis the pleasure produced by pity and fear." Thus tragedy rests on a poetics of mimesis, understood as a true and proper aesthetic of execution and reception in which one central component is the horizon of expectation of the audience. The means of this mimesis are word, music, song, gesture, and dance. Each of these elements becomes the object of a semiotic inquiry in the sense that each of them is significant and performs a precise function in the mimetic process.

The discussions that followed the papers given today converged quite visibly along a single methodological perspective that again confirms the vitality of a philology that is understood not as an end in itself but as a means of understanding antiquity and conversing with antiquity. A dialogue between two cultures enriches both of them at the same time, however distant from each other, and however openly each one preserves its own cultural identity and coherence. The scholar of antiquity is not an antiquarian, tending the cult of the past. Rather, he makes a past that pertains to the present. He is a scientific researcher who makes use of many disciplines—linguistics, semiology, anthropology, sociology, archaeology—while never losing sight of history. He must also be endowed with the creative spirit, or rather (in reference to Nietzsche's warning) he must be a rigorous scientist and at the same time an artist. For these reasons, I do not hide my reservations about a critical approach to texts that is now finding followers also in the United States: the so-called deconstructionism of Derrida, whose motto is "nothing outside the text." It is less a Protagorean relativism or an epistemological nihilism of the Gorgianic type,[2] than an extreme corollary of the Aristarchean motto, alluded to earlier, "interpret Homer by means of Homer." In reality, the relationship between language and the world outside of language is a problem that we must always keep before our eyes in analyzing any text, and especially any ancient Greek text, precisely because of its eminently pragmatic character. This poetry was conceived of as a means to produce an effect—political, social, satirical, or erotic, and so forth— and not to express idiosyncratic states of mind.

To conclude, there remain for me only to praise the efforts and the interpretive abilities of the speakers, and to express my wish that, even after today's *giubilazione*, our productive friendship will continue and result in new studies and new research, to enliven our common intellectual journey.

Translated by Robert W. Wallace

Notes

1. Bruno Gentili, *Poetry and Its Public in Ancient Greece: From Homer to the Fifth Century*, trans. A. Thomas Cole (Baltimore 1988) 3.

2. Ibid., x.

3. J.-J. Rousseau, *Essai sur l'origine des langues*, ed. Charles Porsci (Bordeaux 1968) 89 (= ch. 8, end of first paragraph).

4. The theme of "the performance of wisdom" is now fittingly inspiring classicists: cf. Richard Martin, "The Seven Sages As Performers of Wisdom," in Carol Dougherty and Leslie Kurke, eds., *Cultural Poetics in Archaic Greece* (Cambridge 1993) 108–27.

The Laughter of the Suitors:
A Case of Collective Madness in the Odyssey

1. Joseph Russo, in Joseph Russo, Manuel Fernandez-Gallo, and Alfred Heubeck, *A Commentary on Homer's Odyssey*, vol. 3 (Oxford 1992) 124.

2. *Homer: The Odyssey*, trans. A. T. Murray, vol. 2 (Cambridge, Mass. 1919) 299.

3. Cf. Russo (supra, n. 1); E. R. Dodds, *The Greeks and the Irrational* (Berkeley 1951) 70, according to whom "the symbolic vision of the Apolline hereditary seer Theoclymenus in Book 20 belongs to the same psychological category as the symbolic visions of Cassandra in the *Agamemnon*, and the vision of the Argive prophetess of Apollo who, as Plutarch tells, rushed one day into the streets, crying out that she saw the streets filled with corpses and blood."

4. Cf. Dodds (supra, no. 3) 8–10; Antonella Mauri, "Funzione e lessico della follia guerriera nei poemi omerici," *Acme* 43 (1990) 51–62.

5. For example, *Od.* 9.81; *Il.* 15.464. The metaphoric use of this verb to describe phenomena of psychic disturbance is more widespread in later periods: cf. Pind. *Ol.* 7.31 and especially Nic. *Ther.* 757.

6. Eur. *Bacch.* 33. For this traditional way of describing mental illness, cf. for instance *Il.* 6.234, where Zeus "takes away" the mind of a warrior (φρένας ἐξέλετο). For the Homeric model of mental illness, see B. Simon, *Mind and Madness in Ancient Greece* (Ithaca, N.Y. 1978) 65–78.

7. Xen. *Symp.* 1.10. Other evidence describes, in similar terms, accesses of convulsive crises in the course of rites of trance (e.g., Eur. *Bacch.* 1122) or more pacific cases in which

the exaltation of a poet is described when he is "possessed" (according to Platonic terminology) by the Muses: cf. Pl. *Ion* 535b.

8. Cf. Erika Bourguignon, ed., *Religion: Altered States of Consciousness and Social Change* (Columbus, Ohio 1973); I. M. Lewis, *Ecstatic Religion: An Anthropological Study of Spirit Possession and Shamanism* (Harmondsworth 1971); George Devereux, *Essais d'ethnopsychiatrie générale* (Paris 1973).

9. Henri Jeanmaire, *Dionysos* (Paris 1951) 132–56. On the corybantic cults, the most important contribution is still I. M. Linforth, *The Corybantic Rites in Plato*, University of California Publications in Classical Philology 13, no. 5 (1946) 163–72.

10. Ernesto De Martino, *Il mondo magico²* (Turin 1973) 91.

11. De Martino (supra, no. 10) 92, who cites Sergie Shirokogoroff, *The Psychomental Complex of the Tungus* (London 1935). These phenomena are included in the vaster category called "arctic hysteria," for which cf. D. F. Aberle, "Arctic Hysteria and Latah in Mongolia," *Transactions of the New York Academy of Sciences* 2 (1952) 291–97.

12. Cf. Gilbert Rouget, *La musique et la transe: Ésquisse d'une théorie générale des relations de la musique et de la possession* (Paris 1980) 25–45.

13. Siegfried Laser, *Medizin und Körperpflege* (Göttingen 1983) 75 and n. 204.

14. ἀφραδίη is the word used some verses earlier (288) to describe the arrogant and consequently foolish minds of the suitors, who, blinded by their violence, insult the men who will kill them. The same word is used to describe senseless conduct like that of the Cyclops (*Od.* 9.361).

The Proem of Simonides' Elegy on the Battle of Plataea
(*Sim. Frs. 10–18 W²*) and the Circumstances of the Performance

1. On the same argument see my previous "L'elegia di Simonide dedicata alla battaglia di Platea (Sim. Frs. 10–18 W²) e l'occasione della sua performance." *ZPE* 102 (1994) 9–22.

2. The editio princeps of the new papyrus is in *The Oxyrhynchus Papyri*, vol. 59, ed. E. W. Handley, H. G. Ioannidou, P. J. Parsons, and J. E. G. Whitehorne (London 1992). The editor of papyrus 3965 was P. J. Parsons; the text can be supplemented with some fragments from *P. Oxy.* 2327 already published by Lobel (according to Parsons [ibid., p. 5], *P. Oxy.* 2327 and *P. Oxy.* 3965 are two copies of the same book); in West's first edition of *Iambi et Elegi Graeci*, vol. 2 (Oxford 1972), *P. Oxy.* 2327 figures as *Adesp. Eleg.* 28–60.

Of West's text (in *Iambi et Elegi Graeci ante Alexandrum cantati*,² ed. M. L. West, vol. 2 [Oxford 1992]), fragments 10–17 (and perhaps 18)—largely reconstructed on the basis of *P. Oxy.* 2327 and *P. Oxy.* 3965—might be linked with the Plataea elegy. These include two fragments of indirect transmission (frs. 15–16 W²) quoted by Plutarch (*De Herod. malign.* 872d) which make it possible to attribute the work to Simonides (thanks to a fragment of *P. Oxy.* 3965).

3. One can recognize a parallel in Homer, usually employed to highlight the death of a warrior (*Il.* 13.389–91 and 16.482–84).

4. At the end of the *Odyssey*, Agamemnon in Hades makes a long speech to Achilles, in which he recalls the hero's funeral celebrations (*Od.* 24.36–97) and mentions that the bones of Achilles and Patroclus were put in the same urn. This is a reference to the traditional theme of "the funeral of Achilles," at which the Muses were present. Obviously the connection would be very evocative if the performance of the elegy was itself part of the commemoration of the warriors who had died at Plataea.

5. In Homer, there is no explicit account of the death of Achilles, which is only alluded to, or forecast as the result of the joint action of Apollo and Paris (cf. *Il.* 19.416–17, 22.358–60). Precise reference to the death being the work of Apollo alone is to be found in the tragedies (cf. Aesch. fr. 350, and Soph. *Philoc.* 334–35), which are texts integral to the Athenian tradition.

6. Lines 9–12 can be reconstructed in various ways, but West's seems to fit in best with the rhythm of the narrative (the introduction of the principal gods opposed to Troy and the contraposition of Achilles' death and the fall of the city). In fact, the "chariot of justice" is an unusual image; Dike, the goddess of justice, is usually represented with a rod or a pair of scales, but never seated in a chariot.

7. Obviously the reference is to Homer; what we have here is a veritable exaltation of the role of poetry and the poet as the only means for guaranteeing the continuing fame of men and deeds. Certain key words in early Greek poetry appear here (some clear in the text itself, others very likely suppositions made by the editors): κλέος is the glory conferred by poetry: ἀληθείη is not only the "truth" of the account, it is also the negation of oblivion, the only hope for guaranteeing the survival in time of the transient race of heroes (and the even more transient race of common mortals).

8. The passage is skillfully echoed in Theocritus's *Hymn to the Charites* (16.44–46). The echo is almost a quotation because the Greek poet places it in a passage in which the poetry of Simonides is described as being able to preserve the fame and memory of his contemporaries (just as Homer did for the heroes of the past).

9. These lines are reconstructed on the basis of two of Simonides' epigrams: "Simonides" 16.1 FGE and 20a.3–4 FGE; cf. infra, the section on "Occasion and Commission."

10. The reading cυν[όντεc was suggested by L. Lehnus during a very fruitful discussion of the text along with E. Cingano.

11. Simonides' account of the Spartans' departure, their march to the Isthmus, rendezvous with the other Peloponnesian forces, and subsequent march to Eleusis is rather cursory and vague (and the present state of the text offers no help in filling in the details). Unlike the other sources, there is no mention here of conflicts and quarrels preceding the Spartan departure (this could be taken as evidence that the elegy is a Spartan commission). And, in contrast to what Herodotus says (9.19), it seems that the rendezvous with the other Peloponnesian forces did not take place at the Isthmus but at Megara, a Doric city that was a member of the Peloponnesian League. The extant text makes no mention of the arrival of the Athenians, which according to Herodotus took place at Eleusis. Plutarch says the Athenians went straight to Plataea, and Diodorus places their rendezvous with the other Greek forces at some point between the Isthmus and Boeotia.

12. Another completely conjectural line: Teisamenos was a seer of Elis, a descendant of Iamos, a son of Apollo and nephew of Poseidon, who had been priest and seer at Olympia at the time the games were founded. Teisamenos was hired by the Spartans as official seer for the expedition and, in return, obtained for himself and his brother the much-sought-after and rarely conceded right to Spartan citizenship (cf. Hdt. 9.33–35).

13. The following translation is, with minimal variations, West's in *Greek Lyric Poetry*, trans. M. L. West (Oxford 1993) 168–69.

14. See, above all, M. L. West, *Studies in Greek Elegy and Iambus* (Berlin 1974) 10–21; E. L. Bowie, "Early Greek Elegy, Symposium and Public Festival," *JHS* 106 (1986) 13–35, and "Miles Ludens? The Problem of Martial Exhortation in Early Greek Elegy," in O. Murray, ed., *Sympotica: A Symposium on the Symposion* (Oxford 1990) 221–29; M. Vetta, ed., *Poesia e simposio nella Grecia antica: Guida storica e critica* (Rome 1983), and "Il simposio: la monodia e il giambo," in *Lo spazio letterario della Grecia antica*, vol. 1: *La produzione e la circolazione del testo*, pt. 1: *La polis* (Rome 1992) 177–218; W. Rösler, "Mnemosyne in the Symposion," in Murray (supra) 230–37.

15. This was a wind instrument, usually with two pipes (closer to the oboe than to the flute). The verb "sing" as used here is to be understood in the widest sense to include *recitarcantando* and *recitativo*.

16. Cf. Vetta, "Il simposio" (supra, n. 14) 188–91.

17. This is the case with Solon's *Salamis* (cf. West [supra, n. 14] 12; *contra* Bowie, "Early Greek Elegy" [supra, n. 14] 18–21) and of Archilochus's fr. 1 W^2 (cf. A. Aloni, *Le muse di Archiloco. Ricerche sullo stile archilocheo* [Copenhagen 1981] 32–48).

18. Sources (*SudΣ* 439; *Vit. Pind.* [Ambros.] p. 2.21ff. Drachmann; Plu. *Them.* 15.4) speak of another poem on the Battle of Salamis—but this is more likely to have been a lyric rather than an elegy; cf. M. L. West, "Simonides Redivivus," *ZPE* 98 (1993) 1–14, in particular 2–3.

19. Perhaps Xenophanes' *The Founding of Colophon* should be added to this list of historical elegies; again this seems to have been an enormous poem of more than 2,000 lines. On the historical elegy see Bowie, "Early Greek Elegy" (supra, n. 14) 27–34.

20. Cf. Vetta, "Il simposio" (supra, n. 14) 196–99.

21. A. E. Harvey, "The Classification of Greek Lyric Poetry," *CQ* n.s. 5 (1955) 157–75, in particular 170–71; B. Gentili, "Epigramma ed elegia," in O. Reverdin, ed., *L'épigramme grecque, Entretiens Hardt* 14 (Vandoeuvres-Geneva 1968) 37–70, in particular 50–53.

22. D. L. Page, "The Elegiacs in Euripides' Andromache," in Douglas E. Gerber, ed., *Greek Poetry and Life: Essays Presented to Gilbert Murray on His Seventieth Birthday, January 2, 1936* (Oxford 1936) 206–30.

23. Cf. Schol. *ad* Eur. *Andr.* 103.

24. Eur. *Andr.* 91–93: ἡμεῖς δ' οἷσπερ ἐγκείμεσθ' ἀεὶ / θρήνοισι καὶ γόοισι καὶ δακρύμασι / πρὸς αἰθέρ' ἐκτενοῦμεν· κτλ.

25. Cf. Bowie, "Early Greek Elegy" (supra, n. 14) particularly 27–34. See Ps.-Plu. *De musica* 1134a.

26. Cf. Vetta, "Il simposio" (supra, n. 14) 191–92.

27. Obviously it is an easy criticism to make, after the publication of this previously unknown elegy by Simonides.

28. G. Nagy, *Pindar's Homer: The Lyric Possession of an Epic Past* (Baltimore 1990) 217–24.

29. On the subject of "compensation," see Nagy (supra, n. 28) 118–22, 139–43.

30. To a greater or lesser extent historical narrative remains an essential part of the *logos epitaphios* which in fifth-century Athens replaces and renders "democratic" the previous performances of funeral poetry. Cf. N. Loraux, *The Invention of Athens: The Funeral Oration in the Classical City* (Cambridge, Mass. 1986, translated from *L'invention d'Athènes. Histoire de l'oraison funèbre dans la cité classique* [Paris 1981]) 3–4 and 132–71.

31. Gentili (supra, n. 21) 44–46, 54–56.

32. Cf. Bowie, "Early Greek Elegy" (supra, n. 14) 29.

33. Cf. Bowie, "Early Greek Elegy" (supra, n. 14) 31.

34. Under the definition used here it would be difficult to consider the brief invocation at the beginning of Solon's fr. 13 W² (cf. Bowie, "Early Greek Elegy" [supra, n. 14] n. 85 on p. 29) or those at the beginning of the two books of Theognis (lines 1–8 and 1231–34; cf. West, *Studies* [supra, n. 14] 42) as proems.

35. For a discussion of proems and a bibliography on the subject (above all with regard to lyric poetry), see A. Aloni, "Proemi e funzione proemiale nella poesia greca arcaica," in *Lirica greca e latina*, Ann. Ist. Orient. Napoli (Fil.-Lett) 12 (1990 [but 1992]) 99–130.

36. For a discussion of the structure of the epic proem, see R. Janko, "The Structure of the Homeric Hymns: A Study in Genre," *Hermes* 109 (1981) 9–24.

37. West (supra, n. 18) 5–6, too, points out the exceptional nature of the address to Achilles, a mortal demigod in a context normally reserved for gods, and thence puts forward the theory that the poem was written for some festival or ritual dedicated to Achilles. The unusual nature of this apostrophe to Achilles also raises another point. In proems the poet, present in the first person, traditionally apostrophizes the addressee in the second person (line 19 ἀλλὰ σὺ μὲ]ν νῦν χαῖρε, θεᾶc ἐρικυ[δέοc υἱέ); there is, therefore, a copresence of poet and addressee. The proem to Simonides' elegy shows that the addressee need not be a god: depending on the occasion he can also be a hero. Could not these direct apostrophes to the hero/addressee be the model for those rare second-person apostrophes that are addressed to heroes in epic poetry (where the norm is for the poet to refer to heroes in the third person)?

38. This concept of Panhellenic poetry is developed in Nagy (supra, n. 28), in particular 414–37, and also in G. Nagy, "Early Greek Views of Poets and Poetry" in G. Kennedy, ed., *Cambridge History of Literary Criticism*, vol. 1 (Cambridge 1989) 1–77, in particular 29–35.

39. Cf. Aloni (supra, n. 17) 34–37.

40. On this point West (supra, n. 18) 5 is fairly cautious: "we may guess that these elegiac epyllia were designed to be performed, as entertainment, in that setting in which elegy was usually performed, with aulos accompaniment."

41. As far as I can see, apart from the Trojan epic only three early Greek mythical narratives have a martial theme and involve a conflict between a Greek alliance and an external enemy: those dealing with the Titans, the Centaurs, and the Amazons. During the course of the fifth century these enemies of the Greek heroes were increasingly portrayed as "barbarians." Cf. E. Hall, *Inventing the Barbarian: Greek Self-Definition through Tragedy* (Oxford 1989) 101–59.

42. Nagy (supra, n. 28) 118–21; W. Burkert, *Greek Religion* (Cambridge, Mass. 1985, translated from *Griechische Religion der archaischen und klassischen Epoche* [Stuttgart 1977]) 105–7.

43. The Thermopylae texts are a special case: the sacrifice of Leonidas and his men is not considered in itself but rather as the premise for the subsequent victory of Salamis.

44. Nagy (supra, n. 28) 152–53.

45. M. Alexiou, *The Ritual Lament in Greek Tradition* (Cambridge 1974) 16–23.

46. Loraux (supra, n. 30) 42–56.

47. Cf. also Alexiou (supra, n. 45) 18.

48. Nagy (supra, n. 28) 18 and 152–53 with bibliography.

49. Nagy (supra, n. 28) 152 and 193 with specific reference to the victory of Plataea. Personally I do not see the contradiction—so much emphasized by Loraux (supra, n. 30) 49–50—between *threnos* (a type of performance) and *epainos* (primarily a definition of a function of song). I would suggest that all future discussions of early Greek literary genres be preceded by an accurate distinction between actual occasions (marriages, funerals, symposia, etc.), modes (song or recital; soloist or chorus), and types of performance (epinicia, threnos, etc.), functions (ἔπαινος, ψόγος, etc.) and metrical forms.

50. As Parsons (supra, n. 2) 32 suspects.

51. Cf. D. L. Page, *Further Greek Epigrams* (Cambridge 1981) 197–200, which favors attribution to Simonides.

52. Τόνδε ποθ' Ἕλληνες ῥώμῃ χερὸς ἔργῳ Ἄρηος.
    [εὐτόλμῳ ψυχῆς λήματι πειθόμενοι.]
Πέρςας ἐξελάςαντες, ἐλεύθερον Ἑλλάδι κόςμον
    ἱδρύςαντο Διὸς βωμὸν Ἐλευθερίου.

This altar, the Greeks who by strength of arms and the courage of Ares,
    [Obeying the audacious desires of their soul,]
Having driven off the Persians and freed Hellas,
    by common will, raised to Zeus Eleutherios.

53. Ἑλλάνων ἀρχαγὸς ἐπεὶ cτρατὸν ὤλεςε Μήδων
Παυςανίας. Φοίβῳ μνᾶμ' ἀνέθηκε τόδε.

Commander of the Greeks, after destroying the Medes,
Pausanias dedicated this *mnêma* to Phoebus.

54. At the very least, Simonides' authorship of these two epigrams is unlikely (cf. Page [supra, n. 51] 211–13 and 216–17). However, they are almost certainly contemporary

with the events they refer to and reveal that at the time there was a feeling or, if one prefers, a dominant ideology of Panhellenism.

55. The main source is Herodotus (books 8 and 9): to differing degrees both Diodorus (*Bibliotheca* 11) and Plutarch (*Arist.* and the treatise *De Herod. malign.*) draw upon him. A clear and balanced account of the events connected with the second Persian War, along with a careful evaluation of all the sources, is to be found in Plutarch, *Vita Aristidis*, ed. I. Calabi Limentani (Florence 1964)—cf. in particular pp. xxxi–xxxiv and liii–lix. The fairly extensive bibliography on the subject of Plataea is taken account of in L. Prandi, *Platea: momenti e problemi della storia di una polis* (Padua 1988) in particular 47–77 and 161–73.

56. ταῦτα γὰρ οὐ χορὸν ἐν Κορίνθῳ διδάcκων οὐδ' ἇcμα ποιῶν εἰc τὴν πόλιν. ἄλλωc δὲ τὰc πράξειc ἐκείναc ἐν ἐλεγείᾳ γράφων ἱcτόρηκεν.

57. One should anyway bear in mind that Plutarch would have been much more willing to pick up on evidence that suggested the commission came from Athens rather than elsewhere.

58. The marked pro-Athenian bias in Herodotus's sources is pointed out in A. E. Wardman, "Tactics and the Tradition of the Persian Wars," *Historia* 8 (1959) 49–60.

59. On this point see the predominantly negative views expressed in Prandi (supra, n. 55) 161–73.

60. Once again attribution to Simonides is likely to be wrong (cf. Page [supra, n. 51] 213–15); but scholars are agreed in dating the epigram around 479 B.C. or shortly after.

61. *P. Oxy* 2327 fr. 27 col. ii, originally edited by West among the *Adespota elegiaca* (fr. 58).

62. Simonides, fr. 13.8–10 W²: ὄφρ' ἀπὸ μὲν Μήδ[ων . . . / καὶ Περcῶν, Δώρου δ[ὲ . . . / παιcὶ καὶ Ἡρακλέοc [.

63. Thus it is difficult to accept West's hypothesis (supra, n. 18) 8–9, that the above-mentioned lines 8–9 of fr. 14 W² are an allusion to the foundation of the Delian League. It would indeed be odd for the Spartan soothsayer to be forecasting the establishment of the union that was to be one of the main weapons in the Athenians' anti-Sparta campaign; but even setting that aside, there are problems with making the reading fit the extant text: line 8 can be read]νὴν cυμμ.[ ].ην φιλεω[, with traces of corrections (.α..γε.) over the group ην φιλε. This enables us to recognize with near certainty a reference to a cυμμαχίη (Parsons however does not exclude a cυμμορίη). All the rest is uncertain. The alliance Teisamenos is referring to could well be that sworn in 481 B.C. (Hdt. 7.145), which might well have been renewed during the commemorative rites, which, I am arguing, were the occasion for Simonides' elegy. Plutarch points out that on that occasion an undertaking was given to raise a body of men annually in order to continue the war against the barbarians (*Arist.* 21). This would fit with the references (line 7, ἦ cφε καὶ ἐξ Ἀ]cί[η]c ἐλάcει) to the driving of the barbarians out of Asia—that is, from the Greek-settled coast of Anatolia.

64. Cf. B. Gentili, *Poesia e pubblico nella Grecia antica* (Rome 1989²) 174–75.

65. At the Dionysian Games of Spring 476 B.C.; cf. "Simonides" 28 FGE and the observations in Page (supra, n. 51) 241–43. On the end of his residence in Athens, his

move to Sicily, and subsequent death, see J. H. Molyneux, *Simonides: A Historical Study* (Wauconda, Ill. 1992), 211–36.

66. Harvey (supra, n. 21) 170.

The Seal of Theognis

1. The text of this and subsequent citations of Theognis is that of M. L. West, *Iambi et elegi graeci ante Alexandrum cantati*[2], vol. 1 (Oxford 1989).

2. For reasons explained infra, n. 25, I take the quotation to run to the end of line 23.

3. Gregory Nagy, "Theognis and Megara: A Poet's Vision of His City," in Thomas J. Figueira and Gregory Nagy, eds., *Theognis of Megara: Poetry and the Polis* (Baltimore 1985) 31–34; Andrew Ford, "The Politics of Authorship in Ancient Greece," in the same volume, 82–95.

4. Richard Reitzenstein, *Epigramm und Skolion* (Gießen 1893) 74, pointed out the parallelism between the four short poems with which the Theognidea open (1–18) and the four poems at the beginning of the collection in Athenaeus. Cf. B. A. van Groningen, ed., *Théognis: Le premier livre*, Verhandelingen der koninklijke Nederlandse Akademie van Wetenschappen, afd. Letterkunde, n.s. 72, no. 1 (Amsterdam 1966) 18.

5. First published by Schubart and Wilamowitz in 1907. There are new editions by Franco Ferrari, "*P. Berol.* Inv. 13270: I canti di Elefantina," *Studi Classici e Orientali* 38 (1988) 181–227; and by Cinzia Casagrande et al., "Poesia in un papiro di Elefantina: Edizione critica e commento," *Quaderni di Filologia Classica* 4 (1983) 5–23.

6. References to the relevant scholarship in Franco Ferrari, *Teognide: Elegie* (Milan 1989) 8 n. 8.

7. Next to this line there appears in the margin a birdlike sign. Furthermore, the same sign was found in a third-century B.C. papyrus fragment of a poem by Timotheos, in which the poet's name, if it appeared, is not preserved. See Jakob Diehl, *Sphragis: Eine semasiologische Nachlese* (Diss. Gießen 1938) 50–51. If this sign could be interpreted as the graphic imitation by the copyist of a sphragis in the literal sense, then we would have some evidence that the poet's name had come to be felt as a "seal." At the time Diehl wrote, the nature of this sign in the margin was much in doubt; I do not know if it has been discussed since.

8. Wolf Aly, "Sphragis," *RE* 3A (1929) 1757. Cf. Walther Kranz, "Das Verhältnis des Schöpfers zu seinem Werk in der althellenischen Literatur," *Neue Jahrbücher für Pädagogik* 27 (1924) 75: "der Sänger des kitharodischen Nomos, also uralter sakraler Poesie, nennt in dem Schlussstück des 'Siegels,' . . . Namen und Herkunft." Cf. Kranz, "Sphragis: Ichform und Namensiegel als Eingangs- und Schlussmotiv antiker Dichtung," *RM* 104 (1961) 16. (This article was reprinted in *Studien zur antiken Literatur und ihr Fortwirken* [Heidelberg 1967] 27ff.).

9. Ulrich von Wilamowitz, *Timotheos: Die Perser* (Leipzig 1903) 100.

10. Albin Lesky, *A History of Greece Literature*, trans. J. Willis and C. de Heer (New York 1966) 170.

11. Who also names himself in fr. 27: see Wilamowitz (supra, n. 9) 65.

12. Marcello Durante, "Ricerche sulla preistoria della lingua poetica greca: La terminologia relativa alla creazione poetica," *RendLinc.* Classe di scienze morali, storiche e filologiche 15 (1960) 244–45, groups these passages in *Hymn. Ap.* and Theognis with Ibycus fr. 282 P. Cf. M. Durante in *Sulla preistoria della tradizione poetica greca,* pt. 2 (Rome 1976) 180. *Hymn. Ap.* is important in the argument of Woodbury (infra, n. 13) 31, 30–40.

13. Leonard E. Woodbury, "The Seal of Theognis," in *Studies in Honor of Gilbert Norwood* (Toronto 1952) 28; reprinted in *Collected Writings,* ed. C. G. Brown et al. (Atlanta 1991) 37. (Other references to this article give the page numbers in the form: earlier/later publication). Cf. Pier Angelo Perotti, "A proposito del 'sigillo' di Teognide," *Vichiana* 14 (1985) 335–42; Anastasios A. Niketas, " Ἑρμηνευτικὲς παρατηρήσεις στὴν ⟨⟨σφραγίδα⟩⟩ τοῦ Θεόγνιδος," *EEAth* ser. 2, 27 (1979) 119. The name is also of great importance in the interpretation of Giovanni Cerri, "Il significato di 'sphregìs' in Teognide e la salvaguardia dell'autenticità testuale nel mondo antico," *Quaderni di Storia* 17, no. 33 (1991) 21–34, who understands the seal as the "indicazione del nome dell'autore su copia autentica ufficialmente depositata" (33). An objection to Cerri's interpretation is line 21, where the affixing of the seal (n.b., ὧδε) is linked to the future Panhellenic fame of Theognis. It is difficult to see how a copy of the poet's work deposited in a temple or a state archive could have this result. In an important discussion of the seal, Wolfgang Rösler, *Dichter und Gruppe* (Munich 1980) 78–89, reverts to the older view that the seal was intended to protect the text published by the poet from alterations (esp. 84).

14. Woodbury (supra, n. 13) 24/31. Pietro Giannini, "Il proemio, il sigillo e il libro di Teognide: Alcune osservazioni," in Roberto Pretagostini, ed., *Tradizione e innovazione nella cultura greca da Omero all' età ellenistica: Scritti in onore di Bruno Gentili,* vol. 1 (Rome 1993) 377–91, argues that lines 19–23 express the intention physically to affix a seal to the papyrus roll that contains the work of Theognis (cf. Cerri, supra n. 13).

15. *Archaic Greek Gems* (Evanston, Ill. 1968) 176. (Cf. A. W. Johnston, *Trademarks on Greek Vases* [Warminster 1979] 2: "Impression of marks from a stamp or gem is unknown on decorated vases and rare on plain ware in the archaic period.")

16. For controversial cases, see Zazoff (infra, n. 20) 101–2.

17. L. H. Jeffery, *The Local Scripts of Archaic Greece*[2] (Oxford 1990) 85, 113, 322 (name added later), 346, 360.

18. Rosalind Thomas, *Oral Tradition and Written Record in Classical Athens* (Cambridge 1989) 41.

19. Thomas (supra, n. 18) 41–42.

20. R. J. Bonner, "The Use and Effect of Attic Seals," *CP* 3 (1905) 400: "The chief and original purpose of a seal was to safeguard." (On this page, Bonner also surveys the evidence, mostly from the fourth century B.C., for the use of seals for the purpose of identification.) The law of Solon (D. L. 1.57) that prevented the carver of a sealstone from keeping a copy after he sold the stone, might seem to imply that a seal indicated the owner of the thing sealed, but the fifth-century references to seals, some of which are

cited in the text of my article, suggest that their use was for safeguarding the property of an already known owner. For the disputed date of the law, see Peter Zazoff, *Die antiken Gemmen* (Munich 1983), 99 n. 3.

21. Ar. *Lys.* 1195–1202; *Thesmo.* 414–16, 424–28; Eur. *Or.* 1108. There is much more evidence. See Fraenkel (infra, n. 43) on Aesch. *Ag.* 609 and James Diggle, *Euripides' Phaethon* (Cambridge 1970) on 223.

22. The demand of textual accuracy could be made in the case of an oracle, as in Theognis 805–10. But in these verses it is the integrity of the *theoros* that is in question, and the diction describing the possible tampering with the text of the oracle differs completely from the diction of 20–21.

23. On the μέν . . . δέ construction coordinating 19–23 and 24–26, see M. L. West, *Studies in Greek Elegy and Iambus* (Berlin 1974) 149, and Woodbury (supra, n. 13) 25/33, who compares Theognis 309–12 and 319–22 for multiple δέ's after μέν. See also Sappho fr. 168B Voigt and the explication of this poem by Diskin Clay, "Fragmentum Adespotum 976," *TAPA* 101 (1970) 119–29.

24. van Groningen (supra, n. 4) 447.

25. In his edition (supra, n. 1), M. L. West limits the quotation of what people will say in the future to Θεύγνιδός ἐστιν ἔπη / τοῦ Μεγαρέως (22–23). In the sentence forming the rest of line 23, εἰμί or rather ἔσομαι, in keeping with the future tenses in lines 20–22, would be understood. Cf. West (supra, n. 23) 149. But the ellipse of the first person of the copula would be very abnormal; see Eduard Schwyzer, *Griechische Grammatik*, vol. 2 (Munich 1953), 623. All of line 23 belongs to the quotation. Cf. Woodbury (supra, n. 13) 31/41.

26. Sc. ἔπος. Cf. lines 16, 18, 22. For the syntax of the line, see D. A. Campbell, *Greek Lyric Poetry* (New York 1967) 349; D. E. Gerber, *Euterpe* (Amsterdam 1970) 273. Jasper Svenbro, *La parole et le marbre: Aux origines de la poétique grecque* (Diss. Lund 1976) 84–86, translated as *La parola e il marmo: Alle origini della poesia greca* (Turin 1984) 84–86 (*sic*) gives an idiosyncratic interpretation.

27. Cf. Friedrich Nietzsche, *Sämtliche Werke*, vol. 5, ed. Giorgio Colli and Mazzino Montinari (Munich 1980) 263: "Das . . . Wort ἐσθλός bedeutet der Wurzel nach Einen, der *ist*, der Realität hat, der wirklich ist, der wahr ist; dann, mit einer subjektiven Wendung, den Wahren als den Wahrhaftigen: in dieser Phase der Begriffs-Verwandlung wird es zum Schlag- und Stichwort des Adels und geht ganz und gar in den Sinn 'adelig' über, zur Abgrenzung vom *lügenhaften* gemeinen Mann, so wie Theognis ihn nimmt und schildert."

28. Nagy (supra, n. 3), 31 compares Theognis 24 with Solon fr. 7 W²: ἔργμασιν ἐν μεγάλοις πᾶσιν ἀδεῖν χαλεπόν and develops a comparison of the Theognis of lines 24–25 with lawgivers like Lycurgus and Solon.

29. Antiph. fr. 188 K-A (from *Plousioi*) on a certain Euthynus, a rich merchant (cf. fr. 126 K-A, where he is identified as a dealer in salt fish); *Ar. Nub.* 332 with the schol., who explains that the reference is to ostentatious sophists; *Ar. Vesp.* 585, where Philocleon expresses contempt for the pompous seals on the will of a rich man; *Ar. Eccl.* 632: signet

rings are a mark of the wealthy and arrogant; Eupolis 202 K-A: on the luxury of the Cyrenaeans, the wealthy of whom have signets worth ten minae; Eupolis 204 K-A (from *Marikas*), where the possession of a sphragis is associated with another luxury, myrrh, as in Antiph. fr. 188 K-A.

30. See Campbell (supra, n. 26) 348 on the dative of agent here.

31. Pier Angelo Perotti, "A proposito del 'sigillo' di Teognide." *Vichiana* 14 (1985) 339–40 takes σοφιζομένῳ . . . ἐμοὶ as an example of what in Latin is sometimes called "the *ab urbe condita* construction." It is doubtful, however, that this construction is possible in Greek with the present tense. (The verb οἴχομαι that occurs in one of Perotti's examples is perfective.)

32. Campbell (supra, n. 26) 348; Nagy (supra, n. 3) 29 para. 8 n. 3.

33. Santino Caramella, "Il sigillo di Teognide," *Orpheus* 6 (1959) 139–47, discusses the seal of Theognis in the context of a history of Greek political thought, with emphasis on Plato's *Protagoras*, *Meno*, and *Theaetetus*, and identifies the seal as a moral consciousness of self set against the vicissitudes of the polis. This consciousness is somehow the origin of Platonic ethics. Caramella's interpretation of the seal is thus, like mine, a political one, but Caramella retains a romantic view of the poet. Caramella concludes: "Il 'sigillo' di Teognide, nato dall'ingenuo amore di un poeta dei suoi versi, sta così, nelle origini del pensiero greco, a significare come l'anamnesi e l'ethos avessero per gli antichi affinità profonde, anzi unica radice, nella coscienza eroica della personalità."

34. Lines 681–82, discussed by Lowell Edmunds, "The Genre of Theognidean Poetry," in Figueira and Nagy (supra, n. 3) 105–6. On the text of line 682, I follow Nagy (supra, n. 3) 24–26.

35. Nagy (supra, n. 3) 22–26, 29–30.

36. Cf. Veda Cobb-Stevens, "Opposites, Reversals, and Ambiguities: The Unsettled World of Theognis," in Figueira and Nagy (supra, n. 3) 170–71.

37. "Homer, Odysseus, and the Instruction of Princes," *TAPA* 114 (1984) 41–43.

38. On the poet's use of *ainos* see Nagy (supra, n. 3) 26–29 and Edmunds (supra, n. 34) 105–7.

39. On "synchronic distinction expressed mythically as a diachronic sequence" in Greek and Near Eastern mythology, see Robert Mondi, "Greek Mythic Thought in the Light of the Near East," in Lowell Edmunds, ed., *Approaches to Greek Myth* (Baltimore 1989) 141–98.

40. On 679 and context, see Cobb-Stevens (supra, n. 36) 162–63. On the pattern, see Lowell Edmunds, "Thucydides' Ethics as Reflected in the Description of Stasis (3.82–83)," *HSCP* 79 (1975) 73–92.

41. Verg. *G.* 1.199–200; *TLS* April 22, 1994, p. 16. Cf. Hor. *C.* 3.6.45–48; Cole Porter, "Anything Goes."

42. J. D. Denniston, *The Greek Particles*² (Oxford 1966) 165; Jean Carrière, "Nouvelles remarques sur l'époque et sur le texte de Théognis," *REG* 67 (1954) 44–45.

43. Xenoph. fr. 1.13 W²; Solon fr. 4.9–10 W²; Hom. *Il.* 15.99, *Od.* 9.6, 10.465 and context (cf. Theognis 1256, where the same phrase occurs), 17.531 and context; Theognis 757–66;

Panyassis fr. 12.16–18 Kinkel. See Eduard Fraenkel, *Aeschylus: Agamemnon*, vol. 2 (Oxford 1978) on Aesch. *Ag.* 806, and J. Latacz, *Zum Wortfeld "Freude" in der Sprache Homers.* Bibliothek der klassischen Altertumswissenschaft, 2nd ser., 17 (Heidelberg 1966), 161–73.

44. Xenoph. fr. 1.4 W²; Hom. *Il.* 3.246.

45. Cf. Karl Bielohlawek, "Gastmahls- und Symposionslehren bei griechischen Dichtern (Von Homer bis zur Theognissammlung und Kritias)," *WS* 58 (1940) 11–30, translated as "Precettistica conviviale e simposiale nei poeti greci da Omero fino alla silloge teognidea e a Crizia," in Massimo Vetta, ed., *Poesia e simposio nella Grecia antica* (Bari 1983) 109–14, on the norms of sympotic conduct as reflected in Theognis. *Euphrosunê* also suggests the appropriate mood for the acceptance of Theognis's poetry. Nagy (supra, n. 3) 60 (para. 47 n. 5) explains *euphrosunê* as "a programmatic word for the social harmony of an audience listening to poetry."

46. See the appendix.

47. After the Loeb translation of Bernadotte Perrin (vol. 4 of the *Lives* [Cambridge, Mass. 1916]). The Greek text is that of West² (supra, n. 1).

48. Mauro Tulli, "La σφραγίς di Crizia," *QUCC* n.s. 19 (1985) 189–90.

49. Or, in the terminology of Schwyzer, (supra, n. 25), vol. 2, p. 129, genitive of material.

50. Tulli (supra, n. 48) 194–95.

51. Woodbury (supra, n. 13) 29/37 holds that the seal is the name of Kritias in the preamble to the decree. Andrew Ford has suggested to me *per litteras* that "if he would have gone on to paraphrase the relevant portion of the decree, the 'art' involved may have been converting the language of the Assembly into elegiacs, as Kritias plays with the limits of versification in fr. 4 W²," which is from the poem in honor of Alkibiades.

52. Cf. Nagy (supra, n. 3) 35.

53. D. T. Steiner, *The Tyrant's Writ: Myths and Images of Writing in Ancient Greece* (Princeton 1994) 89–91, discussing the seal of Theognis under the heading, "Enshrining the text," speaks of an "equation between the poetic text and the sealed *agalma*" and thus leaves out the oral dimension of the seal. She follows Woodbury (supra, n. 13) in holding that a function of seals was to name the owner of the sealed property, and she quotes the Thersis inscription. Louise Pratt, "The Seal of Theognis, Writing, and Oral Poetry," *AJP* 116 (1995) 171–84, argues that the seal is the written form of the text.

54. For a survey of the Homeric formula, see G. S. Kirk, *The Iliad: A Commentary*, vol. 2: *Books 5–8* (Cambridge 1990) 222 on 6.459–62. For a survey of imitations of the formula in Greek, see J. R. Wilson, "ΚΑΙ ΚΕ ΤΙΣ ΗΩΔ' ΕΡΕΕΙ: An Homeric Device in Greek Literature," *Illinois Classical Studies* 4 (1979) 1–15.

55. Observed in the case of 6.460 by the exegetical scholia and in the case of 7.89–90 by Kirk (supra, n. 53) 246 ("The style of the comment is that of funerary epigrams . . .") and by Gregory Nagy, "Homeric Questions," *TAPA* 122 (1992) 36, and *Pindar's Homer: The Lyric Possession of an Epic Past* (Baltimore 1990) 18 n. 7. Cf. Paul Friedländer and Herbert B. Hoffleit, *Epigrammata: Greek Inscriptions in Verse* (Berkeley 1948; reprint, Chicago 1987) 11 on the relation of *IG* IV 358 (a hexameter epigram) to *Il.* 7.89. The most extensive discussion is that of Ruth Scodel, "Inscription, Absence and Memory: Epic and

Early Epitaph," *SIFC* 10 (1992) 57–76. She shows that the ambiguities and paradoxes of the *Iliad*'s variants on epitaphs are related to an implicit comparison between the fame conferred by epic and the memory preserved by the inscribed epitaph.

56. Another indication of awareness of writing in this passage may be the implicit parallel between the tumulus as a sign that preserves fame (Hector's more than that of his slain foe, from Hector's point of view) and the function of epic poetry, which is to preserve fame. See Andrew Ford, *Homer: The Poetry of the Past* (Ithaca 1992) 131–57.

57. Robert Renchan, "Progress in Hesiod," *CP* 75 (1980) 339–40.

58. Xenoph. fr. B11 D-K; cf. Heraklitos frs. B56–57 D-K; Hdt. 2.53; Pl. *Ion* 531a–b; Isok. 12 (*Panath.*) 18, 33; *Certamen Homeri et Hesiodi*, cf. Hes. *OD* 650–59. Joseph Farrell, *Vergil's Georgics and the Traditions of Ancient Epic: The Art of Allusion in Literary History* (New York 1991) 40–41, shows that in Bacchylides 5.191–94 the phrase βοιωτὸς ἀνήρ "takes its place in the long tradition linking these two great poets."

59. As argued in Edmunds (supra, n. 34) 96–104. Cf. Gregory Nagy, "Early Greek Views of Poets and Poetry," in George A. Kennedy, ed., *The Cambridge History of Literary Criticism*, vol. 1 (Cambridge 1989) 34: "any poetic tradition other than that of Homer and Hesiod must have a contest of its own with these canonical standards, if it is to stand a chance of becoming canonical on its own terms," and also Nagy, *Pindar's Homer* (supra, n. 55) 53 n. 8.

60. West (supra, n. 23) 80.

61. B. M. W. Knox, in P. E. Easterling and B. M. W. Knox, eds., *The Cambridge History of Classical Literature*, vol. 1: *Greek Literature* (Cambridge 1985) 138.

62. Ford (supra, n. 3) 89.

63. Nagy (supra, n. 3) 33.

64. For a survey, see Ferrari (supra, n. 6) 5–45.

65. Ford (supra, n. 3) 91.

66. Pl. *Hipp.* 228d–229a: cf. Friedländer and Hoffleit (supra, n. 55) 139–40.

67. See Ford (supra, n. 3) 88–92; B. M. Lavelle, "Hipparchos' Herms," *EchCl* 29 n.s. 4 (1985) 419: "[T]he herms were at least partially symbols for Hipparchos, showing the inhabitants of the countryside that at least part of the ruling family in Athens was to be identified with patriotic philosopher [Solon, whom, according to Lavelle, H. was imitating] rather than with opportunistic tyrant."

68. For the Seven Sages as poets and performers, see Richard P. Martin, "The Seven Sages As Performers of Wisdom," in Carol Dougherty and Leslie Kurke, eds., *Cultural Poetics in Archaic Greece* (Cambridge 1993) 108–27.

69. It is the only one in the form of an elegiac couplet. On the problem of whether Phokylides wrote elegiacs see West[2] (supra, n. 1) 95.

70. As is fully argued by M. L. West, "Phocylides," *JHS* 98 (1978) 164–67.

71. Cf. the quip—or proverb?—preserved in a fragment of a comic poet: τουτὶ μὲν ἥδειν πρὶν Θέογνιν γεγονέναι (Plut. *Mor.* 395d, 777c = fr. ad. 461K).

72. Detlev Fehling, "Zur Funktion und Formgeschichte des Prooimiums in der älteren griechischen Prosa," in ΔΩPHMA: *Hans Diller zum 70 Geburtstag*, Griechische Humanistische Gesellschaft, 2nd ser.: Studien und Untersuchungen 27 (1975) 66: "Der

Verfasser war offenbar nur fähig, irgend etwas Altertümliches zu bieten, und vermengte die Gattungen, indem er eine Anleihe bei gnomischer Literatur machte." Cf. Alcmaeon B1 D-K.

73. The first fifteen lines of the passage I shall discuss can be found at the beginning of the B frs. of Epicharmus in D-K, with commentary. The entire fr. can be found in W. Crönert, "Die Sprüche des Epicharm," *Hermes* 47 (1912) 402–3. The papyrus, from a mummy wrapping, on which this fragment is preserved, can be dated to 280–240 B.C.: Crönert 402. The text I shall quote is Crönert's. The fragment is also printed in *CGFPap* (fr. 86).

74. Fehling (supra, n. 72), 65–66.

75. One can compare Empedocles' "oracle of Necessity, old psephisma of the gods," which is πλατέεσσι κατεσφρηγισμένον ὅρκοις (B115.1–2 D-K), "sealed with broad oaths." (According to this oracle, those who have committed murder or who have sworn a false oath must wander for thrice ten thousand years apart from the blessed.) Here, the seal establishes the authority of the instrument in question; the source or authorship of the instrument, that is, Necessity and the gods, has already been asserted.

76. The *Banquet of the Seven Sages* may have taken shape already in the fifth century: see Stefano Jedrkiewicz, *Sapere e paradosso nell'Antichità: Esopo e la favola* (Rome 1989) 136 n. 104 for references.

77. A valuable list of mythological *hupothêkai* attested for the fifth century is provided by Leslie Kurke in the appendix to "Pindar's *Sixth Pythian* and the Tradition of Advice Poetry," *HSCP* 120 (1990) 104–7. For *hupothêkai* as a genre, see Kurke 90–91.

78. Martin (supra, n. 68) 115–19.

79. On the traditional narrative frame, see Gregory Nagy, *The Best of the Achaeans* (Baltimore 1979) 281–83, and add to Nagy's evidence Arist. *Rhet.* 1393b23, where Aristotle clearly regards the frame as integral to the fable. Note also that the narrative frame of "The Book of Ahikar" is the basis of the assimilation of Ahikar to Aesop in the *Vita Aesopi* 101–23. On Ahikar, see W. R. Halliday, *Indo-European Folktales and Greek Legend* (Cambridge 1933) 143–52; Jedrkiewicz (supra, n. 76) 127–35; Francisco R. Adrados, "The 'Life of Aesop' and the Origin of the Novel in Antiquity," *QUCC* n.s. 1 (1979) 98–106.

80. Martin (supra, n. 68) 115–19.

81. Kurke (supra, n. 77) 106 n. 79. (Griffith's suggestion was in the form of an oral communication.)

82. E. L. Bowie, "Early Greek Elegy, Symposium and Public Festival," *JHS* 106 (1986) 27–34, argues for elegiac narratives of city history composed for competition at public festivals. For a survey of agonistic mannerisms and "awareness of (an) immediately present judge(s) . . . and the challenge of a viable but contradictory alternative to the poet's present statement" in archaic and early classical literature, see Mark Griffith, "Contest and Contradiction in Early Greek Poetry," in Mark Griffith and Donald Mastronarde, eds., *Cabinet of the Muses: Essays on Classical and Comparative Literature in Honor of Thomas G. Rosenmeyer* (Atlanta 1990) 191–200.

83. See the list in Jedrkiewicz (supra, n. 76) 140–43. For an excellent account of the

competitive aspect of Aesopic wisdom, see Stefano Jedrkiewicz, "The Last Champion of Play-Wisdom: Aesop," *Itaca* 6–8 (1990–92) 115–30.

84. Kurke (supra, n. 77) 106.

85. As a skolion: Praxilla fr. 3 = *PMG* carm. conviv. 14; cf. Ar. *Vesp.* 1238; *Pelargoi* fr. 430K = fr. 444 K-A; Kratinos *Kheirones* fr. 236K = fr. 254 K-A. See 3. in Kurke's list for further evidence: Kurke (supra, n. 77) 104. For parallels with Theognis, see Ruth Scodel, " Ἀδμήτου λόγος and the *Alcestis.*" *HSCP* 83 (1979) 51–54.

86. Evidence surveyed by Joseph Fontenrose, *The Delphic Oracle: Its Responses and Operations, with a Catalogue of Responses* (Berkeley 1978) ch. 5 ("Chresmologues and Oracle Collections").

87. *ARV²*, p. 329 (134). Cf. J. D. Beazley, "Hymn to Hermes," *AJA* 52 (1948) 337. He takes ΧΙΡΟΝΕΙΑ as feminine singular (cf. Ὀδύσσεια and similar titles): it could also be neuter plural. Cf. also H. R. Immerwahr, "Book Rolls on Attic Vases," in Charles Henderson Jr., ed., *Classical, Mediaeval, and Renaissance Studies in Honor of B. L. Ullman,* vol. 1 (Rome 1964) 21 (4); Kurke (supra, n. 77) 92. For an index of related school scenes, see F. A. G. Beck, *Album of Greek Education* (Sydney 1975); the kuathos in question is 75a–b (with illustrations pl. 14).

88. For the semantics and history of γνωμολογία, see Konstantin Horna, "Gnome," *RE* suppl. 6 (1935) 74–75. "Gnomology" is one of those words, like "myth" or "historian," that we use with deliberate anachronism in speaking of the classical and archaic periods. Karl Bielohlawek, "Hypotheke und Gnome: Untersuchungen über die griechische Weisheitsdichtung der vorhellenistischen Zeit," *Philologus* suppl. 32, no. 3 (1940) 4–6, discusses early evidence of gnomology in Homeric epic.

89. See Vetta (supra, n. 45) 117–31, 149–55.

90. West (supra, n. 23) 54.

91. See Nagy (supra, n. 3) 46–51 for a critique of West in this matter.

92. This essay was originally written in the spring of 1987. I am grateful to Gregory Nagy for discussing it with me at that time; to Emmett Bennett for a set of detailed comments; and to *intervenuti* at the University of Venice, where it was delivered orally. I am grateful to J. P. Small for help with the present revised version; to Andrew Ford for a set of detailed comments; to Shifra Rubin for comments on style; and to my fellow editor Robert Wallace for both meticulous proofreading and challenging questions on presentation of evidence. Never was it truer that any remaining faults, etc.

Prose Genres for the Performance of Traditional Wisdom in Ancient Greece: Proverb, Maxim, Apothegm

1. As Roman Jakobson says, "Any attempt to reduce the sphere of poetic function to poetry [alone] . . . would be a delusive oversimplification"; "Closing Statement: Linguistics and Poetics," in T. A. Sebeok, ed., *Style in Language* (New York 1960) 356. On this and the following page Jakobson gives good examples of poetic structuring devices used to shape everyday prose discourse, including his now famous analysis of the political

slogan, "I like Ike." My attempts below to trace poetic expressiveness in Greek wisdom speech have been inspired in part by Jakobson (cf. also his *Selected Writings*, vol. 4 [The Hague 1966] 637–38, and R. Jakobson and L. Waugh, *The Sound Shape of Language* [Bloomington 1979]) and by the helpful comments of this chapter's anonymous referee.

2. The distinction between speech event and speech act is a staple of sociolinguistic research. See, for example, D. Hymes, *Foundations of Sociolinguistics* (Philadelphia 1979) 52–53. Speech act itself is a concept associated with the linguist-philosopher J. L. Austin and his seminal book *How to Do Things with Words* (Oxford 1962).

3. Most influential for my orientation have been D. Hymes, "Breakthrough into Performance," in D. Ben-Amos and K. Goldstein, eds., *Folklore: Performance and Communication* (The Hague 1975), and reprinted in Hymes's *In Vain I Tried to Tell You: Essays in Native American Ethnopoetics* (Philadelphia 1981); R. Bauman, *Verbal Art As Performance* (Rowley, Mass. 1977), and *Story, Performance, and Event* (Cambridge 1986); and C. L. Briggs, *Competence in Performance* (Philadelphia 1988). For the successful use of performance-centered scholarship to direct our search for meaning away from ancient Greek speech as purely text and toward its context, see R. P. Martin, *The Language of Heroes* (Ithaca, N.Y. 1989) esp. pp. 4–10, for a statement of method and further bibliography; and his essay "The Seven Sages As Performers of Wisdom," in C. Dogherty and L. Kurke, eds., *Cultural Poetics in Archaic Greece* (Cambridge 1993) esp. 115–19.

4. I am aware of the existence of other Greek wisdom genres generally called "precepts" in English, the Greek *hypothêkai* and *chreiai*. The former are commonly attributed to traditional wise men like the Seven Sages, and the latter to professional philosophers of late antiquity (see Hock and O'Neil infra, n. 22). Neither belongs to the realm of *emergent* wisdom speech as defined below.

5. The best definitions of anecdote offered by recent scholarship confirm their characteristic tendency to combine two key components: the brief *story* about an important or familiar personage and his memorable *utterance* at a key dramatic juncture. See A. Taylor, "The Anecdote: A Neglected Genre," in J. Mandel and B. Rosenberg, eds., *Medieval Literature and Folklore Studies: Essays in Honor of Frances P. Utley* (New Brunswick, N.J. 1970); B. Botkin, "Anecdote," in M. Leach, ed., *Standard Dictionary of Folklore and Mythology*, vol. 1 (New York 1950) 56; and Bauman (supra, n. 3) 54–55. The presence of dialogue and of a final noteworthy "saying" is seen as characteristic of the best anecdotes but not strictly required of the genre—exactly the situation we find for the ancient *apophthegma*, as discussed below.

6. There have been, to be sure, some rewarding studies of the proverb (J. F. Kindstrand, "The Greek Concept of Proverbs," *Eranos* 76 [1978] 71–85; R. Strömberg, *On Some Greek Proverbial Phrases* [Göteborg 1947], and *Greek Proverbs* [Göteborg 1954]; A. M. Ieraci-Bio, "Le concept de *paroimia*: *Proverbium* dans la haute et la basse antiquité" in F. Suard and C. Buridant, eds., *Richesse du proverbe*, vol. 2 [Lille 1984] 83–94; J. Russo, "The Poetics of the Ancient Greek Proverb," *Journal of Folklore Research* 20 [1983] 121–30). Studies of the *gnômê* have tended to be collections of sententious quotes from authors like Menander, or from earlier poets (e.g., E. Ahrens, *Gnomen in griechischer Dichtung (Homer, Hesiod, Aeschylus)* [Halle 1937]); but the recent dissertation of A. P. M. H.

Lardinois, *Wisdom in Context: The Use of Gnomic Statements in Archaic Greek Poetry* (Diss. Princeton University 1995), is exemplary in incorporating modern methodology and literature in its analysis of *gnômai*. The apothegm and anecdote remain only minimally investigated. W. Gemoll's *Das Apophthegma* (Leipzig 1924), the only serious investigation of the Greek apothegm, in fact devotes most of its space to other topics.

7. It may come as a surprise to classical philologists to learn that scholars in folklore have long accorded serious research and full genre status to jokes, tall tales, taunts and jeers, curses and blessings, lullabies, jump-rope and hand-clap rhymes, gossip, "memorates," monologues, "novelles," ghost stories, and personal experience narratives, in addition to the better-known legends, Märchen, and ballads that are commonly thought of as the staples of oral folk literature. Although some native Greek genres can perhaps never be uncovered from our limited surviving records, a few forms comparable with those named in English may await our discovery. What to call them will of course pose a challenge, except in those lucky instances where the "native category" has been internally labeled (e.g., *ainos, psogos, ainigma*). For good methodological and theoretical discussion of this issue see D. Ben-Amos, "Analytical Categories and Ethnic Genres," *Genre* 2 (1969) 275–301.

8. "Emergence" essentially characterizes performance that evolves as the natural and unpremeditated result of social interaction. See Bauman, *Verbal Art* (supra, n. 3), esp. pp. 37–45 on the "emergent" quality and structures of "optional" performance (such as wisdom speech) in contrast to "conventional" performance (such as formal recitation); see also Bauman, *Story* (supra, n. 3). Hymes, *In Vain* (supra, n. 3) 79–82, reviewing the development in recent scholarship of a technical sense of "performance," notes the different approaches taken by linguistics and folklore: "In contemporary transformational generative grammar the term performance treats overt behavior as a realization, quite likely imperfect, of an underlying knowledge on the part of a speaker. In contemporary folklore the term performance has reference to the realization of known traditional material, but the emphasis is on the constitution of a social event, quite likely with emergent properties."

9. Hymes, *In Vain* (supra, n. 3) 81.

10. Martin (supra, n. 3). Martin's groundbreaking application of recent anthropological and folkloristic scholarship to ancient Greek cultural "performance" has to some extent inspired my own investigation.

11. This definitional problem leads even the most knowledgeable proverb scholars to positions that essentially straddle both views. Cf. Peter Seitel, *Proverbs and the Structure of Metaphor among the Haya of Tanzania* (Diss. University of Pennsylvania 1972) 14: "A proverb is a metaphorical representation, or description, of the situation about which it is spoken. . . . Metaphor is a central feature of the phenomenon of proverb use. . . . Metaphorical proverbs are taken to be the most general proverbial type. Literal proverbs (aphorisms, apothegms) may be seen as a special case of the more general metaphorical type."

12. As recently as 1988, the folklorist Briggs (supra, n. 3, 101–4) complains about the inadequacy of current definitions, noting that most focus on either textual or contextual

features without doing justice to both; that many scholars still cannot reconcile culture-specific types with their desire for a cross-cultural comparative model; and that almost all definitions are tautological and imbued with a priori and intuitive assumptions.

13. Roger D. Abrahams, "Proverbs and Proverbial Expressions," in R. M. Dorson, ed., *Folklore and Folklife: An Introduction* (Chicago 1972) 119, 121.

14. For further description of universal characteristics of proverbs, with abundant examples, see the early fundamental studies of A. Taylor, *The Proverb* (Cambridge, Mass. 1931) and B. J. Whiting, "The Origin of the Proverb," *Harvard Studies and Notes in Philology and Literature* 13 (1931) 45–91, and the excellent recent articles of Abrahams (supra, n. 13) and F. A. de Caro, "Riddles and Proverbs," in E. Oring, ed., *Folk Groups and Folklore Genres: An Introduction* (Logan, Utah 1986).

15. The well-known κοινὰ τὰ τῶν φίλων at the end of Plato's *Phaedrus* (279c6), for example, simply illustrates the point being argued. Even when Plato is more involuted, as at Symp. 174b4–5 when he has a speaker give us only a distorted version of a known proverb which includes additionally a pun on Agathon's name, the speaker's purpose is playful but not particularly complicated on the semiotic level. Similarly Aristophanes often gets a laugh by having one of his characters pun on a proverb or deliberately distort it. For further discussion see D. Tarrant, "Colloquialisms, Semi-Proverbs, and Word-Play in Plato," *CQ* 40 (1946) 109–17, and its sequel in *CQ* n.s. 8 (1958) 158–60.

16. This is not listed as a proverb in Strömberg, *Proverbial Phrases* (supra, n. 6), whereas Gyges' two proverbs are. Yet one close echo in Heraclitus, ὀφθαλμοὶ τῶν ὤτων ἀκριβέστεροι μάρτυρες (101a D-K), and one more distant one, κακοὶ μάρτυρες ἀνθρώ-ποισιν ὀφθαλμοὶ καὶ ὦτα βαρβάρους ψυχὰς ἐχόντων (107 D-K), suggest we have a familiar proverbial topic and phrasing. Its use here in a context of overt association with two distinct proverbs should make its proverbial status evident. Strömberg (pp. 8–9) acknowledges the unclear boundary between proverbs and maxims and other "winged words," but understands Gyges' utterances to be proverbs not maxims because they are treated as familiar traditional wisdom. For discussion of the unusual concentration of three proverbs in this one episode and the resulting problematic of reconciling conflicting modes of traditional wisdom, see Russo (supra, n. 6).

17. My colleague Lowell Edmunds has kindly supplied me with parallel phraseology in Arist. *Rhet.* 1.7.34, 3.10.17; Athen. 3.99d (attributed to the orator Demades); and Eur. *Suppl.* 447, which show that the "springtime" is a commonly understood Greek metaphor for "the pick of" or choice part of anything.

18. Good analysis of the difference between the metaphorical and general qualities of proverbs and maxims—following Aristotle—is offered by N. Barley, "A Structural Approach to the Proverb and Maxim with Special Reference to the Anglo-Saxon Corpus," *Proverbium* 20 (1972) 737–50; and of the distinctly metaphorical quality of proverbs, by P. Seitel, "Proverbs: A Social Use of Metaphor," *Genre* 2 (1969) 143–61, and his dissertation (supra, n. 11).

19. Beginning with the scholiasts, this proverb has been interpreted negatively to mean that an Athenian neighbor is a restless or troublesome one. See the well-known description of the Athenian character given by the Corinthian delegate at Thuc. 1.70 (cf.

further 3.13 and 4.92.4), and Isoc. *Antid.* 299–300 (cited by William M. A. Grimaldi, *Aristotle, Rhetoric,* vol. 2: *A Commentary* [New York 1988] 271).

20. The problem of distinguishing *paroimiai* from *gnômai* according to Aristotle's criteria is pursued further by Lardinois (supra, n. 6, 15–17). He observes that Aristotle, in the *Rhetoric* and elsewhere, cites several proverbs that are nonmetaphorical, contradicting his own stated criterion. Noting that Aristotle once refers to those who "coin" *gnômai* (*gnômotypoi, Rhet.* 1395a 7), Lardinois concludes that while both proverbs and maxims are "generalizing statements about particular actions," maxims do not have to be traditional but can be striking original formulations. Then it would follow that those maxims that are also proverbs would be those that have long become familiar and are therefore perceived as traditional. A similar view, less clearly stated, may be gleaned from Strömberg, *Proverbial Phrases* (supra, n. 6) 8–9. Kindstrand, "Greek Concept" (supra, n. 6) 74, would make the distinguishing criterion not so much traditionality as ethical content, suggesting that it was because many proverbs "were too popular in character without any ethical content and did not express the ancient wisdom" that Aristotle judged some proverbs not to be maxims.

21. It is of curious interest that this traditional association is continued by K. Rupprecht, "Paroimia," *RE* 18, pt. 2 (1949) 1707–35, where it is claimed (1708) that proverbs (not maxims) are naturally spoken by farmers. Aristotle would probably have agreed that proverbs, *instead* of maxims, are what farmers *ought to* be speaking.

22. It is well known that the playwright Menander captured Greek traditional wisdom so aptly in well-turned phrases that many of his verses became traditionally cited maxims. Collections of his iambic trimeters were made in later antiquity and valued as compendia of sententious wisdom, a tradition that has continued even into modern times, when *Menandri Sententiae* are available in various editions.

23. D. Lateiner, *The Historical Method of Herodotus* (Toronto 1989) 26–30, calls special attention to this author's many vivid representations of nonverbal communication, thus demonstrating the importance, in principle, of giving both word and gesture equal status within the kind of performance we have been discussing. Martin's definition of performance quoted earlier, and his study of the Seven Sages (supra, n. 3), rightly includes gestural along with verbal behavior, a topic I could not include in my own study.

24. M. Lang, *Herodotean Narrative and Discourse* (Cambridge, Mass. 1984) 58–67, claims to find sixty-two maxims in Herodotus and is tempted to add twelve more. A few of these maxims deserve rather to be identified as nonmetaphorical proverbs, since they are specifically introduced by their speakers as familiar sayings (e.g., "Everyone should mind his own affairs" [discussed earlier], or "Not every end is seen in the beginning," 7.51.3). But most of the others are simply general statements of principle, like "injustice is the enemy of justice," "all human life is brief," or "the Spartans think one thing and say another," and Lang allows no means of distinguishing between any general statement and the maxim as a formal entity. Her discussion suffers from an inconsistency and plurality of definitions: on the one hand, she freely equates proverbs with maxims, while on the other she attempts to make fine distinctions between "proverb-like sayings,"

"sentences," "true maxims," "proverb-like maxims," expressions that are "truly proverbial," "maxims that are most like proverbs," the "uncrystalized expression of a *senten-
tia* or *gnômê*," and phrases that "seem to be *gnômai*, but no one is proverbial." Such fluid
criteria allow her to equate maxims with an excessively broad range of general statements, so that all boundaries between ordinary speech and special wisdom performance
seem lost. The investigation of Herodotus's use of maxims, proverbs, and apothegms
presents a special challenge, because while he does not provide labels for these genres, he
is nevertheless inclined to represent speech acts and speech events that contain them.
The subject needs a rigorous and thorough investigation with modern linguistic and
paroemiological methods.

25. For recent discussions of the emergence of literate habits against a cultural background that was pervasively oral, see R. Thomas, *Literacy and Orality in Ancient Greece*
(Cambridge 1992), and W. V. Harris, *Ancient Literacy* (Cambridge, Mass. 1989).

26. This conception of discourse occurs in Bakhtin's writings, and is best presented
in his essay "The Problem of Speech Genres," included in C. Emerson and M. Holquist,
eds., *Speech Genres and Other Late Essays* (Austin 1986).

27. This sequence is essentially that put forward by W. Gemoll in *Das Apophthegma*
(Leipzig 1924) 4–6, although with minimal discussion of the process of development
and no attempt at explaining it. He observes briefly that for Plutarch *apophthegma* and
apomnêmoneuma have become synonymous: in the more narrowly philosophic tradition represented by Hermogenes the Cynic (late second century A.D.) it is *apomnêmoneuma* and *chreia* that are similar; but more often in the philosophical and biographical
traditions it is *chreia* and *apophthegma* that are virtually synonymous, both referring to
the memorable action and saying, usually in combination, of a famous wise person. I
have omitted the *chreia* from my study because it belongs essentially to the post-Platonic
written anecdotal tradition. The most recent full discussion, R. F. Hock and E. N.
O'Neill, *The Chreia in Ancient Rhetoric*, vol. 1: *The Prolegomena* (Atlanta 1986) 3–10,
locates the origins of the *chreia* in the Socratic circle and understands all the sayings and
anecdotes reported in Diogenes Laertius to be essentially *chreiai*, although Diogenes
himself never applies this term to the anecdotal material he quotes.

28. This process of abstraction from context followed by circulation as an independent saying is described as early as Herodotus (1.129), who concludes his anecdote about
Hippokleides dancing away his marriage to Kleisthenes' daughter by quoting the protagonist saying "Hippokleides doesn't care," οὐ φροντὶς Ἱπποκλείδῃ, and then com-
menting "it is from this that this is quoted," ἀπὸ τούτου μὲν τοῦτο οὐνομάζεται.

29. One likely indicator that Herodotus lacks the vocabulary for identifying his
apothegms and anecdotes as the formal genres ἀπόφθεγμα and ἀπομνημόνευμα is his
use of the general word τοῦτο to refer to *both of them* (1.129, quoted in n. 28). The Greek
ἀνέκδοτος (= "not given out," i.e., unpublished or unmarried) has nothing to do with
our modern concept of the anecdote. See K. J. Dover, "Anecdotes, Gossip, and Scandal,"
in *The Greeks and Their Legacy*, Collected Papers, vol. 2 (Oxford 1988) 45.

30. G. M. A. Grube, *A Greek Critic: Demetrius on Style* (Toronto 1961) 85, 96.

31. Gemoll (supra, n. 27) 3 suggests a threefold division into *Lakonika* (Chilonian, thoughtful, short and striking); *asteia* ("urbane," playful, riddling); and *Kynika* ("of the Cynics," serious-amusing).

32. For good discussion of the wider sociological reality, as well as the extension of "performance" to include nonverbal behavior, see Martin (supra, n. 3).

Chorus and Community in Euripides' Bacchae

I gratefully acknowledge a fellowship at the National Humanities Center in 1993–94, funded by the National Endowment for the Humanities, during which this study was written; and I thank the editors and anonymous reader of this volume for helpful comments.

1. See C. Segal, *Dionysiac Poetics and Euripides' Bacchae* (Princeton 1982) ch. 4, esp. 89–93.

2. See, e.g., Eur. *Med.* 824–45 and *Hipp.* 30–33; and Soph. *Ant.* 152–54, 1015–18, 1246–49; *OT* 19–23 and 159–63; *El.* 4–8; *OC* 14–18, 55–63, 668–719.

3. E. R. Dodds, ed., *Euripides, Bacchae*[2] (Oxford 1960) ad loc. (p. 165) compares *Orestes* 902ff.

4. The battle that Dionysus threatens, of course, never occurs, one of the false leads that Euripides sometimes injects into his prologues: see Richard Hamilton, "*Bacchae* 47–52; Dionysus' Plan," *TAPA* 104 (1974) 39–49.

5. For some of these themes of group and isolation, with different emphasis, see A. J. Podlecki, "Individual and Group in Euripides' *Bacchae*," *AntCl* 43 (1974) 144–45, 164.

6. See Segal (supra, n. 1) 242–47. On the elusiveness of the chorus in the play, see also S. Goldhill, "Doubling and Recognition in the *Bacchae*," *Metis* 3 (1988) 137–56 at 143–44. M. Arthur's excellent study, "The Choral Odes of the Bacchae of Euripides," *YCS* 22 (1972) 145–79, emphasizes the ambiguity of the chorus, but concentrates on its gnomic morality rather than its role in the expression of a civic ethos.

7. See Arthur (supra, n. 6) 169 and Segal (supra, n. 1) 242, 247. It would be interesting to know how Aeschylus presented his chorus in his lost Pentheus and Lycurgus dramas.

8. See C. Segal, *Euripides and the Poetics of Sorrow* (Durham, N.C. 1993) 120–35.

9. We may compare also the chorus's horror of Medea's deed in *Med.* 1251–93, where it expresses the sentiment, if not of the city, at least of ordinary women in the city (cf. 1090–1115). Our judgment of the chorus in the *Bacchae*, of course, must be qualified by the lacuna near the end; and it is possible that it uttered some statement of compassion after Agave's funeral lament. Given the present state of the text, we can only establish large probabilities and base our conclusions on the words and gestures of the chorus in the text that survives.

10. J. March, "Euripides the Misogynist," in Anton Powell, ed., *Euripides, Women, and Sexuality* (New York 1990) 61–62, attempts to give as positive an interpretation as

is possible of the closing scene. For the mixture of tones see Segal (supra, n. 1) 317–18, 323–27.

11. See G. Ieranò, "Zeus e Dioniso: In margine a Eur. *Bacch.* 1349," *RFIC* 120 (1992) 286–91.

12. Such is the direction of the reading by Richard Seaford, *Reciprocity and Ritual* (Oxford 1994) ch. 7, esp. 255–56; also 311ff. But the play does not in fact particularly develop "the contradiction between royal family and polis" (256). Elements of the royal family are quite sympathetic to Dionysus, and it is not clear just who or what represents "the polis" on Seaford's view. His attempt to read Pentheus's death in terms of the foundation of a hero cult (312), however valid as an interpretation of the structure of a foundation myth in Dionysus's relation to Thebes, receives little support from the text of the play. See my review in *BMCR* 6 (1995) 651–57.

13. The foreign appearance of a chorus, of course, has precedents in Greek tragedy, notably in Aeschylus's *Suppliants* and *Eumenides* and in Euripides' *Phoenician Women* and perhaps in some of the Trojan plays. Euripides may also have been influenced by Aeschylus's lost *Pentheus*.

14. For other aspects of the lack of a sense of civic solidarity in the *Bacchae* see J.-P. Vernant, "The Masked Dionysus of Euripides' *Bacchae*," in J.-P. Vernant and P. Vidal-Naquet, *Myth and Tragedy in Ancient Greece*, trans. J. Lloyd (New York 1990) 401–2.

15. See, e.g., P. E. Easterling, "The Second Stasimon of *Antigone*," in R. D. Dawe, J. Diggle, and P. E. Easterling, eds., *Dionysiaca: Nine Studies in Greek Poetry by Former Pupils Presented to Sir Denys Page on His Seventieth Birthday* (Cambridge 1978) 158.

16. For the problem of the chorus's gnomic moralizing, see Arthur (supra, n. 6) esp. 147–48, 154–55, 164–65; A. F. H. Bierl, *Dionysos und die griechische Tragödie* (Tübingen 1991) 71–72; also Podlecki (supra, n. 5) 145.

17. On the ambiguities of Dionysus, see Segal (supra, n. 1) 7–26; Bierl (supra, n. 16) 13–20; A. Henrichs, " 'He Has a God in Him': Human and Divine in the Modern Perception of Dionysus," in T. H. Carpenter and C. A. Faraone, eds., *Masks of Dionysus* (Ithaca, N.Y. 1993) 13–43, with recent bibliography. On the issue of his accommodation in the city, see Arthur (supra, n. 6) 154–55, 174–75; Segal (supra, n. 1) 328–36, 344–47. As Vernant, "Masked Dionysus" (supra, n. 14) 406–9, eloquently points out, the maenadic savagery of the Theban woman, of course, enacts only one side of the Dionysiac experience.

18. For these positive functions of Dionysiac cult within the polis, see, e.g., A. Henrichs, "Changing Dionysiac Identities," in B. F. Meyer and E. P. Sanders, eds., *Jewish and Christian Self-Definition* (London 1982) 140–41 and 151–55; "Between Country and City: Cultic Dimensions of Dionysus in Athens and Attica," in M. Griffth and D. J. Mastronarde, eds., *Cabinet of the Muses*, Festschrift T. G. Rosenmeyer (Atlanta 1990) 262–71; also Henrichs (supra, n. 17); M. Detienne, *Dionysus at Large*, trans. A. Goldhammer (Cambridge, Mass. 1989) 34–41, 53–56, 60–63.

19. See Henrichs, "Changing Dionysiac Identities" (supra, n. 18) 257–77; Bierl (supra, n. 16) 17–20, 28–29, 51–54, 125–32.

20. Interpreters have been (and probably will continue to be) divided between pro- and anti-Dionysus views of the play. For useful surveys of the various positions, see

H. Rohdich, *Die Euripideische Tragödie* (Heidelberg 1968) 162–67, and Bierl (supra, n. 16) 177–78.

21. See, e.g., Dodds (supra, n. 3) introduction, xxii–xxiii; also his *The Greeks and the Irrational*, Sather Classical Lectures 25 (Berkeley 1951) 275.

22. See R. Friedrich, "Medea Apolis: On Euripides' Dramatization of the Crisis of the Polis," in A. H. Sommerstein, S. Halliwell, J. Henderson, and B. Zimmermann, eds., *Tragedy, Comedy and the Polis, Papers from the Greek Drama Conference, Nottingham, 18–20 July 1990* (Bari 1993) 233.

23. The phrase τὸ δὲ κατ' ἦμαρ refers to continuity in time (i.e., every day) but also includes a notion of the uncertainty of human life and the importance of knowing mortal limitations. For a good discussion and references, see M. McDonald, *Terms for Happiness in Euripides*, Hypomnemata 54 (Göttingen 1978) 261–62.

24. On the shifts and nuances of the terms for happiness in this ode, see McDonald (supra, n. 23) 258–63, and J. de Romilly, "Le thème du bonheur dans les *Bacchantes*," *REG* 76 (1963) 361–80, esp. 366–69.

25. Lines 877–80 have been much discussed, and I follow Dodds (supra, n. 3) ad loc. (pp. 187–88), who keeps the manuscript reading, with the deletion of the problematical second τό (i.e., τί τὸ σοφόν, ἢ τί κάλλιον παρὰ θεῶν γέρας ἐν βροτοῖς ἢ χειρ' ὑπὲρ κορυφᾶς, etc.) with the sense, "What is wisdom, or what nobler (lovelier) prize is there from the gods for mortals than to hold one's hand over the head of one's enemies in greater power?" J. Roux, *Les Bacchantes d'Euripide* (Paris 1972) ad loc. (II, 514–17), however, accepts an emendation proposed independently by W. E. Blake and A. J. Festugière: she punctuates with a question mark after βροτοῖς and introduces the following clause with the interrogative particle ἦ (ἦ χειρ' ὑπὲρ κορυφᾶς . . .). The sense would then be, "What is wisdom, or what finer prize is there from the gods for mortals? Is it to hold one's hand over the head of one's enemies in greater power? [No, for] what is beautiful [noble, *kalon*] is always loved." Dodds (ad loc.) discusses this text and interpretation and dismisses them (rightly, I think), on the ground that they put too much weight on αἰεί ("always") in the last clause (881). The emendation also requires a strong adversative sense in 881, which is possible, of course, but not given in the text. J. Diggle in his recent Oxford Classical Text, *Euripidis Fabulae*, vol. 3 (Oxford 1994) obelizes 877, largely on metrical grounds: see his *Euripidea: Collected Essays* (Oxford 1994) 471. The emended text makes this ode an expression of moral generalities more like that of "normal" choral moralizing. But, even with this reading, there remains the sharp contrast with the chorus's call for bloody justice in the fourth stasimon. As Lowell Edmunds reminds me (*per litteras*), the proverbial ring of ὅτι καλὸν φίλον (noted by Dodds [supra, n. 3] p. 187; see Theognis 17, Pl. *Lysis* 216c) adds a further irony to the chorus's use of traditional wisdom for its own purposes. Seaford (supra, n. 12) 402–4 accepts the emended text of Roux and Blake, and interprets αἰεί as a reference to the "*permanent happiness*" brought by initiation into the Dionysiac mysteries. This view solves some of the problems of αἰεί but, even leaving aside the hypothetical nature of the mystic allusion, still leaves the problem of why the chorus should specifically list power over one's enemies as its major term of contrast with the *eudaimonia* of the following lines. It

also does not take account of the chorus's explicit indulgence in the pleasure of violent revenge in the fourth stasimon.

26. On this feature of the ode see Segal (supra, n. 1) 203, 243–44.

27. The interpretation and text of this entire passage (1005–10) are unsure and have been the subject of intense discussion. I follow, essentially, Dodds (supra, n. 3) and Roux (supra, n. 25) ad loc.

28. See Segal (supra, n. 1) 331–32.

29. On this scene see R. P. Winnington-Ingram, *Euripides and Dionysus* (Cambridge 1948) 127–28.

30. More literally, "You have brought about a glorious victory song, (but made it) into lament, into tears," reading γόον with Dodds (supra, n. 3), after Canter. This reading is also adopted by Diggle in his Oxford Classical Text (supra, n. 25). For the interpretation of the phrase, see Dodds ad loc. For the ritual structure involved in the irony of the inverted epinikion, see H. Foley, *Ritual Irony: Poetry and Sacrifice in Euripides* (Ithaca, N.Y. 1985) 210–16; M. Hose, *Studien zum Chor bei Euripides* (Stuttgart 1990) 1:192–93 and 2:388.

31. With Dodds, *Bacchae* (supra, n. 3) on lines 1163–64, I follow Wecklein's conjecture, reading ἐν αἵματι στάζουσαν χέρα βαλεῖν τέκνου. On the various meanings and ironies in the uses of *kalon* in the play, see Winnington-Ingram (supra, n. 29) 24, 108–9.

32. See μακάριον θήραν, 1171; μάκαιρ' Ἀγαύη, 1180; εὐτυχής, 1184. Compare the language of happiness in 902–11 and the beatitudes of the chorus's opening ode, 72–82.

33. For further discussion see C. Segal, "Female Mourning and Dionysiac Lament in Euripides' *Bacchae*," in A. H. F. Bierl and Peter von Möllendorff, eds., *Orchestra: Drama, Mythos, Bühne: Festschrift für Helmut Flashar* (Leipzig 1994) 12–18, esp. 13–15. M. Alexiou, *The Ritual Lament in Greek Tradition* (Cambridge 1974) 134–39, provides indications that this antiphonal form of lamentation has great antiquity; see also C. N. Serematakis, *The Last Word: Women, Death, and Divination in Inner Mani* (Chicago 1991) 99–125, cited and discussed in more detail below.

34. For the details of gender reversal in the play, see Segal (supra, n. 1) ch. 6.

35. Interpreters have been divided about the meaning of *tlamon*. Dodds (supra, n. 3) ad loc. argues for a tone of sympathy, whereas Winnington-Ingram (supra, n. 29) 136, with n. 3 and 144 n. 1, thinks that the word is merely an objective expression of Agave's misery. For discussion see Hose (supra, n. 30) 1:209 and 2:388–89, who allows for both possibilities but leaves the issue open, and Segal (supra, n. 33), where I argue for Dodds' position, that *tlamon* expresses pity. Cf. Eur. *IT* 1420, e.g., with the comment of Hose 1:203–4. See also Segal (supra, n. 1) 244.

36. On these passages from Euripides' *Suppliants* and *Phoenissae*, see R. Seaford, "Dionysus As Destroyer of the Household: Homer, Tragedy, and the Polis," in Carpenter and Faraone (supra, n. 17) 119–20 and 125–26, who, however, is concerned with negated wedding ritual and destruction in the household, not rites of mourning.

37. On this passage and its Dionysiac affinities, though from a different point of view, see Seaford (supra, n. 36) 116–19.

38. See especially *HF* 896–97, οὔποτ' ἄκραντα δόμοισι Λύσσα βακχεύσει, "Never

will Lyssa rage in bacchantic madness without effect for the house." On this passage see Bierl (supra, n. 16) 86–87. For further details see Segal (supra, n. 33).

39. R. Schlesier, "Mixtures of Masks: Maenads As Tragic Models," in Carpenter and Faraone (supra, n. 17) 89–114, esp. 99–103; Seaford (supra, n. 36). Both of these important studies show how easily the "Dionysiac metaphor" (Seaford 115) can be transferred to other areas of highly emotional experience, especially involving women and fraught with disorder and destruction for the household.

40. See N. Loraux, *The Invention of Athens*, trans. A. Sheridan (Cambridge, Mass. 1986) 45–49; also Alexiou (supra, n. 33) 108. For a cross-cultural approach see G. Holst-Wahrhaft, *Dangerous Voices: Women's Laments and Greek Literature* (London 1992) 20–29, 119–24.

41. For cross-cultural parallels see Holst-Wahrhaft (supra, n. 40) esp. ch. 1.

42. See Alexiou (supra, n. 33) 122–28, 131–205.

43. That this scene may represent actual practice in bringing such celebrants out of their ecstasy has been argued on very different lines by G. Devereux, "The Psychotherapy Scene in Euripides' *Bacchae*," *JHS* 90 (1970) 35–48.

44. On the contrasting movement of *pompê, agôn,* and *kômos* in the play, see R. Seaford, "Dionysiac Drama and the Dionysiac Mysteries," *CQ* 31 (1981) 267; Foley (supra, n. 30) 208–16, 230–31.

45. This speech is also important, of course, in arousing our sympathies for Pentheus at the end: see Winnington-Ingram (supra, n. 29) 143.

46. My interpretation is not seriously affected by the much discussed problem of the Palace Miracle, whether the house really or only figuratively collapses or whether it is all allusion.

47. I cannot agree with the optimistic view of the play's ending suggested by Seaford's emphasis on the arrival of the Dionysiac cult in Thebes: Seaford (supra, n. 12) 255–57, 353–54, and (supra, n. 36) 138. On the problem of integrating Dionysus into the city, see Segal (supra, n. 1) 303–9, 339–47; Foley (supra, n. 30) 244–45, 254–58; F. I. Zeitlin, "Thebes: Theater of Self and Society in Athenian Drama," in J. J. Winkler and F. I. Zeitlin, eds., *Nothing to Do with Dionysus?* (Princeton 1990) 135–36, 148–50.

48. Lines 13–26 of the prologue are the play's most emphatic passage for Dionysus's journey between East and West and barbarian and Greek. Their authenticity has been questioned by A. Dihle, "Der Prolog der 'Bacchen' und die antike Überlieferungsphase des Euripides-Textes," *SBHeid* (1981) 11–27, but his objections are now vigorously and convincingly refuted by Diggle, *Euripidea* (supra, n. 25) 444–61.

49. For the cosmopolitanism of Dionysus, see A. Henrichs, "Greek and Roman Glimpses of Dionysus," in Caroline Houser, ed., *Dionysus and His Circle: Ancient through Modern* (Cambridge, Mass. 1979) 8–11, with further references there cited.

The Ion of Euripides and Its Audience(s)

1. A "sentimental but very fine" specimen of the genre, in the judgment of H. J. Rose, *A Handbook of Greek Literature* (London 1934) 189. Cf. W. H. Friedrich, *Euripides*

und Diphilos, Zetemata 5 (Munich 1953) 10: "Keine der erhaltenen attischen Tragödien ist geeigneter als diese den Übergang zur Komödie, insbesondere zu Menander, zu bilden," with the detailed analysis of the *Ion* that follows (pp. 10–29).

2. Compare Thucydides' analysis (1.3.2) of the way the sons of Hellen served as mercenaries in various cities of the partially Pelasgian territory that would subsequently be called Hellas, thereby contributing to the spread of the designation *Hellênes*, with Herodotus's account (7.94; 8.44.2) of how the Pelasgians in Attica, the Peloponnesus, and the islands came to be called Ionians once Xuthus's son Ion arrived in their midst and was chosen as their commander. Thucydides is concerned with the general onomastic consequences of the activities of Hellen and his descendants; Herodotus with a particular aspect of the renaming process in which a crucial role was played by one of Hellen's grandchildren.

3. Aeolians from Methymna, Tenedos, and Ainos appear between Ionians and Dorians in the list of Athens' Aegean allies at Thuc. 7.58.5–6, but more as offshoots of the Boeotians than as representatives of a major ethnic subgroup. Their unwilling presence at Syracuse in a battle that pitted them against contingents from their mother cities on the mainland is there contrasted with the behavior of another group of Boeotians, Athens's willing allies, the Plataeans.

4. This is, of course, the hypothesis of H. Grégoire (*Euripide Suppliantes, Ion, Iphigénie en Tauride* [Paris 1933] 165–67), taken over with minor additions and modifications by E. Delebeque (*Euripide et la guerre du Péloponnèse* [Paris 1951] 225–41) and R. Goosens (*Euripide et Athènes*, Académie Royale de Belgique, Classe des Lettres, Mémoires 54, no. 4 [Brussels 1962] 486–500).

5. Cf. V. Di Benedetti, *Euripide: Teatro e società* (Turin 1971) 297.

6. See, in particular, G. B. Walsh, "The Rhetoric of Birthright and Race in Euripides' *Ion*," *Hermes* 106 (1978) 313–15, and Bernhard Smarczyk, *Untersuchungen zur Religionspolitik und politischen Propaganda Athens im Delisch-Attischen Seebund*, Quellen und Forschungen zur Antiken Welt 5 (Munich 1990) 615–18. A hitherto neglected piece of evidence is the special emphasis given in the description of the colonization of Ionia (lines 1581–87) to settlements in the vicinity of the Hellespont (lines 1585–87). Though maintaining control over this region had always been essential to Athenian interests, it was only with the battles of Cynossema (September 411), Abydus (October–November 411) and Cyzicus (April 410) that the mounting, for the first time, of a serious Spartan challenge to that control made the area the focal point of the entire war.

7. The most authoritative proponent of this view is Wilamowitz, *Euripides, Ion* (Berlin 1926) 8–9, followed by, e.g., D. J. Conacher, *Euripidean Drama* (Toronto 1967) 271ff., and A. Pippin Burnett, *Euripides, Ion: A Translation with Commentary* (Englewood Cliffs, N.J.: 1970) 1–2. A. S. Owen (*Euripides, Ion: Edited with Introduction and Commentary* [Oxford 1939] xi–xiv) regards Euripides' version as a late fifth-century invention but allows for the possibility that it first appeared in the Sophoclean play discussed infra, nn. 12 and 18.

8. The solution to the problem which Euripides has Creusa offer to Ion—that she was too young at the time of the war, still an infant in her mother's arms, to share the fate

of her sisters (*Ion* 280)—involves further difficulties. For if Creusa was still an infant during the war in which her father perished, how was Apollo's intervention necessary to ensure that her subsequent pregnancy remained ἀγνῶς . . . πατρί (line 14)? One suspects that such complications would not have arisen had mention of a daughter named Creusa appeared in any earlier Athenian tradition concerning the reign of Erechtheus. Euripides would simply have situated her marriage—like, presumably, those of her sister Procris to Cephalus and her sister Oreithyia to Boreas—in the time before their father's death.

9. See also *Ath. Pol.* fr. 1 (notices coming from Harpocration and the epitome of Heraclides).

10. See H. v. Geisau, "Xouthos," *RE* A9 (1967) 2157–59.

11. On the origin of these versions, see C. Robert, *Die griechische Heldensage* (Berlin 1921) 147 n. 1.

12. It is tempting to suppose that this genealogy first appeared in a play of Sophocles, the one variously referred to as the *Ion* (frs. 319–22 Radt) or the *Creusa* (frs. 350–59). But our evidence contains nothing that would allow us to date the drama, reconstruct its plot, or even be sure that the two sets of surviving fragments come from the same play. The *Creusa* of the second title may be (as Robert [supra, n. 11] 146–47 believed) the Corinthian princess betrothed to Jason.

13. The same may be said of Aristotle's reference (*Ath. Pol.* fr. 1) to a cult of *Apollo patrôios* established by Ion after his settling in Attica—if in fact this cult was conceived in the tradition as a means of honoring the founder's own father. Ion's choice of Apollo may have reflected nothing more than the desire to find a god "suitable . . . to preside over his kinship organization" (P. J. Rhodes, *A Commentary on the Aristotelian* Athenaion Politeia [Oxford 1981] 67).

14. In the *Euthydemus* passage just cited, it is unclear whether the reference is to all Ionians or simply to the citizens of the Ionian metropolis, Athens; and even if the more inclusive attribution is the one intended, it may rest on nothing more than inference from what existed at Athens—as the appearance of *Athênaia fratria* alongside *Apollôn patrôios* and *Zeus herkeios* in the instances of "Ionian" usage cited by Socrates at 302d might suggest.

15. Cf. M. P. Nilsson, *Geschichte der griechischen Religion*, vol. 1 (Munich 1941) 525: "Bei ihm [Euripides] ist . . . der Vater des Ion der in einer Höhle an der Nordseite der Burg . . . verehrte Apollo, der ὑπακραῖος, nicht Patroos genannt wird. Diese Identifikation ist also recht späte genealogische Mache, obgleich sie schon im vierten Jahrhundert geläufig war." It should also be pointed out that "dass Ion mit dem Apollon βοηδρομιος in Verbindung gebracht wird . . . spricht eher gegen als für seine Beziehung zu Apollon πατρῷος" (Robert [supra, n. 11] 148 n. 1).

16. Much the same may be true, as Lowell Edmunds points out to me, of the circumstances of Oedipus's death at Colonus: unknown, or contradicted by a tradition (cf. Paus. 1.28.7) that had him buried on the Areopagus—before the premiere of Sophocles' play, whose dramatis personae are accordingly pledged to silence (*Od. Cl.* 1760–67) as to the existence and whereabouts of the tomb.

17. The possibility that poets were, in general, "licensed and expected to tell tall

stories and thereby *un* tell well-founded traditions" (M. Griffith, "Contest and Contradiction in Early Greek Poetry," in D. Mastronarde and M. Griffith, eds., *Cabinet of the Muses: Essays in Classical and Comparative Literature in Honor of Thomas E. Rosenmayer* [Atlanta 1990] 200) should certainly be borne in mind in analyzing the various excursions into "revisionist" mythology which occur in Stesichorus, Pindar, and the dramatists. But the license and the expectation, if they existed, were not ones of which the poet was likely to have availed himself in the present instance.

18. Several scholars (e.g., Grégoire [supra, n. 4] 162, and A. Pippin Burnett, *Catastrophe Survived* [Oxford 1971] 103) have found traces in the *Ion* of a polemic against an earlier dramatic version of the legend, which could only be that of Sophocles. If they are right, and if, as has been suggested (supra, n. 12), Sophocles' innovation consisted in making Ion the son of Xuthus and Creusa rather than of Xuthus alone, the superiority—from the point of view of probability—of Euripides' version is obvious. There was no conceivable reason why Attic tradition should have been unaware of the existence of a son of Xuthus and Creusa, and, on the other hand, very good reasons for its knowing nothing of a son of Creusa and Apollo. But all hypotheses based on a reconstruction of the plot of the *Ion* (or *Creusa*) of Sophocles are very risky ones.

19. For the position of Ion according to the provisions of Attic law, see Burnett (supra, n. 18) 106 n. 6, and F. E. Zeitlin, "Mysteries of Identity and Designs of the Self in Euripides' *Ion*," *PCPS* n.s. 35 (1989) 80 with n. 143. The attitudes he could expect to encounter among his fellow citizens may be inferred from Eupolis *Demes* fr. 110 K-A: the shade of Pericles asks information from a new arrival in Hades about the child he had by Aspasia and is told καὶ πάλαι γ' ἂν ἦν ἀνήρ, εἰ μὴ τὸ τῆς πόρνης ὑπωρρώδει κακόν.

20. This long passage has struck many readers as inorganic, which it certainly is if one fails to take into account the function it may have had in suggesting reasons for the absence of any record of public achievements that might have justified Ion's ultimate role as *Stammvater*. Such achievements were part of the earlier tradition—it was successful generalship that won Ion his citizenship and political importance. But Euripides has eliminated this possibility by making him already heir apparent by adoption when he arrives in Athens.

21. For a survey of various conclusions reached, see Conacher (supra, n. 7) 277–79.

22. See H. R. Immerwahr, " 'Αθηναικές εἰκόνες στόν "Ιωνα τοῦ Εὐριπίδη," *Hellenika* 25 (1972) 277–97.

23. It is unlikely that the inaccuracies in the description of Apollo's temple at Delphi indicated by C. H. Whitman, *Euripides and the Full Cycle of Myth* (Cambridge, Mass. 1974) 76–77, would have been noticed or felt as such by the audience.

24. See the discussions of Verrall, Murray, and Norwood cited by Conacher (supra, n. 7) 277 n. 33.

25. Livy *Ab urbe condita*, pref. 6.

26. There were doubtless those in the audience who would have favored, as Maurizio Bettini pointed out during the discussion following the presentation of this paper, a third interpretation—one that gave Ion, like Heracles, both a divine and a human father. (Enrico Montanari, *Il mito dell'autoctonia*[2] [Rome 1981] 171–72, argues in similar fashion

for the coexistence of "due genealogie . . . 'tragicamente' sospese e. quasi, reciproca-mente elise.") But had Euripides himself been interested in encouraging this approach he could easily have created a sequence of events that made it at least chronologically possible for Ion to be the son of Xuthus and Creusa—and so to be regarded correctly by Xuthus as, in some sense at any rate, his own child.

27. The uniqueness of the *Ion* in this respect means that there is no danger—as there could be otherwise—that the "Verrallism" of the analysis offered here might become contagious.

28. It would have needed them in the case of Dorus (son of Xuthus and Creusa, according to Athena, rather than Xuthus's brother, as in the traditional genealogy). But of all the revelations that occur in the course of the drama, this is certainly the least important. It is also the least credible, which probably explains why Athena is the one that makes it. Its inclusion in the "human" portion of the play would have made the latter seem less believable.

29. Leaving the question of paternity unresolved makes it easier to follow Nicole Loraux in seeing Ion as continuator in a certain sense of the Athenian tradition of autochthonous kings, and Creusa as a kind of virgin mother to whom—along with Athena—the Athenian people owes its origin and prosperity. See the Creusa chapter in *The Children of Athena*, trans. C. Levine (Princeton 1993).

30. For the two terms "dramatic" and "theatrical" space as used here, see the discussion in Maria Grazia Bonanno's contribution to this volume.

31. Upon his initial entry Ion is identified by Hermes, who thereby becomes not simply the first person to refer to him by name but the first *among the gods* to do so (ὄνομα δ' οὗ μέλλει τυχεῖν / Ἴων' ἐγώ ⟨ ⟩ πρῶτος ὀνομάζω θεῶν [80–81]). *Theôn* here serves asd a means of indicating that Hermes is performing his traditional role as divine πρῶτος ὀνοματοθέτης, the god charged with correctly naming everything (in this case the son of Creusa and Apollo) when it first comes to the attention of mankind. The fact that before the moment of performance the name was already in use to designate another personage (a son of Xuthus who never existed) detracts in no way from Hermes' priority in applying it correctly.

32. That the play's conciliatory agenda was directed as much toward Delphi as toward Ionia—a response to the "necessità che Atene riassorbisse il dio delfico nelle proprie forme culturali (tragediografiche) proprio per assicurare la sopravvivenza della *polis* autoctona mediante il meccanismo protettivo della sua egemonizzazione" (Montanari [supra, n. 26] 178–79)—strikes me as possible, but less likely, given the relative unimportance of the identity of Ion's true father for one of the two interpretations, mythicizing and rationalizing, that its message allows.

Poet, Public, and "Theatrocracy":
Audience Performance in Classical Athens

1. On judging music see also *Laws* 658e–659a, and 655d: "it is commonly said that the standard of rightness in music is its pleasure-giving effect. That, however, is an

intolerable sentiment; in fact, it is a piece of flat blasphemy." According to *Laws* 670b–c, "the general public are simply ridiculous in their belief that men are adequate judges of what is good or otherwise in melody and rhythm, if they have merely been drilled into singing to the pipe and marching in step, though it never occurs to them that they do these acts without understanding anything about them." Translations of *Laws* are adapted from A. E. Taylor; that of *Gorgias* is by W. D. Woodhead.

2. In the fifth and fourth centuries, judges in Athenian dramatic festivals were chosen by lot before the plays' performance, and hence could be influenced by audience reactions. See A. W. Pickard-Cambridge, *The Dramatic Festivals of Athens*[2], rev. J. Gould and D. Lewis (Oxford 1968) 95–99.

3. See *Laws* 876b, condemning the *thorubos* of Athens's dikastic jurors "like in theaters." In *Republ.* 492b–c Sokrates asks how any young man could not be swept away when the crowd, "seated together in assemblies or courtrooms or theaters or camps," with great *thorubos* roars its approval or condemnation, "both clapping and shouting out so that the rocks and the region around reecho the *thorubos* of censure and praise."

4. Plut. *Phoc.* 8.5; see also Pl. *Gorg.* 502d–503a, *Pol.* 296d–297c.

5. *Elem. Harm.* 41.4–5 M. See A. Belis, *Aristoxène de Tarente et Aristote: Le traité d'harmonique* (Paris 1986) 99. According to *Aristoxenos's Drinking-Party Miscellanies* (ap. Athen. 632b), "now the theaters have become utterly barbarised, and this vulgar music has advanced into the extremity of corruption" (trans. Barker).

6. Plato's musical biases largely shaped the interpretive scheme of [Plut.] *De musica* and other texts; see I. Henderson, *New Oxford History of Music*, vol. 1: *Ancient and Oriental Music*, ed. E. Wellesz (Oxford 1957) 396.

For a similar debate in the early church, between the search for applause and the importance of content, see A. Roncoroni, 'Origini della retorica cristiana dell'applauso," in *Studi in onore di F. Rittatore Vonwiller*, vol. 2 (Como 1980) 411–23, and, more briefly, A. Stuiber, "Beifall," *Reallex. f. Ant. u. Christ.* 2 (1954) cols. 98–102.

7. B. Marzullo, "Die visuelle Dimension des Theaters bei Aristoteles," *Philologus* 124 (1980) 189–200, interprets the discussion of tragedy in *Poetics* as a reaction against the developments of Aristotle's own time.

8. B. Gentili and G. Cerri, *History and Biography in Ancient Thought* (Amsterdam 1988) 13 with n. 27 (Euripides, Thucydides [see esp. 1.22], and Plato "all place at the center of their polemical propositions the rigid contrast between the usefulness (*ophelimon*) of a rational account, and the pleasure (*hêdonê, terpein*) inherent in the practice of the performance. Thus for the first time that antinomy between the useful and the delightful which was destined to remain one of the typical characteristics of European culture, was outlined"). See also B. Gentili, "Lirica greca arcaica e tardo arcaica," in F. Della Corte, ed., *Introduzione allo Studio della Cultura Classica*, vol. 1 (Milan 1972) 63.

9. Henderson (supra, n. 6) 395. By contrast, Plato states that fifth-century popular audiences were willing *not* to raise a *thorubos*: to plêthos êthelen archesthai (*Laws* 700d).

10. Two texts indicate the existence of attendants or beadles in the theater. In Ar. *Pax* 734, the chorus states that "the rod-bearers" (*rhabdouchoi*) "ought to beat any poet who

praises himself to the theater." (The R scholiast is uncertain whether these were beadles instructed to maintain order among the audience, or else judges of the contest "whom Homer calls *aisumnêtai.*") In 349 B.C., Demosthenes (21.179) mentions the existence of "assistants" (*hyperêtai*) who removed if necessary those who had taken a wrong seat in the theater. Since *hyperetai* could be a general term for public slaves, it is not quite certain that Demosthenes' *hyperêtai* differed from the *rhabdouchoi,* or that these *hyperêtai* had at some point replaced the *rhabdouchoi.* However, Plato's reference to *rhabdouchoi* in the past tense, and the probable shift in nomenclature (unless Demosthenes is not speaking precisely), support these two hypotheses. The *rhabdouchoi* were presumably noncitizens (see Dem. 21.178–80), and held the equivalent of billy-clubs. They may have been abolished at the same time as the Scythian police, who kept order in the Ekklesia and Boule and who disappear from the sources between 403 and 390. Possibly both institutions were seen to be fundamentally undemocratic. It cannot, I think, be decided if the *rhabdouchoi* were Scythian policemen. There certainly is no indication that their function was to silence audience reactions in the theater.

11. C. Segal, in P. E. Easterling and B. M. W. Knox, eds., *Cambridge History of Classical Literature,* vol. 1: *Greek Literature* (Cambridge 1985) 244.

12. P. Ghiron-Bistagne, "Die Krise des Theaters in der griechischen Welt im 4. Jh. v. u. Z.," in E. C. Welskopf, ed., *Hellenische Poleis, Krise-Wandlung-Wirkung,* vol. 3 (Berlin 1974) 1335–56: quotations are taken from pp. 1353 and 1335. See also P. Ghiron-Bistagne, *Recherches sur les acteurs dans la Grèce antique* (Paris 1976) 195: "les manifestations de toute cette foule [of spectators] étaient difficilement contrôlables"; and similarly H. Kindermann, *Das Theaterpublikum der Antike* (Salzburg 1979) 22.

13. See A. Barker, *Greek Musical Writings,* vol. 1: *The Musician and His Art* (Cambridge 1984) 93–98 ("The musical revolution of the later fifth century"). Barker translates the Pherekrates passage on pp. 236–37.

14. See, e.g., G. Vlastos, "Does Slavery Exist in Plato's Republic?," *CP* 63 (1968) 294 n. 18 (reprinted in *Platonic Studies*[2] [Princeton 1981] 145–46 n. 18). So also G. Grote, *Plato and the Other Companions of Sokrates*[3], vol. 3 (London 1875) 346. Grote vigorously rejects Plato's statement in *Laws* that the Athenians ever sat quietly and decorously in the theater.

15. See, e.g., A. Lesky, *Greek Tragic Poetry* (New Haven 1983) 400, and Henderson (supra, n. 6) 339 ("for the history of music, the decisive event was the fall of Athens in 404 B.C.").

16. In what follows I do not discuss the audience reactions of tears (see, e.g., Eur. fr. 407 N., Pl. *Phil.* 48a, Isoc. 4.168) and laughter (see S. Halliwell, *CQ* 41 [1991] 279–96, esp. 290–96) but not because these may be largely involuntary and free from significant cultural variables. Rather, the literary record is unable adequately to reflect any variables in these responses. From what follows we might conclude that in the fourth-century theater both laughter and tears increased. This would be difficult to prove.

17. On audience response in antiquity, see A. Müller, *Lehrbuch der griechischen Bühnenalterthümer* (Freiburg 1886) 305–8 (a full and concise discussion of ancient sources),

Pickard-Cambridge (supra, n. 2) 272–78 (another detailed overview, which also does not evaluate the evidence chronologically), and W. Arnott, *An Introduction to the Greek Theatre* (Bloomington, Ind. 1959), ch. 4 ("The Audience"), a vivid but less scholarly treatment. Kindermann (supra, n. 12), esp. ch. 1 pt. 2 ("Zuschauerraum, Publikumsstruktur, und Reaktionsfähigkeit") is more general yet. F. B. Ferrari, *De veterum acclamationibus et plausu libri septem* (Milan 1627), reprinted in J. G. Graevius, *Thesaurus antiquitatum Romanarum*, vol. 6 (Vienna 1732) 4–230, collects much material, though (inevitably) without modern textual references. See also Stuiber (supra, n. 6) cols. 92–103, especially on Roman and Christian materials.

18. Cf. the acute remarks of O. Taplin, "Fifth-Century Tragedy and Comedy: A *Synkrisis,*" *JHS* 106 (1986) 172–73, on the differences in *intended* audience response between comedy and tragedy. For example, "it was essential for comedy, if it was to succeed, that the audience should interrupt; it was essential for tragedy, if it was to succeed, that the audience should not interrupt."

19. According to D. L. 2.34, Sokrates walked out when in the *Auge* someone said, "it is best to let [virtue] roam at will."

20. See also the story of Euripides' response, to those who "railed at" (*loidorein*) his character Ixion as "impious" and *miaros* (Plut. *Mor.* 19e = frs. 424–27 N.), that Ixion would be punished. However, it is not explicitly said that this occurred in the theater. For the unreliability of such anecdotes, see (among recent discussions) A. Momigliano, *The Development of Greek Biography* (Cambridge, Mass. 1971) 70, M. R. Lefkowitz, "Aristophanes and Other Historians of the Fifth-Century Theatre," *Hermes* 112 (1984) 143–53, and (especially on Euripides) M. Delcourt, "Les biographies anciennes d'Euripide," *AC* 2 (1933) 279–80, and P. T. Stevens, "Euripides and the Athenians," *JHS* 76 (1956) 89.

21. J. D. Beazley, *Attic Black-Figured Vase Painters* (Oxford 1956) 36 and 681 (= Athens Nat. Mus. 15499, and fig. 64 in Ghiron-Bistagne, *Recherches* [supra, n. 12] 199).

22. I omit Herodotos's famous story (6.21.2) of the theater audience bursting into tears at Phrynichos's *Capture of Miletos,* which resulted in a fine for the playwright, because in the theater itself only tears are attested. Plutarch (*Cim.* 8) records that when the young Sophokles first presented plays at the Dionysia, "contentiousness [*philoneikia*] and partisanship [*parataxis*] among that *theatai*" was so intense that the archon appointed the ten generals as judges. Whatever the historicity of this episode, however, Plutarch thought that the strife he describes occurred before the plays' performances.

23. For the meaning of *exepeson,* see LSJ s.v. 12 with examples (Dem. 18.265 is especially clear).

24. In "Dikastic *thorubos,*" in P. Cartledge and F. D. Harvey, eds., *Crux: Essays Presented to G. E. M. de Ste. Croix* (Exeter 1985), V. Bers shows that "fairly early in the fifth century *thorubos* was common at large official meetings" (p. 3), including courtrooms and assembly.

25. See also Aelian *VH* 2.13, that at the first performance of Aristophanes' *Clouds* the audience noisily demanded that the judges give Aristophanes first prize, but they refused. This story would illustrate Plato's point, but its attestation is inadequate. (I owe

the reference to Franca Perusino.) Cf. also the first hypothesis to *Frogs*, reporting that the audience demanded that the play be repeated because of the political wisdom contained in the *parabasis*.

26. Athen. 406f. On Chamaileon, see Momigliano (supra, n. 20) 70. This is the same man who claimed that Aeschylus wrote his plays while drunk.

27. C. T. Murphy, "Popular Comedy in Aristophanes," *AJP* 93 (1972) 173–75, traces this and other practices to the genre of popular farce widespread throughout Greece.

28. Though Hesychios once defines *krotoi* (s.v.) more widely as *euphêmiai, epainoi* (but cf. id. s.v. *krotêsas: ktuptêsas tais chersin*), its regular pairing with *boê* argues that its meaning was generally restricted to clapping. Several texts specify "*krotein* with the hands" (Paus. 10.31.8, Pallad. *Hist. Lausiac.* 83 col. 1185c–d)—although that expression could be thought ambiguous.

29. Bers (supra, n. 24) collects a large number of references to *thorubos* in the courts.

30. L. Edmunds, in an appendix ("Life of Sophocles and Reception of *Oedipus at Colonus*") to *Theatrical Space and Historical Place in Sophocles' Oedipus at Colonus* (Lanham, Md. 1996). Various exclamations by fifth-century jurors ("You're singing!" "Get down!"), are noted by Bers (supra, n. 24) 3 and n. 10. Bers argues that the first of these may be documented as early as the 450s.

31. See [Pl.] *Axioch.* 368d, Philod. *Acad. Ind.* p. 14 M., Plut. *Mor.* 545c.

32. A. S. F. Gow, *Theocritus*, vol. 2 (Cambridge 1965) 107; cf. 96.

33. Photios, Hesychios (ss. v.), and schol. [Pl.] *Ax.* 368d (ed. W. Greene) all report the usefulness of this word for calming horses. According to Ar. *Vesp.* 625, when someone saw lightning he was supposed to *poppuzein*—presumably to avert a bad omen.

34. See e.g. Ar. *Eccles.* 431 (in the Assembly), Dem. 19.195 (in Philip's court), 21.14 (in the Assembly), and Isok. 12.264.

35. Epic. fr. 143 = D. L. 10.5, Plut. *Mor.* 45f (also in connection with Epicurus) and 1117a, Eun. *Hist.* p. 259 D.

36. Dio Cass. 63.20.5; Epictet. *Diss.* 3.23, 24, and see Struiber (supra, n. 6) col. 94.

37. Dio Cass. 61.20, Philostr. *VS* 2.32, p. 274.2, Luc. *Salt.* 83; see C. Sittl, *Die Gebärden der Griechen und Römer* (Leipzig 1890) 62. Aurelian first donated handkerchiefs to the Roman people to be waved in showing approval (*HA Aurel.* 48.5).

38. For audiences jumping to their feet, see Mart. 10.10.9–10, Hor. *AP* 429, Plin. *Ep.* 6.17, and W. Kroll, "Rhetorik," *RE* Suppl. 7 (1940) 1076 (for further Roman references).

39. Pollux 4.88 refers to an incident in which an actor named Hermon, who expected not to perform and had set off home, was called back by the herald "after all those before him had been hissed off the stage." For hissing off the stage, see also Antiphanes ap. Athen. 223a. At the opening night of his musical "The World of Paul Slickey" (1959), John Osborne was chased down Charing Cross Road by angry members of the audience.

40. See Harpokr. s.v. *eklôzete* (also *Souda* and *Et. Mag.* ss.v., which are similar), and Hesych. *klôzein*.

41. See Alkiphr. 3.35.3, Synes. *De provid.* 1.13 p. 106c.

42. Cf. Petron. 90.1.3, Luc. *Pseudomant.* 25, Euseb. *HE* 5.1.7, and Macrob. 2.6.1 (lapi-

datus a populo Vatinius . . . obtinuerat ut aediles edicerent ne quis in arenam nisi pomum misisse vellet).

43. Cf. Ghiron-Bistagne, *Recherches* (supra, n. 12) 197, stating that fourth-century audiences threw "eggs and tomatoes"; cf. Ghiron-Bistagne, "Krise" (supra, n. 12) 1354: "Sie [the actors] wurden mit Tomaten oder Eiern beworfen, das ist sicher." Apparently Ghiron-Bistagne had not tasted "la cucina prima del pomodoro" at Venice's Corte Sconta.

44. See Pickard-Cambridge (supra, n. 2) 280 n. 1.

45. See Sittl (supra, n. 37) 90, and Ferrari (supra, n. 17) 77–79. The offensive noise which imitates "breaking wind," and which in cockney rhyming slang is called a rasp-berry (from "raspberry tart")—in Greek *pordê*—is attested as a gesture of contempt (*kataperdomai tinos*) in Ar. *Vesp.* 619 cf. 1305, *Pax* 547, *Plut.* 618 and (in the fourth century) in the comic poet Epikrates (ap. Athen. 59f), but not in the theater or by a theater audience.

46. See, e.g., C. W. Dearden, *The Stage of Aristophanes* (London 1976) 13–18. By contrast, for us modern lighting, the higher stage, and the orchestra pit reinforce the illusion that the audience is not present. See generally P. D. Arnott, *Public and Performance in the Greek Theater* (London 1989) 10–16.

47. See D. Bain, "Audience Address in Greek Tragedy," *CQ* 25 (1975) 13–25; T. K. Hubbard, *The Mask of Comedy: Aristophanes and the Intertextual Parabasis* (Ithaca, N.Y. 1991); P. Thiercy, "Le rôle du public dans la comédie d'Aristophane," *Dioniso* 57 (1987) 169–85. For examples of addresses to the audience outside the *parabasis*, see Ar. *Pax* 50–53 and 664.

48. W. B. Stanford begins *Greek Tragedy and the Emotions* (London 1983) with a dialogue summarizing his questions to other scholars: "Q. What was the aim of the dramatists of the classical period in Athens? A. To win a prize at the Dionysian festival. Q. How did they do that? A. By being best at giving their audiences the pleasure of laughing and crying." (I note that he applies this to the fifth century.)

49. However, between 1912 and 1948 the modern Olympic Games sponsored contests in architecture, painting, sculpture, music, and literature.

50. Ar. *Vesp.* 1410–11. Herodotos (6.129) had earlier told the famous story of Hippo-kleides, who in the sixth century danced upside down on tables and, when rejected, replied *ou phrontis Hippokleidêi*.

51. See O. Taplin, "Tragedy and Trugedy," *CQ* 33 (1983) 331–33, and J. Henderson, "The Demos and the Comic Competition," in J. J. Winkler and F. Zeitlin, eds., *Nothing to Do with Dionysos?* (Princeton 1990) 271–313.

52. See also Pl. *Gorg.* 462c–d, *Phaidr.* 259e–260a, *Republ.* 493a–d.

53. On this see H. Flasher, "Die Poetik des Aristoteles und die griechische Tragödie," *Poetica* 16 (1984) 3–7; G. Xanthakis-Karamanos, *Studies in Fourth-Century Tragedy* (Athens 1980) 3–4; and T. B. L. Webster, *Art and Literature in Fourth Century Athens* (London 1956) 51, 65–67; cf. 68–69.

54. See R. W. Wallace, "Frammentarietà e trasformazione: evoluzioni nei modi della comunicazione nella cultura ateniese fra V e IV sec.," *QUCC* 46 (1994) 14–16.

55. T. B. L. Webster, "Fourth Century Tragedy and the *Poetics*," *Hermes* 82 (1954) 297 (reprinted in Webster [supra, n. 53] 31).

56. Lesky (supra, n. 15) 401. He adds, "Undoubtedly, we are also justified in assuming that diction became more heavily rhetorical, and that further advances were made in the line of musical virtuosity, which Plato (*Laws* 3, 700d) condemned as the main reason for the corruption of theatre."

57. See D. Page, *Actors' Interpolations in Greek Tragedy* (Oxford 1934) 15–20.

58. See esp. Ghiron-Bistagne, "Krise" (supra, n. 12) 1348–52.

59. Ael. *VH* 14.40; Plut. *Mor.* 334a, *Pelop.* 29.

60. M. H. Hansen, "The Number of *Rhetores* in the Athenian *Ekklesia*, 355–322," *GRBS* 25 (1984) 123–55, reprinted in *The Athenian Ekklesia*, vol. 2: *A Collection of Articles, 1983–89* (Copenhagen 1989) 93–125. See generally W. Eder, ed., *Die athenische Democratie im 4. Jh. v. Chr.* (Stuttgart 1995).

61. I also note that accusations of pandering to the crowd are not limited to dramatic poets and democratic politicians and orators. In *Nauagos* (Athen. 509b–c = fr. 14 K. = fr. 14 K-A) the fourth-century comic poet Ephippos thus describes the young student of Plato in politics: "he consorts with art—the art of making money by speaking, and he cannot say anything incautious. . . . His hair is carefully cut, his beard is long, but his words are only clichés."

62. Again, an antecedent to Plato's objection may be found in Thucydides, in his judgment that as each of the politicians who came after Perikles "strove to become first, they tended to abandon affairs to the people to gratify the demos's pleasures [*hêdonas*]" (2.65.10, trans. Rhodes [adapted]).

63. See *Dysk.* 966–99, *Mis.* 464–65, *Sam.* 733–74, *Sik.* 420–22, and fr. 771 = schol. Ar. *Plut.* 689 (ἐξάραντες ἐπικροτήσατε). Afterward, of course, such requests become common. On his deathbed Augustus asked his friends "if he had played the comedy [*mimus*] of life fitly," and added in Greek a two-line tag asking for *krotos* (Suet. *Aug.* 99).

64. See generally my two articles, "Frammentarietà" (supra, n. 54), and "Speech, Song, and Text, Public and Private: Evolutions in Communications Media and Fora in Fourth-Century Athens," in Eder (supra, n. 60).

65. See, e.g., *Gorg.* 462d–e. *Republ.* 390a.

66. Aristox. *Elem. Harm.* 30–31; see also Themist. *Or.* 21.245c–d, Procl. *In Parmen.* 127c.

67. For comparative evidence, when Anglo-American theater divided into elite and popular audiences, the latter similarly rejected wit, in-jokes, satire and intellectual content in favor of the variety of vaudeville, a collection of acts, sentiment, spectacle, and humanized drama. See R. Porter, *English Society in the Eighteenth Century* (London 1982) 241, 257; G. Rowell, *The Victorian Theatre, 1792–1914: A Survey* (Cambridge 1978) 2, 38; F. Hodge, *Yankee Theatre: The Image of America on Stage, 1825–1850* (Austin, Tex. 1964); and R. Toll, *On with the Show* (Oxford 1976).

68. Thanks to Lowell Edmunds, the anonymous referee for this paper, and my audiences in Rome and Florence for useful comments and suggestions.

All the (Greek) World's a Stage:
Notes on (Not Just Dramatic) Greek Staging

1. *European Literature and the Latin Middle Ages*, trans. W. Trask (Princeton 1990) 158–64.

2. Cf. E. A. Havelock, *Preface to Plato* (Cambridge, Mass. 1963) 27.

3. B. Gentili, *Poesia e pubblico nella Grecia antica* (Rome 1984), translated by T. Cole as *Poetry and Its Public in Ancient Greece* (Baltimore 1988) 40. For some qualifications of Havelock's views, see G. Cerri, "Il passaggio dalla cultura orale alla cultura di comunicazione scritta nell'età di Platone," *QUCC* 8 (1969) 119–33.

4. *Poetry* (supra, n. 3) 42.

5. Cf. respectively, V. Bérard, *Introduction à l'Odyssée*, vol. 1: *L'épos homérique. Le poème réprésenté* (Paris 1933) 75; M. Valgimigli, *Poeti e filosofi di Grecia*, vol. 2: *Interpretazioni* (Florence 1964) 563–83 (the work dates back to 1928).

6. Cf. moreover C. F. Russo, *Aristofane autore di teatro* (Florence 1984, translated by K. Wren as *Aristophanes, an Author for the Stage* [London 1994]) x–xi; "Platone è competente . . . :—se in Omero cancelli le parti del poeta che stanno fra le parti dei personaggi, avrai una forma opposta: la forma della tragedia—così si dialoga in una scuola di strumenti critici situata nell'Atene di Platone, *Repubblica* 394b."

7. J. Herington, *Poetry into Drama: Early Tragedy and the Greek Poetic Tradition* (Berkeley 1985) x.

8. Herington (supra, n. 7) 39.

9. Cf., respectively, W. Rösler, "Die Entdeckung der Fiktionalität in der Antike," *Poetica* 12 (1980) 283–319; W. Rösler, "Über Deixis und einige Aspekte mündlichen und schriftlichen Stils in antiken Lyrikern," *WürzJbb* 9 (1983) 7–28; and J. Latacz, "Realität und Imagination. Eine neue Lyrik-Theorie und Sapphos φαίνεταί μοι κῆνος-Lied," *MusHelv* 42 (1985) 67–94.

10. I am referring in particular to the drastic statement made by M. R. Lefkowitz, "Τῶ καὶ ἐγώ: The First Person in Pindar," *HSCP* 67 (1963) 177–253, for whom the "I" of Pindaric poetry was always choral; a statement that has been mellowed in the more recent "Who Sang Pindar's Victory Odes?," *AJP* 109 (1988) 10–11. On this topic, cf. most recently, J. M. Bremmer, "Pindar's Paradoxical ἐγώ and a Recent Controversy about the Performance of His Epinicia," in S. R. Slings, ed., *The Poet's I in Archaic Greek Lyric* (Amsterdam 1990), as well as M. Fantuzzi, "Preistoria di un genere letterario: A proposito degli inni V e VI di Callimaco," in R. Pretagostini, ed., *Scritti in onore di B. Gentili*, vol. 3 (Rome 1993) 935–38, which rightly puts us on guard against the equally unjustifiable statement "per cui la prima persona singolare degli epinici esprimerebbe sempre la 'voce' dell'autore" (935, n. 24).

11. Cf. Pretagostini (supra, n. 10), vol. 1, 347–61 and 129–40, as well as A. Aloni, "Proemio e funzione proemiale nella poesia greca arcaica," *A.I.O.N.* 12 (1990) 99–130.

12. Cf. Pretagostini (supra, n. 10), vol. 1, 131.

13. Cf. M. Fantuzzi, "Preistoria di un genere letterario: a proposito degli inni V e VI di Callimaco," in Pretagostini (supra, n. 10), vol. 3, 927; as well as R. Pretagostini, "Rito e

letteratura negli inni 'drammatici' di Callimaco," *A.I.O.N.* 13 (1991) 253–63, which, with the expression "literary drama" (Bulloch) indicates "una nuova e inedita categoria poetica della cultura alessandrina," to which, without doubt, the mimetic (or dramatic) hymn of Callimachus should be attributed.

14. Cf. Rösler, "Über Deixis" (supra, n. 9) 14–23 (and for the specific updating in the environment of the symposium, see pp. 19–20).

15. Cf., on this subject, Fantuzzi (supra, n. 13) 941, who refers to W. Albert, *Das mimetische Gedicht in der Antike* (Frankfurt 1988).

16. Cf. G. Mastromarco, *Il pubblico di Eronda* (Padua 1979) 22–105, as well as his *The Public of Herondas* (Amsterdam 1984) 5–63.

17. N. W. Slater, "From Ancient Performance to New Historicism," *DRAMA* 2 (1993) 2. Unfortunately, among the most illustrious names he mentions, from Newiger to Whitman and from W. G. Arnott to Taplin, the name of C. F. Russo is missing—whose *Aristofane attore di teatro* (supra, n. 6), first published in Florence in 1962, was important and ahead of its time.

18. Cf., respectively, Herington (supra, n. 7) 22; M. G. Bonanno, *L'allusione necessaria* (Rome 1990) 60–69. For the sociopragmatic context, reference should be made to the important research by C. Calame, *Les choeurs de jeunes filles en Grèce archaïque*, vols. 1–2 (Rome 1977).

19. For this idea see M. Puelma, "Die Selbstbeschreibung des Chores in Alkmans grossem Partheneion-Fragment (fr. 1 P. = 23 B., 1 D. v. 36–105)," *MusHelv* 34 (1977) 30.

20. P. Brook, *The Empty Space* (London 1968) 11.

21. Cf. L. Edmunds, "The Blame of Karkinos: Theorizing Theatrical Space," *DRAMA* 1 (1992) 222.

22. Cf. M. Heidegger, *L'arte e lo spazio* (Genoa 1979), translated from *Die Kunst und der Raum* (St. Gallen 1969) 11, 15–17.

23. For a clarification of such a productive-communicative (and thus pragmatic) notion relative to the "art of the performance" (distinct, according to Kowzan, from the thing obligatorily communicated in space and time), cf. M. De Marinis, *Semiotica del teatro. L'analisi testuale dello spettacolo* (Milan 1982) 63–64.

24. Slater (supra, n. 17) 8.

25. Cited by De Marinis (supra, n. 23) 60, to whom I refer for the specific attention dedicated to the notions of technical replicability, repeatability, and reproducibility (64–67).

26. Edmunds (supra, n. 21) 223.

27. Cf., on this subject, M. D'Amico, *Scena e parola in Shakespeare* (Turin 1974).

28. B. Marzullo, *I sofismi di Prometeo* (Florence 1993) 131 n. 81 ("un' attuazione non più che virtuale di siffatti movimenti"), appropriately recalls Taplin's solution (*The Stagecraft of Aeschylus* [Oxford 1977] 274–75), which is among other things about an emblematic scene, "che costituisce un indiscutibile esempio di impossibilità di realismo": thus G. Monaco, "La scena allargata," *Dioniso* 53 (1982) 16 (who cites precisely the same view as A. W. Pickard-Cambridge and P. Arnott).

29. Cf., respectively, D. Del Corno, in E. Corsini, ed., *La polis e il suo teatro* (Padua

1986) 205–13; D. L. Page, *Actors' Interpolations in Greek Tragedy* (Oxford 1934) 112; D. Bain, *Actors and Audience: A Study of Asides and Related Conventions in Greek Drama* (Oxford 1977) 53 n. 2.

30. Cf. O. Taplin, "Did Greek Dramatists Write Stage Instructions?," *PCPS* n.s. 23 (1977) 121–32.

31. Del Corno (supra, n. 29) 208: "La soluzione andrà in effetti, io credo, ricercata in questa direzione; ma accentuando in essa non tanto la rilevanza di quel che accadeva sulla scena, bensì quello che agli spettatori era richiesto di immaginare che accadesse, integrando con l'apporto della loro fantasia il mero dato visivo." For a clarification of the Aristophanic stage convention, cf. G. Mastromarco, *Commedie di Aristofane*, vol. 1 (Turin 1983) 26–31, as well as *Introduzione a Aristofane* (Rome 1994), where in the chapter "Un testo per la scena" (105–41) among other things various problems concerning stage-words are examined in depth, also in analogy with Shakespearean theater (111–16). For the use of tragedy of the stage-word, cf. B. Marzullo, "La parola scenica," *QUCC* 22 (1986) 95–104; "La parola scenica, II," *QUCC* 30 (1988) 79–85; "La parodos dell'Alcesti (Eur. *Alc.* 77–140)," *MusCr* 23–24 (1988–89) 123–83; as well as Marzullo (supra, n. 28), esp. 164–68 n. 42.

32. Dale's study, which dates back to 1956, is included in her *Collected Papers* (Cambridge 1969) 119–29. Cf. two almost contemporary works by Swiss anglicists, not by chance on Shakespeare: R. Stamm, *Shakespeare's Word-Scenery (with Some Remarks on Stage-History and the Interpretation of His Plays)* (Zurich 1954), and A. Müller-Bellingshausen, "Die Wortkulisse bei Shakespeare," *Shakespeare-Jahrbuch* 91 (1955) 183–95. Both are mentioned by Marzullo, "Parodos" (supra, n. 31) 123 n. 1.

33. Aristotle adds later the gestural dimension (1455a29, καὶ τοῖς σχήμασι συναπεργαζόμενος sc. ὁ ποιητής). Cf. D. W. Lucas, *Aristotle Poetics* (Oxford 1968) 177, who mentions other, less persuasive interpretations. Chapter 17, which in the first two paragraphs refers to the introduction of 1454b15 on the αἰσθήσεις of the audience that the poet must not disappoint, is much debated. In particular the error of Karkinos has given rise to the most diverse interpretations (cf. R. Dupont-Roc and J. Lallot, *Aristote. La Poétique* [Paris 1980] 278–81: more recently, and especially, see J. R. Green, "Carcinus and the Temple: A Lesson in the Staging of Tragedy," *GRBS* 31 [1990] 281–85, and Edmunds (supra, n. 21) 224–25), starting from the text itself, where for example on the basis of ὁρῶν at line 24, μὴ ὁρῶντα at line 27 is understood as addressed to the poet and not to the spectator (if so, then τὸν θεατήν would be a mistaken gloss), but the negation μή "should give a conditional or generic force" as Lucas (174) correctly objects. The problem (only touched on here), which needs further study, is about the relationship between ὄψις and λέξις in the perspective of the audience's enjoyment: (μή) ὁρῶντα should however refer to whoever watches the actual stage, that is, the spectator. The preceding ὁρῶν refers to the poet in "virtual" conditions, that is as if he watched the stage from the spectator's point of view; cf. moreover the parallel 1453b3, δεῖ γὰρ καὶ ἄνευ τοῦ ὁρᾶν οὕτω συνεστάναι τὸν μῦθον ὥστε κτλ., where the effect of the tragedy is claimed even without performance, ἄνευ τοῦ ὁρᾶν indicating the absence of the spectator, as well as 1460a13, where, with reference to a certain absurdity (ἄλογον) allowed by

the epic διὰ τὸ μὴ ὁρᾶν εἰς πράττοντα, the (here still absent) condition of dramatic spectator is also defined technically.

34. On this subject cf. M. Di Marco, " "Οψις nella *Poetica* di Aristotele e nel *Tractatus Coislinianus*," in L. De Finis, ed., *Scena e spettacolo nell'antichità* (Florence 1989) 140.

35. B. Marzullo affirms a distinction between the first, with an essential (and structural) function, and the second, with a secondary (and decorative) function. Cf. Marzullo (supra, n. 28) 146 n. 15, that synthesizes his previous work.

36. Thus D. Lanza, "L'attor comico sulla scena," *Dioniso* 59 (1989) 297–312, whose line of argument is set out most effectively in "Lo spazio scenico dell'attore comico," in De Finis (supra, n. 34) 179–91.

37. Thus Lanza, "Lo spazio" (supra, n. 36) 182.

38. Thus D. Del Corno, *Aristofane. Le Rane* (Milan 1985) xviii.

39. Cf. B. Marzullo, "Die visuelle Dimension des Theaters bei Aristoteles," *Philologus* 124 (1980) 190.

40. This is the successful translation of ὄψις by Taplin, *Greek Tragedy in Action* (London 1978), ch. 1: "The Visual Dimension of Tragedy," whose title Marzullo borrowed (supra, n. 39), and by Di Marco (supra, n. 34) 129. For a semantic analysis of the term, cf. F. Donadi, "Nota al cap. VI della *Poetica* di Aristotele: Il problema dell'ὄψις," *AttiPatAcc* 83, no. 3 (1970–71) 414–24, as well as Di Marco (supra, n. 34) 129 n. 3.

41. This effective definition is by D. Lanza, *Aristotele. Poetica* (Milan 1987) 18.

42. Thus C. Gallavotti, *Aristotele. Dell'arte poetica* (Milan 1974) 25, correctly entitles the passage in question.

43. Thus M. De Marinis, "Aristotele teorico dello spettacolo," in *Teoria e storia della messinscena nel teatro antico*, Atti del Convegno Internazionale Torino, 17–19 April 1989 (Genoa 1991) 13.

44. Thus Lanza (supra, n. 41) 141.

45. Thus De Marinis (supra, n. 43) 14.

46. Thus Lanza (supra, n. 41) 13.

47. This is the title of a famous essay by Pasolini, published in *Empirismo eretico* (Milan 1972) 198.

48. Pasolini (supra, n. 47) 294.

49. Pasolini (supra, n. 47) 206.

50. On the other hand, the institutional affirmation of the book—Aristotle was noticeable as a willingly lone "reader" (cf. Lanza [supra, n. 41] 11)—insinuated concretely (historically) the possibility and the necessity of a κτῆμα, and also aesthetic, ἐς ἀεί.

Remarks at the American Academy in Rome, February 12, 1994

Editor's note: Professor Gentili's remarks have been edited for inclusion in this volume.

1. "Tragédie, oralité, écriture," *Poétique* 10 (1982) 135ff.

2. As J. P. Sullivan acutely observed in I. J. F. de Jong and J. P. Sullivan, eds., *Modern Critical Theory and Classical Literature* (New York 1994) 16.

Contributors

ANTONIO ALONI is Professor Ordinarius of Greek Literature at the Università degli Studi di Torino.

MAURIZIO BETTINI is Professor Ordinarius of Greek and Latin Philology and Preside of the Facoltà di Lettere at the Università degli Studi di Siena.

MARIA GRAZIA BONANNO is Professor Ordinarius of Greek Literature at the Università degli Studi di Roma II.

A. THOMAS COLE is Professor of Classics at Yale University.

LOWELL EDMUNDS is Professor of Classics at Rutgers University.

GIULIO GUIDORIZZI is Associate Professor of Greek Grammar at the Università degli Studi di Milano.

JOSEPH RUSSO is Professor of Classics at Haverford College.

CHARLES SEGAL is Professor of Classics at Harvard University.

ROBERT W. WALLACE is Associate Professor of Classics at Northwestern University.

9 780801 867354